D0895361

Lowell Mason
His Life and Work

Studies in Musicology, No. 86

George Buelow, Series Editor

Professor of Music
Indiana University

Other Titles in This Series

780.92
M399L
P395l

Lowell Mason
His Life and Work

by
Carol A. Pemberton
Instructor in English
Normandale Community College
Bloomington, Minnesota

72298

U·M·I Research Press

Ann Arbor / London

Copyright © 1985, 1971
Carol Ann Pemberton
All rights reserved

Produced and distributed by
UMI Research Press
an imprint of
University Microfilms Inc.
Ann Arbor, Michigan 48106

Library of Congress Cataloging in Publication Data

Pemberton, Carol A. (Carol Ann), 1939-
Lowell Mason: his life and work.

(Studies in musicology ; no. 86)
Revision of thesis (Ph.D)—University of Minnesota,
1971
"Lowell Mason's music publications": p.
Bibliography: p.
Includes index.
1. Mason, Lowell, 1792-1872. 2. Composers—United
States—Biography. I. Title. II. Series.
ML410.M4P45 1985   783'.092'4 [B]   84-28121
ISBN 0-8357-1650-3 (alk. paper)

To my mother and dad

Lowell Mason

Lowell Mason in the Boston Years, c. 1840.
Engraving by H. Wright Smith
(Used by courtesy of the Trustees of the Boston Public Library)

Contents

Preface

Lowell Mason: The Father of Public School Music. The Founder of American Protestant Hymnody. Empire Builder. The First American to Make a Fortune as a Musician. The Head of a Musical Dynasty. Founder of American National Music. Recipient of an Honorary Doctorate in Music from an American University. . . .

Though tributes to Lowell Mason make a long, impressive list, this book is the first complete biography. The best-known previous study is Arthur L. Rich's *Lowell Mason, "the Father of Singing Among the Children,"* dealing chiefly with Mason's work as an educator. Doctoral dissertations and master's theses offer detailed information on certain aspects of his life and work, but these studies remain in the obscurity of university libraries. As a result, Mason's life and work are usually discussed only in generalities.

It is, therefore, my first objective to tell Mason's story in detail within the context of his era. To the extent that it is possible, I have tried to make any judgments of Mason in light of the standards of his day, not the standards of our day; better yet, when possible, the judgments of his contemporaries are included. The man will be revealed as a perceptive, skilled leader whose personal charm balanced an authoritative and sometimes domineering side. A masterful assimilator and implementer of ideas, Mason helped transform the aimless American music culture of the early 1800s into a culture in which composition, church music, music education, music publishing, music scholarship, and music organizations have flourished.

Another objective of this study is to attract other researchers to American music of the 1800s. Those pioneers whose efforts complemented Mason's deserve more study. Trends in nineteenth-century America deserve more attention by musicologists and interdisciplinary scholars to correlate our music with other cultural expressions. The rise of instrument manufacturing, music publishing, and music criticism are also worth further study with reference to the Mason family and others. The fields in which Mason pioneered, American Protestant church music and American music education, warrant continuing research. A thorough understanding of our cultural heritage will provide insight into current problems as well as historical perspective.

This biography should also dispel some of the condescension with which Lowell Mason has often been regarded. The glamor associated with composition has too frequently obscured the fact that music culture—no matter what the time or place—is profoundly shaped by people besides composers. Mason's accomplishments are often credited grudgingly with the reminder that, despite what he accomplished, he was, at best, a mediocre composer. (If he could be asked, Mason would almost certainly agree with that assessment of his composing.)

This book tells the story of an American family whose experiences parallel those of many others. From the time of Robert Mason, an English immigrant in 1628, through the present day, typical trends appear: from a rural to an urban life; from individual to corporate enterprises; from provincial interests to ever wider, more cosmopolitan ones; from a relatively simple to a highly complex life. Lowell Mason's personal story is part of this adaptation to change. His success follows a typical pattern of American fact and fiction: a man of humble beginnings, meager formal education, and little contact with the famous figures of his time, he nevertheless rose to distinction in his chosen field, changing our cultural climate as a consequence.

Lowell Mason is best known for instigating music programs as part of the public school curriculum, beginning in the Boston Public Schools in 1838. Others might have accomplished this; certainly many of his contemporaries were as intelligent and creative as he was, if not more so. But he succeeded where others could not or did not. The reasons for that success became evident to me as this biography took shape.

To deal with the practical problems of teaching music to *all* children, Mason had to evolve a workable philosophy, suitable textbooks, effective teacher-training programs, and a rationale that the public would accept. To win public support, he also had to have the personal and professional stature to command respect, plus the relentless drive and stamina to persevere despite opposition. To convince the public, he had to speak and write in terms musicians and nonmusicians alike would understand, using a variety of arguments to overcome a variety of obstacles.

In short, he first had to be an established, respected music leader, and he attained that stature as a comparatively young man. He had to be a realistic, systematic, and determined leader, and he was all those things. His values had to be in harmony with the standards of his day, and they were. Most of all, he had to be politically astute, and he was.

Because Lowell Mason's successes reveal a good deal about American culture, this book is more than a recital of one man's achievements. In Mason's example, we see success made possible by a pragmatic approach, by his almost intuitive sense of what the American public could handle educationally and aesthetically. His career was based on such practical considerations as these and on the inherent American desire to extend the "good life" to all, including music for all schoolchildren, congregational singing for all churchgoers, singable music for all choral groups, and music publications for all performers at prices all could afford.

This biography provides a summary of Mason materials for specialists in music education, church music, American studies, and music history, but it is also suitable for the general reader. Insofar as possible, I have avoided technical jargon so that laymen, as well as musicians, can understand Mason's story. I have included background material to acquaint the nonhistorian with American music culture in Mason's time.

Most of the material upon which this book is based is generally inaccessible: nineteenth-century periodicals; Mason's published writings and collections of music; his surviving letters and diaries; the manuscript biography by Henry Lowell Mason; unpublished theses and dissertations which, in turn, drew upon rare books, manuscripts, letters, and other archival items. I believe that subsequent scholars of Mason's period will find this book a shortcut to pertinent materials.

This book makes no attempt to magnify Mason as a composer. To imply that he was a great or major composer would not only be inaccurate, but would also distort his career. Though many of his hymn tunes are a lasting part of America's musical heritage, their popularity is not confused with aesthetic worth.

I made no attempt to analyze Mason's compositions in detail. Harmonic, melodic, and rhythmic qualities are summarized, but detailed analysis lies beyond the scope of this book. Such analysis would be especially meaningful if undertaken as a comparison of musical practices among contemporaries, both American and European, but that, too, lies beyond the scope of this work. Nor did I attempt to trace the sources from which Mason drew music for his many anthologies. Such an undertaking is impossible until a data bank of thematic materials is created to include not only Mason's materials, but those of his contemporaries and precursors.

I have avoided intensive examination of Mason's educational theories and his statements about them. Information about Mason as a teacher and education theorist is more readily available than is information on other aspects of his work. This book covers Mason's teaching career not as fresh material (though that may sometimes be the case), but rather as an essential portion of a complete biography.

Much of this book is organized in accord with the various threads of Mason's career within fairly large blocks of time. This arrangement is especially important for the Boston years, 1827 through 1851, the peak of his work in church music, music organizations, the music education movement, private and public school teaching, teacher training programs, and publication of music books. These activities are discussed separately so that developments in each one can be followed without interruption. Though this method suspends straightforward chronology and, in some instances, necessitates more than one reference to a particular event, I believe the topical approach allows readers to understand specific aspects of Mason's career more easily. At the same time, I have tried to keep the chronology as clear as possible throughout, and I have provided a chronological listing of major events in appendix A.

Most quoted material appears as it did in the original source without comment about the antiquated spelling, punctuation, sentence structure, and diction. In a few instances, I have modernized the material slightly for reading ease, but never at the expense of the meaning or the flavor of the original.

The expression "American music" as used in this book refers to music in the United States of America, a usage that has become standard among writers in the United States.

I refer to the tunebooks Mason produced as "collections," "anthologies," or simply "music books." The miscellaneous nature of their contents justifies these terms, and they are used interchangeably. Because complete titles are often cumbersome, I have used abbreviated titles unless a full title was useful for reasons other than identification. The abbreviation usually consists of the first full phrase of the given title.

This book takes readers into the nineteenth century, into a world inhabited by Americans who loved music as much as we do today. But, unlike us, they had only two ways to hear music: perform it themselves or be in the presence of performers. Today we take much of the music around us for granted; such variety and abundance (not to mention the technological aspects) would have been unimaginable to our forebears; conversely, their limited access to music is all but unimaginable for us.

Through this biography you will meet a representative of that world, Lowell Mason, and consider the ways in which his work brought music into the lives of his countrymen. I believe that you will come to respect him as did his distinguished contemporary, music critic John Sullivan Dwight, who wrote in 1881 in *The Memorial History of Boston:*

> The passion of his youth, and of all his life, was music, with which were coupled a life-long religious zeal and great business enterprise and shrewdness. He was a manager of men, an organizer of movements educational and popular,—some of them of lasting influence....[He was] one of the most prominent figures in our musical activity...whose influence was long, wide-spread, and various, *on the whole for good.*

Acknowledgments

One of the pleasures of writing this biography has been the development of friendships with others who share an interest in Lowell Mason's life and work. It is a privilege now to acknowledge the kindnesses extended to me by members of the Mason family, by leaders of historical societies and countless librarians, and by other scholars of American music. Special thanks are due my correspondents at the Savannah, Georgia Public Library, the Orange, New Jersey Public Library, and the historical societies of Medfield and Westborough, Massachusetts, all of whom provided archival materials pertaining to aspects of Mason's life.

All the librarians who responded to surveys and inquiries were helpful. The staffs of the Sibley Music Library of the Eastman School of Music at Rochester, New York, the Newberry Library in Chicago, the Boston Public Library, Loeb Music Library at Harvard University, and the Minneapolis Public Library deserve special recognition, including the Interlibrary Loan Division of the Minneapolis Public Library that arranged many loans for me. Thanks are due as well to the many libraries across the nation that shared materials through the Interlibrary Loan system.

Because Lowell Mason's personal library and papers were donated to Yale University after his death, the materials at Yale were central to my work. Alfred B. Kuhn and Harold E. Samuel, librarians, and Isabel Clark and Victor Cardell, assistant librarians, helped me in the Music Library and at the Beinecke Rare Book and Manuscript Library while I researched Mason materials at Yale in July 1970 and August 1984. A particular debt of gratitude is due the late Eva J. O'Meara, former librarian. During the early 1970s she helped by finding answers to puzzling questions and by sharing perspectives she gained through years of work with the Mason materials at Yale. Mason correspondence and diaries quoted in this book are found in the Yale collection unless otherwise indicated.

This book is based upon a study completed in 1971 at the University of Minnesota. I owe a great deal to those who helped me in its preparation: Johannes Riedel, Mary C. Turpie, Robert T. Laudon, Robert L. Borg and the late Roy Schuessler, all of whom spent hours reading, evaluating, and encouraging my work.

The libraries mentioned above have graciously granted me permission to quote from archival materials in their possession. In this regard, special recognition is due to the Boston Public Library and the Beinecke Rare Book and Manuscript Library at Yale University. Photographs are used with the kind permission of these institutions and other owners, including Elizabeth Mason Ginnel, one of Lowell Mason's great-granddaughters.

I am particularly indebted to the devoted scholarship of the late Henry Lowell Mason, a grandson of Lowell Mason. Mr. Mason began about 1908 collecting materials for a definitive biography of his grandfather. By consulting people who could recall Lowell Mason from their early years, Mr. Mason collected priceless personal recollections, some of which are incorporated into the manuscript he left incomplete upon his death in 1957. Through the generosity of his heirs, Henry Lowell Mason's manuscript, his correspondence, and other materials gathered over the years are now with the Lowell Mason Papers at Yale. Mr. Mason's meticulous research provided details which would otherwise have been difficult or impossible to trace.

Finally, I am personally indebted to teachers who instilled the love of learning that inspired my graduate studies and to family and friends who supported me with unwavering encouragement during the preparation of this work.

1

The Formative Years

The Johnson Masons of Medfield, Massachusetts

The quiet village of Medfield, Massachusetts lies about eighteen miles southwest of Boston. Located on the east side of the Charles River, Medfield is nestled in gently rolling hills and rich lowlands; its original name, "Meadfield," referring to "meads" or meadows, is easily understood by any observer. The lush vegetation indigenous to the area was largely stripped back by settlers before 1800 because Indians had used the many trees as hiding places from which to attack. By 1800 the village had about seven hundred residents, among them Johnson and Catherine Hartshorn Mason, active, well-respected members of the community.

Johnson Mason (b. August 7, 1767) was one of the two sons of Barachais and Love Battelle Mason. With his brother Arnold, Johnson grew up in Medfield during the turbulent Revolutionary War period. Too young to fight during the war, Johnson volunteered for military service after the Revolution at age sixteen. By 1800 he was commissioned as a captain, and in 1803 he achieved the rank of lieutenant colonel. Johnson was a resolute leader, as was his forebear, Robert Mason (1590–1667), an immigrant with the John Winthrop Company whose sons were among the original settlers of Medfield about 1650. Generation after generation, the sturdy, hard-working, brave men and women of the Mason family helped build Medfield; some of them died defending their homes and community.[1]

In 1791 Johnson Mason married Catherine Hartshorn, the twenty-two year-old daughter of Moses and Elizabeth Smith Hartshorn. Like the Masons, the Hartshorns and the Smiths were long-established Medfield residents. Catherine's ancestry can be traced back to Henry and Elizabeth Smith, who emigrated from England to Massachusetts in 1637 and moved to Medfield in 1651. Catherine ("Caty") Mason came to assume many responsibilities, rearing five children while Johnson became a business and civic leader.

As newlyweds, Johnson and Caty Mason moved into an addition that he had built onto the Mason family home. There they remained near Johnson's aging parents while enjoying their own quarters. They lived for decades in the family home, long after his parents had died. The homestead, located east of the Medfield town square on North Street, consisted of the house, a barn, and several small sheds on a five-acre plot of land. The house was a plain, two-story, white frame structure, bespeaking the Masons' modest but comfortable means.

On a cold, windy Sunday, January 8, 1792, Caty Mason gave birth to her first child, Lowell. In 1793 Lowell's only sister, Lucretia, was born. Later three brothers joined the family: the twins, Johnson and Arnold, born in 1796, and Timothy Battelle, born in 1801.

The Mason children had many playmates. On one side the Reverend and Mrs. Thomas Prentiss lived with their nine children, and on the other side, the Adams family included additional playmates. The Prentiss children included Thomas Jr. (1793–1817), who became a schoolmate and close friend of Lowell Mason's, and Mercy (1801–1877), the youngest child, who helped care for Johnson and Caty Mason in their old age.

The Reverend Dr. Prentiss, a Harvard graduate of 1766, was not only the pastor of Medfield's Congregational church, but also the supervisor of the Medfield schools. In addition, he taught at North School and privately tutored a small group of boys in his home to prepare them for college.

The Adams family also offered intellectual stimulation and examples of high achievement. One of the daughters, Hannah (1755–1831), became a distinguished writer. When in 1799 she issued her *Summary History of New England* (a pioneer work of its type), Johnson Mason proudly subscribed to it. Lowell knew Hannah well, though he spent a good deal more time with her younger brother, George Whitefield Adams. George had a thriving business that fascinated Lowell: in a workshop attached to the Adams house, George built small pipe organs, repaired and tuned pianos, and generally repaired other musical instruments upon request. Lowell probably spent many hours in that shop, chatting, watching George work, and perhaps helping him at times.

Young people in Medfield, like their contemporaries in other small American towns, had certain advantages in that day. "The temptations to vice and idleness were reduced to their lowest terms, and the boys, rarely enjoying the advantages of schooling more than two or three months in the winter, had abundant leisure to devote to their favorite pursuits."[2] Indeed, the school that Lowell and his friends attended held only brief sessions, but those sessions must have been productive. Lowell attended North School and was taught by Mr. Prentiss. By contemporary accounts, Lowell was a fine scholar, as well as a popular, talented, and handsome young man.

When Lowell recalled his school days in later years, he pictured this scene as typical: Mary and Abigail Prentiss and Lucretia Mason walked home from school in front of Tom Prentiss and Lowell, who stayed behind and teased the girls. They met Joseph Allen (another friend and classmate who went on to prominence as a Unitarian clergyman) with a book under his arm as he returned from a tutoring session with Mr. Prentiss. As they walked along, the children saw farmers hoeing corn in nearby fields. On one occasion Lowell and Thomas quarreled on the way, but by the time they reached the Prentiss house, Tom's father had heard about it. He called them into his study and talked to them. Very soon he had "melted us both in contrition...ashamed and mortified we shook hands and were soon good friends again."[3]

The Masons were influenced by Mr. Prentiss in several ways. In 1800 Caty Mason joined the church where he was pastor, and on May 4 of that year, she had all her children (four at that time) baptized. Johnson deferred joining the church until later in life. Although he attended regularly with his family, he had reservations about such precepts as total depravity and eternal damnation. Caty requested that, for the children's sake, he not stir up religious controversy, and he acquiesced in the matter.

Caty herself was devoted to her church and its teachings. When Lowell was almost seventy years old, he recalled his mother's faith and its effect on him: "I cannot be too grateful to my Parents, and especially to my Mother for the religious instruction she gave me when I was a child. I suppose if my Mother had not tried to instruct me in religious things I should never have known the comparative peace I now enjoy, or looked forward as I can now, with a good hope of blessedness to come."[4]

Lowell's father's faith was less overt. At Johnson's funeral, the Reverend Andrew Bigelow characterized him as a man of "retiring modesty and great integrity... prudent, patient, and honest, a devoted Christian [who] had neither the confidence, nor early training which prepares men to speak eloquently in popular assemblies. His piety rather found expression in his example and his life."[5] During his lifetime Johnson Mason worked at many jobs, but his chief income came from the dry goods store he ran with his partner George Ellis on North Street, opposite Dale Street, and from the manufacturing enterprise he and Ellis started about 1801. They began to make straw bonnets using rye straw. Some of these bonnets were for ladies, designed in the latest fashions, and others were for field horses to shield their heads from the sun. If family legend is accurate, Johnson Mason invented the bonnet for horses. The rye used in this operation was cut when in bloom, then prepared by scalding or bleaching. It was then braided by families who exchanged the braid for dry goods at the Mason-Ellis store. Bonnet manufacturing soon grew into Medfield's leading industry.

Johnson also had mechanical talents. After spending many long hours trimming, pressing, and bleaching straw, he developed a machine to handle some of these operations. In his later years he built an apparatus described in family records as "an appliance for the comfort of his bedridden wife." (Caty spent many years as an invalid prior to her death in 1852.) But family records provide an explanation neither of the "appliance" nor of the cause of her invalidism.[6]

While the bonnet industry grew, Johnson became more involved in civic affairs. He was town clerk from 1803 through 1821, treasurer for one year, and selectman for three years. In 1842 he was elected as a representative to the state legislature. In his spare time, Johnson also pursued musical interests. He and Caty sang in their church choir for more than thirty years. He led the basses in a chorus of townspeople in a special July 4 celebration in 1840, even though he was nearly seventy-three years old. He played the bass viol, sometimes in public; for instance, in 1836 he played to assist singing during installation of a new minister at his church.[7] Johnson's seemingly inexhaustible energy, ingenuity, and zest for life (even in his old age) set examples that his son Lowell copied and surpassed in his own long, active life.

Little is known concerning Lowell's boyhood experiences. He grew up around educated people and, because his parents were in fairly comfortable circumstances, he had the freedom to pursue his natural inclination—music. He also spent many hours helping in the dry goods store, gaining experience in dealing with people. He undoubtedly participated in the games and recreational activities of Medfield young people. In a letter to his friend Mercy Prentiss Davis years later, he recalled going to a pasture with Tom Prentiss where there was "good frog catching," but he also spoke of chores, such as cows to be brought home and horses to be cared for. Once when left alone to tend the store, young Mason was interrupted by a friend who invited him along on an excursion to the woods. Forgetting his responsibility, Lowell locked the door and went along with the key in his pocket. His father's reaction is not recorded, but it can easily be imagined.

A more serious episode occurred one hot summer day when Lowell was sixteen. Returning from an errand for his father, he refreshed himself by swimming in the Charles River. He ran into difficulties, nearly drowned, but was rescued by two young boys whose quick thinking and courage won the community's acclaim.[8]

In discussing his early years, Lowell said that he had spent twenty years "doing nothing save playing upon all manner of instruments that came within my reach."[9] As a teenager, he taught his first singing school at Athol, Massachusetts, a town about forty-five miles from Medfield. Recalling the experience years later (1864) in a letter to Mrs. Daniel Bliss, daughter of one of his pupils at Athol, he called the clarinet "my instrument." But he was also at ease playing the violin, cello, flute, piano, and organ, even as a teenager.

By age twenty, Lowell had studied music with several local teachers, the most important of whom was Amos Albee, born in Medfield in 1772. Albee was a member of the Norfolk Musical Society active in Medfield and nearby Dedham. In 1805 he published *The Norfolk Collection of Sacred Harmony*, a tunebook of forty-eight oblong pages. Lowell's copy of this book bears this inscription in his own penmanship: "This is the Book used at the first singing-school I ever attended which was taught by Amos Albee, the compiler. I must have been 13 years old then . . . sixty years have passed away and I am now 73."

Lowell's lifelong respect for Albee prompted such remarks as this one, taken from a letter to his friend, book publisher Melvin Lord in Boston, dated February 9, 1864: "Albee was my first teacher; he was a man 50 years before his time; from him I obtained some of the most valuable books from which I made the H. & H. Coll.—I always esteemed him very highly."[10] Albee must have esteemed Mason highly, too, because Mason apparently absorbed his music lessons with exceptional talent and enthusiasm.

Sometime before 1807 Lowell studied in Dedham with Oliver Shaw (1779–1848), the blind composer-singer of popular psalm tunes and ballads, such as "Mary's Tears," "Sweet Little Ann," and others. So popular were Shaw's songs that he made $1,500 from one alone, namely, "There's Nothing True but Heaven."[11] Shaw settled in Providence, Rhode Island in 1807 and worked as a teacher and organist and as proprietor of a music store. Shaw, an American whose music compared favorably with the imported music popular after 1800, was one of the first and foremost supporters of the "chaste" musical style.[12] His ideas undoubtedly made a deep impression on young Lowell Mason; in fact, Mason later said that he was indebted to him [Shaw] for his start in life, that he owed all to him.[13]

In addition, Lowell learned from his friend and distant relative, Libbeus Smith. Though Smith was a local singing master, it cannot be proved that Lowell ever enrolled in one of Smith's schools. More likely their association was one of friendly, informal contact, as was Mason's association with local violinist James Clark who reputedly welcomed questions Lowell posed.

Lowell probably raised many questions with local musicians, especially when, as a teenager, he agreed to lead a band at Athol. According to one story, Lowell found in his band several instruments he had not learned to play. On the pretext of tuning them, he kept them during the week between rehearsals and learned to play them well enough for his needs as a director. Having found this ploy successful, it is likely he used it more than once.

Lowell's talents found outlets in Medfield also. By age sixteen he led his church choir, an unusually large and capable group for a small, country town. Four years later, he wrote his first composition for this choir, the anthem "Ordination" for the ordination of Dr. Ralph Sanger (1786–1860) as pastor of the Unitarian church in Dover, Massachusetts on September 16, 1812. Lowell took members of his choir to Dover to perform this composition. As a teenager, Mason also played the flute or clarinet in the Medfield band, a group that he led by age eighteen. In short, his "remarkable fondness for music was manifested . . . at an early age, and this passion was directed with care and judgment."[14]

Though talent and interest were apparent, Johnson and Caty Mason did not encourage Lowell to pursue music as a career. Conscientious parents of that time could not encourage children to undertake careers in the arts. The general mood of the times was summed up by Benjamin Franklin who remarked that in America "the invention of a machine or the improvement of an implement is of more importance than a masterpiece by Raphael."[15] Nonetheless, Johnson and Caty Mason encouraged their children to participate in musical activities and to develop their talents as far as possible. Ultimately, three of their sons became music leaders: Lowell, Johnson, and Timothy, the latter two with careers in Louisville, Kentucky and Cincinnati, Ohio, respectively.

While the Masons were raising their children, the new nation was undergoing rapid social and cultural changes, many of them significant in the shaping of American culture. The ferment of those times reached Medfield quickly but quietly from nearby Boston. The changes that affected Lowell's developing personality, as well as those that prepared for his later career in Boston, form the backdrop behind his closely knit, comfortable Medfield associations.

The New England Cultural Environment

When Lowell Mason was growing up, New England's population was spread over a large area with nearly everyone living on farms or in small towns. Even Boston, large in comparison with Medfield, had only 18,038 residents in 1790, according to U.S. Government Census figures. By contemporary accounts, Boston looked much like a typical small town, except for a greater number of private homes, most of which had a woodshed, stable, and garden in the back, often with paths between buildings and nearby houses.

Boston was prospering, as were New England and the new nation in general. The Revolutionary War had left no lasting effect on commerce and industry in Boston; shipping and manufacturing were thriving. But at the same time, this quasi-pastoral community was undergoing marked change and cultural ferment, a part of which grew from commercial dealings with other cultures and a part of which was indigenous.

Those who lived in or near Boston felt some discomfort at the birth of that culturally rich period roughly contemporaneous with Lowell Mason's life. For one thing, the Unitarian-Universalist movements challenged New England theology. The Boston-based new theology reached Medfield in the early years of the nineteenth century. The parish church of which the Johnson Masons were a part became predominantly Unitarian, but a number of members, including the Masons, broke away and formed a second congregation that was emphatically orthodox, i.e., Trinitarian in theology. Lowell did not attend this second church because by that time he had moved away from Medfield permanently.

Adding to the religious fervor of the times were the revival meetings that peaked in the early decades of the century. Beginning in New England, the revival movement that came to be called another "Great Awakening" moved steadily south and west. This "awakening," like the major revivals of the 1700s, spawned new Protestant sects and with them new musical practices and styles. Meanwhile, in New England religious controversy continued, and with it, spirited debates over new types of church music and hymnody.

Quickening cultural interest in New England around 1800 took other forms as well. Artists were beginning to find opportunities in America and to accept the challenges of the new environment. Whereas Revolutionary War era painters Benjamin West (1738-1820) and John Singleton Copley (1737-1815) had built their careers in England, the leading artist of the next generation, Washington Allston (1779-1843) returned to America at age thirty-six, saying that artists "owe something to [their] country when she is disposed to foster...[their] talents."[16]

As part of this heightened cultural interest, new music societies appeared, most of them made up of amateurs under semiprofessional leadership. These groups often proposed to improve some aspect of music in their communities. They were almost always choral groups and almost certainly presented public concerts. In many cases, they also issued collections of music.

One example following this general pattern was the Massachusetts Musical Society, formed in 1807 by fifteen people who wanted to improve the performance of sacred music. This group was a precursor of the famous Boston Handel and Haydn Society, one of a few pioneering music societies to have survived to the present day. Though the Massachusetts Musical Society dissolved within three years, it symbolized growing interest in church music reform.

The Boston Handel and Haydn Society grew directly from the work of an exceptional church choir at the Park Street Church at Park and Tremont Streets, Boston. The group consisted of about fifty singers. Their accompaniment was flute, bassoon, and cello because there was no organ in the church at that time. Keyboard instruments existed in some churches, of course, but, according to a contemporary account, in all of Boston around 1810 to 1815 (a community of at least six thousand families) no more than fifty pianos could have been found; even fewer organs existed there at the time.

A Peace Jubilee celebrating the end of the War of 1812 included a performance by this choir. When reviewing the jubilee, critics urged more public performances by this and comparable music groups. The choir had two members who became noted musicians: Jonas Chickering, founder of the first major American piano manufacturing company in 1823, and H. K. Oliver, composer best known for a hymn tune named Federal Street. Oliver wrote admiringly of the Park Street Church choir's rendering of church music, its "ignoring the prevalent fuguing tunes [such as those by Billings and other eighteenth-century Americans]... and giving the more appropriate and correct hymn-tunes and anthems of the best English composers."[17]

On March 15, 1815, Gottlieb Graupner, Asa Peabody, and Thomas Webb (all Bostonians) sent out circulars, inviting the choir members and others to join a group to form "a correct taste in Sacred Musick [*sic*]."[18] About forty people responded. On April 20, 1815, the group ratified a formal constitution under the name "The Boston Handel and Haydn Society." Most of these early members were musical amateurs who worked as bankers, lawyers, construction workers, teachers, and merchants.

On December 25, 1815, the new organization presented excerpts of Handel's works and Part I of Haydn's *Creation* to an audience of 945 people. Previous performances of oratorio selections had been under the aegis of the leading church musicians, such as Dr. George K. Jackson of Boston's Brattle Square Church, but such performances were occasional, whereas the Handel and Haydn Society provided regular performances.

Other musical organizations, singing societies especially, sprang up in communities large and small. Many of these groups were short-lived; others merged into succeeding groups. Their existence, along with the upsurge of singing schools and church choirs around 1800, demonstrated that many people, dissatisfied with church music as it was, welcomed steps promising improvement. Reforms were widely discussed, and reform movements quickened interest in secular as well as sacred music. This interest was not only conducive to the forming of music societies, but also led to public support for widespread music instruction on a regular basis, specifically, music in the public schools.

Heightened musical interest also inspired a dramatic increase in the production of tunebooks, typically oblong books with vocal music in three or four parts, unaccompanied but provided with figured bass notation. America surpassed England and Europe in the volume of such publications. Over two hundred separate books of sacred music appeared between 1800 and 1838, many of them compiled and promoted by musical societies as money-making ventures. Though few of these books made great amounts of money, they were seldom financial losses.

Lowell Mason absorbed these religious and cultural currents during his early years. The close relationships between religion and music central to his thinking grew out of the cultural climate in general and from his Boston associations during the winter of 1810-11 in particular.

A young minister named Joseph Stevens Buckminster (1784–1812) had moved to Boston to serve the Brattle Square Church in 1805. He soon developed an enthusiastic following as a brilliant orator. More important to Mason was Buckminster's interest in music; Buckminster, who played the flute, cello, violin, and organ, yearned to improve music in his church. To that end, he prepared a hymn and psalm tunebook for his congregation with congregational singing in mind. Published in 1810, its official title was *LXXX Psalm and Hymn Tunes for Public Worship,* but it became known as *The Brattle Square Collection.*

Well-intentioned though they were, Buckminster's efforts were but one more example of a sincere yet frustrated attempt to improve music in the churches. Music had hit a low point around 1800 in American churches. Congregational singing, for centuries the heart of Protestant church music, had degenerated because few churchgoers could read music and consequently the majority knew—at most—only a few tunes by rote. And often they had learned those few tunes imperfectly, having heard only faltering renditions or free improvisations. Congregations with organs were somewhat better off, provided an able organist could be found and the instrument could be kept in repair. Choirs had too few singers with reading ability and too few directors with adequate skills. Itinerant singing school teachers (often amateurs both as teachers and as musicians) taught with widely varying, but usually limited success. All things considered, it is no wonder that both clergy and laymen called for reform, issued books, and established organizations dedicated to improving church music.

Young Mr. Buckminster, then, was not unusual except that he had more musical background than some would-be reformers. Lowell Mason, who had been introduced to Buckminster by their mutual friend Hannah Adams, probably found his ideas about church music rather strange. The young man from Medfield had never heard congregational singing in his youth and had known mostly weak, ineffectual choirs.

Little is known about Mason's other associations and activities in Boston that winter. It is not even certain how long he stayed in the city. He did have at least two Medfield friends in school nearby, namely, Thomas Prentiss, Jr. and Joseph Allen, both of whom were graduated from Harvard in 1811. But by graduation time that spring, Lowell had resumed his Medfield residence; records show that he traveled to Cambridge with a party of townspeople for the commencement exercises.

By about this time, many of Mason's friends and associates launched their careers. For instance, Tom Prentiss taught for several years after graduation, then became a minister in 1814. Tragedy followed him, however, and after a few years' service to the Second Congregational Society, Charlestown, Massachusetts (a Unitarian group), he died of typhus fever in October 1817.

Though he was reaching maturity, Mason was unsettled as to his goals. He had many interests, reflecting his varied experiences in Medfield. Despite his music experiences, he did not plan to become a professional musician; despite his business experience in the family store, he had no enthusiasm for a future in business. After his return from Boston, Lowell could see that Medfield offered few opportunities for him and that his future career, whatever it might be, would have to be found elsewhere.

The Move to Savannah, Georgia

Lowell Mason's uncertainty about his future career made his parents uneasy; they feared their son might disregard the difficulties and pursue music. In 1812, when Johnson Mason learned that two of Lowell's friends planned to go to Savannah, Georgia to find work, he encouraged Lowell to go along, assuming the young man would apply himself there to something practical.

One of these friends, a Mr. Boswell, undertook the move with greater expectations than actually materialized. The other, a Mr. Hall, either lacked definite plans for working in Georgia or changed his plans during the trip, for he traveled only as far as Fayetteville, North Carolina, where he remained to teach music. Lowell's attitudes in anticipation of his move to Georgia are not recorded, but a detailed letter he wrote soon after his arrival suggests a reserved enjoyment of his trip and excitement in finding a new home.

The city of Savannah, one of the most inviting of American cities for a newcomer, offered many attractions, beginning with its beauty. Neat, pale yellow brick houses lined the sidewalks. Many homes were surrounded by walled gardens in which giant live oaks, garlanded with Spanish moss, provided shade. The fragrance of flowers perfumed the wide, tree-lined streets. Pioneer Governor James Edward Oglethorpe (1696-1785), one of Savannah's founders, had ensured that many plots of land were reserved for parks. In these areas magnolias, azaleas, palmettos, and other semitropical vegetation have flourished to this day.[19]

Though the city had suffered much during the Revolutionary War, damages were almost entirely repaired by 1800. The city's trade had not only resumed, but surpassed previous levels. Census figures in 1810 show only a modest population of 5,195 persons, but Savannah was important beyond its numbers as a commercial center. In 1805 it shipped to Liverpool 27,600 bales of cotton, a full quarter of the American crop. After the War of 1812, both the cotton plantations and the shipping industries were booming, so that by 1826, for instance, Savannah shipped 190,000 bales of cotton. It was unquestionably one of the nation's most important seaports.[20]

Savannah's eminence in religious affairs may also have attracted newcomers; certainly that aspect of Savannah's history appealed to Lowell Mason. Governor Oglethorpe had persuaded John Wesley (1703–1791) to move to Georgia, tend the spiritual needs of the colonists there, and spread the gospel to the Indians. Charles Wesley (1707-1788), John's brother, accompanied John to Georgia as the governor's secretary, but became unhappy and returned to England within a few months.

As it turned out, the two most notable aspects of John Wesley's experience had little to do with his original objectives. For one thing, in Savannah, John Wesley established the first Protestant Sunday school in the world in 1736. For another, the trip to America had important ramifications: en route to the New World, Wesley met emigrant Moravians whose ideas about theology and music colored all of the Wesleys' subsequent thinking, thereby affecting the entire Methodist movement. Though a sincere and godly man, John Wesley apparently did not get along well with either his colonial parishioners or the Indians. After two years of exasperating difficulties, he returned to England.

During his years in Savannah, Wesley invited a young English evangelist named George Whitefield (1714-1770) to spend three months there. Whitefield accepted and launched his dynamic American ministry in Savannah. This ministry invigorated American congregations in subsequent years and was partially responsible for the religious stirrings around 1800. A powerful evangelist, Whitefield visited America seven times between 1739 and 1769. He worked all across the land, often preaching forty hours per week. While in Savannah, Whitefield preached at the Independent Presbyterian Church, the congregation that was to be of importance years later to Lowell Mason.

It has been claimed that the lure of opportunity, rather than the city's attractions, drew Lowell Mason to Savannah. Whether or not that is true, Savannah did offer pleasant, refreshingly new surroundings for the young New Englander. Furthermore, the city was culturally alive with musical and other artistic activities. Operas and oratorios were presented occasionally. Societies of local amateur musicians, such as the Old Hundred and the Apollonian, flourished in Savannah, just as did similar groups in New England.

Precisely what prompted Mason's move to Savannah is impossible to ascertain. The common contention that he went there to work in a bank has been disproved, though he held a bank position during the latter part of his stay there. Writing to a former associate, Mr. B. Mallon of Atlanta on September 20, 1869, Lowell recalled, "I was for seven or eight years a clerk in the Planter's Bank, in Savannah, during the latter part of which time—Mr. Geo. W. Anderson was President [Anderson took that post January 7, 1824]. Previous to that time I was for a few years in the dry goods business." It appears that Mason had no particular kind of work in mind and no job lined up in advance of his arrival in Georgia.

Johnson Mason revealed his fatherly thinking in a personal letter written just before Lowell's move to Georgia. It reflects a warm, open father-son relationship and reveals some of the Masons' attitudes and values:

Medfield, November 22, 1812

My Son As you are about seting out on a long & I fear furteagueing journey I cannot refrain from making a few observations to you by way of advice before your departure—Your abilities and address in many particulars I think sufficient to recomend you (at least) to the second class in society the prinsipal indowments in which I think you defisient in (as it respects the present life) is *Prudence and Economy* in the first of these particulars I should not only include a prudential care of your own property but a strict Assiduity and carefull attention in whatever you may be called on to transact for others—by Economy I do not mean to be understood selfisness but a mediom between extravigence and meanness which are both detestable in the minds of the wise and good. If it should please a kind Providence to prosper you in any undertaking so that you should be accumulating a small property to your self you will find plenty of Wolves in Sheaps Clothing to devower it if by inticing flattery, or fals statements it can be obtained by especially in the cience of Music for that will probably make your circile of acquaintance larger in a short space of time so there will not be that chance to distinguish the real characters of your acquaintance that there would be in some other occupations where you would be more deliberate and longer in forming connections. In a word you cannot be too cautious about joining parties and I should recommend you to evade them as much as possable—You will find the manners of the People very different at the Southward from what it is here or in New York I expect Gaming and Sabbath Braking are among the many bad practices which you will find prevalent in Georgia and the Southern States which I hope by the care of a kind Providence you will be able to withstand also numerious other Vices which it is not necessary to enumerate—If you should not meet with success at your journey's end which you expect (which I am fearfull may be the case) you ought not to dispond but maintain steady habbits and have A particular eye to devine providence in all you do.

November 25. I hope there will be some opening here next Spring which will be to your advantage and mine If so I shall inform you but if things should not prove more favourable in the Spring than they are now should not advise you by any means to stay at the Southward dureing Summer shall write you as soon as I can be informed of your Arrival in Savannah—wish you to write me without fail from New York and Alexandria give my respects to Mr. Kellogg and request Mr. D. Metcalf to give you the proceeds of the last Box of Bonnets if they are sold—I am with esteem your

Affectionate father,
Johnson Mason

Mr. Metcalf will give you all the proceeds of my Bonnets except 50 Dollars which I owe Mr. Baxter of Boston.

The journey began on Friday, November 27, 1812 and was completed on Thursday, January 21, 1813, a total of fifty-five days. By Lowell's calculations, the trip covered 1088 miles. A typical day's travel consisted of about twenty-five miles. The mode of transportation was, presumably, horse-drawn wagon. That the journey was more expensive than anticipated is evident from his references to additional money that his father forwarded along the way.

Immediately upon arriving in Savannah, Lowell wrote his parents a lengthy description of the trip. The letter provides not only a detailed itinerary, but also insights into his personality and habits: he was impressed with historical sites; he showed concern for people he met along the way; he recorded his faithful church attendance. The spelling and punctuation preserve the flavor of the original and indicate his level of education in 1812–13, thus providing a reference point for comparison with his later writing:

Savannah January 21, 1813
Thursday

Dear Parents I am at length able to inform you of my arrival this day at this place after an unpleasant, agreeable, fatiguing, fine, long, tedious journey of fifty five days. Having left you on Friday 27th Nov. 1812—we passed through Medway and Belingham to Mendon 17 miles. We staid the night with Mr. Jackson. Saturday 28th. Passed through Uxbridge and Douglass to Thompson in the state of Conecticut 21 miles. Sunday 29th. Went to meeting & heard Rev. Daniel Dow—a high calvinist. Monday 30th. Through Pomfret & Ashford to Mansfield 23 miles. Tuesday Dec. 1st. Through Coventry, Bolton and East Hartford to the city of Hartford 23 miles. Wednesday 2nd. Through Weathersfield and Berlin to Marridon 17 miles. Thursday 3rd. Through Walingford, Hamden and North Haven to the city of New Haven 17 Miles. Friday 4th. We remained at N. Haven on account of rain. Saturday 5th. Through Milford and Stratford to Bridgeport 18 miles. Sunday 6th. Went to meeting. Monday 7th. Through Middlesex, Sokunteek, Norwalk, Stamford, Greenwich, Rye, to Mamaroneck in the State of New York 32 miles. Tuesday 8th. Through New Rochel, East Chester, West Chester, Harleim, to the city of New York 22 miles. 9th and 10th we staid in New York. Friday 11th. Crossed Hudsons river in a steam boat and passed through Powlershook in the State of New Jersey—Barbadoes, Elizabethtown, Bridgetown, Woodbridge to the city of New Brunswick the Capital of New Jersey, 32 miles. Saturday 12th. From New Brunswick to Trenton 27 miles. Here we saw the ground on which the famous Battle was fought in the revolutionary war. Sunday 13th. Crossed Trenton bridge across the Delaware river & passed through Morrisville & Bristol to the city of Philadelphia in the State of Pennsylvania 30 miles. Evening went to church. Monday 14th. Remain in Philadelphia. Tuesday 15th. Crossed the Schuylkill—passed through Darby, Ridley, Chester, to the city of Wilmington the principal place in the State of Delaware. Bristol, Stanford, Cristiania to Elktown 36 miles. Wednesday 16th. North East, Charlestown, Crossed the Susquehannah to Havre de Grace 31 miles. As we were ascending a very steep hill in North East Town Mr. Bosworth's Trunk fell out unperceived by us. We proceeded about three quarters of a mile before we discovered our loss—and we had met only one Negro—we knew it must have fell out at the hill—accordingly we turned about and drove immediately to the place—but behold the trunk was gone—there were two houses in sight—we enquired at both of them but without effect—We therefore concluded that the Negro we had met must have hid it in the woods—which were on all sides of us. Mr. Bosworth took the Pistol, Mr. Hall a club & myself a Dagger and we went in different directions in the woods—after about two hours search I found it in a Ditch covered up with leaves—but no negro—we were in a great hurry or we should have hid ourselves and taken him when he came after it—Thursday 17th. Through Bush and Abbington to the city of Baltimore in the State of Maryland 36 miles. Friday 18th. Remained in Baltimore—went to see the remains of the house that the Federalists defended in Charles Street against the fury of a Democratic mob, and the spot where Genl Lingan was barbarously murdered. Saturday 19th. Through Blensburgh to the City of Washington in the District of Columbia—the capitol of the U. States. Sunday 20th. At Washington. Monday 21st. Through Georgetown, crossed the Potomac river, through Alexandria, by Mount Vernon to Colchester in the State of Virginia 25 miles. At Mount Vernon we saw the seat of Genl Washington which is beautiful beyond any description I can give—it is on a high piece of ground on the banks of the Potomac. The tomb of the American hero stands under a cluster of cedars about one hundred yards from the house. There is no monument of any description whatever—it is 8 miles from Alexandria and 16 from Washington city. William Lee a black man, servant of Genl Washington in the American army is yet living. The seat is now occupied by Judge Bushrod Washington. Tuesday 22nd. Through Dumfries and Aqua to Stafford 25 miles. Wednesday 23rd. Falmouth, crossed the Rappahannock to Bowling Green 31 m. Thursday 24th. Through Hanover to [illegible] 31 miles. Friday 25th. Passed through no town today untill we arrived at the city of Richmond 26 miles. Here we saw the ruins of the Theatre that was burnt in Decr. 1811. A Church is now building on the spot—and directly underneath it is the tomb of about 60 of the unfortunate persons who perished at that time. Saturday 26th. Through Petersburgh 26 miles, Sunday 27th. (no town to-day) 31 miles. Monday 28th. Crossed the Roanoke into the State of North Carolina 24 miles. Tuesday 29th. Went a-hunting. Wednesday 30th. Through Warrenton 24 miles. Thursday 31st. Through Louisburg 31 miles. Friday January 1st 1813. Through the city of Raleigh the capitol of North Carolina 39 miles. Saturday 2nd. To Averysborough 18 miles. Sunday 3rd. To Fayetteville 25 miles. Here Mr. Hall concluded to stay and teach musick we left him on Monday 4th. (no town today) 23 miles. Tuesday 5th (no town) 26 miles. Wednesay 6th. Hunting deer. Thursday 7th (No Town) passed into the State of South Carolina. 15 miles. Friday 8th. Crossed Pede river. Passed through Greenville over Long Bluff 20 miles. Saturday 9th (No Town) 23 miles. Sunday 10th to Stateburgh on the high hills of Santee 15 miles, 11th and 12th. Staid at Stateburgh. Wednesday 13th. Crossed the Lakes [?], the Congree and Wateree rivers and went to Belle Ville 23 miles. 14th. Staid at Belle Ville on the account of rain. Friday 15th. To Orangeburgh 25 miles. Here we found Mr. Cummins. 16th. Staid with Mr. Cummins. Sunday 17th. Went 23 miles (No Town). Monday 18th. Went 30 miles—through water so deep that it came into the waggon. Tuesday 19th. Went 33 miles (no town, house, or any thing else). Wednesday 20th. Crossed Savannah river at the Two Sisters ferry—went 27 miles. Thursday 21st. Arrived at Savannah 16 miles.

The whole distance if I have added it right is one thousand and eightyeight miles. Although we have generally found good entertainment on the road—yet we have several times put up at a little log house where there was but one room, a large family of children and fifteen or twenty negroes—this was not altogether comfortable. Our horses have held out remarkably well and are in good order at present. I board at a very good house kept by Mrs. Battey. Mr. B. and myself occupy three rooms—one apiece for a bed and one between us for musick. I have called on Doc. Kollock [pastor of the Independent Presbyterian Church]—who is an extremely fine man. He thinks I shall meet with encouragement. I find however that my prospects are materially different from what I expected by Mr. Bosworths account—if I make two hundred dollars in all I shall think I do well—indeed I have offered to let myself for $150 to Mr. B. and he will not give it. But it is certain I must make 2 or 300 before I can return home. I wrote to you from New York and informed you of the money I had received there on your account. When we got to Alexandria we found we should be deficient and I got $20 of Mr. Metcalf which I shall consider myself indebted to you for. I shall expect to receive a letter from you as soon as this reaches you [illegible] write on one sheet to prevent postage. I hope by the time I write you again I can give you a more pleasant account of my business.

It is very warm here—so as to be some days quite uncomfortable—and amongst imprudent people it is unhealthy (there has a number died within a few days after having been sick but two or three days) I suppose there is about 8 to 10 die weekly. I shall not think of staying in the city next summer if I do not come home—but shall probably return as far as some part of South or North Carolina. From New York we shipped the guns by Water and they arrived here in four days. Mr. Bosworth is willing to acknowledge now that it would have been much better if we had come by Water.

N. Underwood is at No. 30 North 2nd St. Philadelphia—he said he would attend to business you wished him to do.—I wrote to Mr. Hill from Washington and requested him to give you this information. Lucretia will remember me to all my young friends and thank Mary Prentiss for the Poem.

Goodbye for the present
   L. Mason[21]

A New Life in Savannah

Upon arrival in Savannah, Lowell Mason chose to join the Independent Presbyterian Church. Founded in 1755, it was thriving under the leadership of Henry Kollock, mentioned in Lowell's letter to his parents. Like many of the clergy with whom Mason became associated, Kollock was well educated and capable. After graduation from the College of New Jersey (now Princeton University) at age sixteen, Kollock remained for further study in French and theology. Just before his move to Savannah in 1806, he was a theology professor at the College of New Jersey and the recipient of an honorary Doctor of Divinity degree from Harvard.

Edward Stebbins, chairman of the board of trustees at the church, also played an important role in Mason's life. Stebbins, another native of Massachusetts, was twenty-eight years older than Mason. He employed the young man in his dry goods store and, after a few years, made him a partner. The January 21, 1817 issue of the *Savannah Gazette* carried the first advertisement for the firm of Stebbins & Mason. It announced that the store had just received, among other things, boxes of straw bonnets and three pianofortes—both indicating the Mason influence. Subsequent ads point to a wide range of merchandise: Irish linens, French silks and ribbons, velvet "indispensables" with gilt clasps, silk nets for the head, buckskin and beaver fleecy-lined gloves, ostrich and down feathers, artificial flowers, pianos, lamb's wool hose for men.[22]

From all indications, Stebbins & Mason prospered. The firm ran regular ads, sometimes sizable ones, in contemporary newspapers. But in 1819 or 1820, Stebbins died, and Mason went to work at the Planter's Bank as a clerk. Little is known about his responsibilities there, but upon his resignation in 1827, President George W. Anderson wrote a letter commending his "ability, industry, and faithfulness."

Masons's leadership in the Independent Presbyterian Church in Savannah is but one example of lifelong devotion to his church. Confusion has surrounded his denominational affiliation: he has been regarded as either a Congregationalist or a Presbyterian. The Savannah church was in accord with Presbyterian doctrine but followed the congregational (autonomous) plan of organization. Mason, with his rigorous Calvinistic background and his preference for the congregational approach, felt completely at home at the Independent Presbyterian Church.

More important than denominational labels were Mason's evangelicalism and his preference for simple, straightforward preaching and nonliturgical services. According to his own accounts, young Mason (who had been a faithful churchgoer all his life) reached a crisis point in his religious faith and underwent an emotional experience which he regarded as his "conversion." As a climax, in a diary entry for October 20, 1814, he wrote, "I have been looking over this book and reflecting upon my journey from Mass. to Georgia. I give up myself to God, resting my soul on the merit of Jesus for Salvation. O receive me my blessed Saviour for in this is my hope, my only hope."[23] Such piety and sentimentality were not uncommon among believers at the time, and certainly not uncommon in Mason's personal writings.

By 1804 the church operated a Sunday school as part of its program. Children of the congregation met in the basement of the Chatham Academy building until about 1807. Records show that in December 1815 a new school was organized for all children regardless of their religious affiliations. Mason helped plan the new school. The first Sunday seven students, all boys, attended. Apparently the classes were for white children only. According to information published by the church in 1926, the first Negro Sunday shool in North America was started in 1826 by that church through the initiative of Lowell Mason, then Sunday school superintendent.

The school established in 1815 was the only such school in Savannah at the time. Mason was elected superintendent from the beginning and held the post almost continuously until he left Savannah in 1827. To assist the school and its staff, he formed in November 1816 an organization called the Savannah Sunday School Union Society. Under the auspices of this organization, the school moved to the Chatham Academy building. Meanwhile, Mason extended his own influence and that of the school through writings in circulars and periodic reports.

This organizing, leading, and writing foreshadowed Mason's later work. Here in Savannah, on a small scale, Mason was testing his ideas and leadership abilities. After a modest start, his work grew steadily with increased enrollments and objectives. By 1817 the superintendent's report indicated that 120 pupils had been enrolled in the several classes. In addition to moral and religious precepts, the children were learning reading and spelling.

The Sunday school met several needs because when it was first established, there was no public school in Savannah. When the first public school was opened in 1817, Mason was one of its several advocates; he also distributed information about it to the Sunday school students. At the same time, he continued to promote the Sunday school itself. Unabashed appeals for community support were necessary because the Savannah Sunday school, like its English prototype, reached destitute children and helped them in many ways besides offering religious and other instruction. A women's group called The Industrious Circle provided clothing for needy children to enable them to attend the Sunday school, church services, and (after 1817) the public school. Community support also took the form of some funding from the Savannah city council.

Records of the Sunday school confirm Superintendent Mason's methodical, imaginative, and tireless pursuit of success. One example of his ingenuity was his "Black Book Plan" for handling discipline. A student's name was recorded in Mason's black book when he committed such offenses as swearing, stealing, fighting, telling lies, disobeying authorities, or being absent on three successive Sundays without good reason. The student whose name was entered into the book could be pardoned by his teacher with the consent of the superintendent, but upon receiving three unexcused offenses, was expelled. The book was open to the inspection of students, teachers, and visitors. Those whose names were listed could not use the library, a private collection containing at least 110 volumes by the end of 1818. The Black Book Plan apparently kept discipline problems to a minimum.

Management—planning, organizing, and superintending details—was Mason's forte. In addition to organizing the schools and the teachers' association, he helped establish the Savannah Missionary Society in 1818 to reach other parts of Georgia with religious instruction. The acting secretary at the first meeting, he was elected secretary thereafter.

It has been stated that Mason's "soul was in this work his whole life...and...at a meeting held under its auspices...his tune for Bishop Heber's grand missionary hymn ["From Greenland's Icy Mountains"] was first used."[24] The music was composed in 1824. According to family history, a young woman named Mary Wallace Howard, a recent immigrant from England, brought the poem to Lowell's attention. As an assistant in the Sunday school and a soprano soloist at the Independent Presbyterian Church, she knew him well. Supposedly she sent an errand boy to the Planter's Bank, hoping that Mason could take time to suggest appropriate music for the poem. Within a half-hour, the boy returned with the music Mason had composed on the spot. It was first written as a soprano solo, and when first sung at the church, Miss Howard was the soloist.[25]

In addition to organizations he helped found, Mason took an active part in several existing charitable groups. One of these was the Georgia Bible Society, founded in Savannah in 1810, just two years after the first such society was formed in Philadelphia and six years before the American Bible Society was formed in New York. In this respect, as in others, Savannah was in the forefront of contemporary movements. Mason also belonged to the Savannah Religious Tract Society and the Union Society (organized in 1750 as the St. George Society) which provided care for orphaned boys. Published notices indicate that Mason acted as secretary for the latter group. And as a representative of the Union Society, he greeted General Lafayette during his visit to Savannah.[26]

During all his years in Savannah, Mason sought supplemental income. He was paid for his work with the Union Society, but his other church and charitable work was unpaid service. He said years later that he had busied himself where he could in order to have an honest income, adding that he had arrived in Savannah with but ten dollars to his name. The sense of financial uncertainty he felt as a newcomer to Georgia persisted in spite of his success at Stebbins & Mason and his steady job at the bank. Years later, in reflecting on the Georgia years, he said that he had "eked out a living" by the various jobs he took.[27]

One of his part-time salaried jobs was with the Savannah Public Library. Though ordinarily efficient, apparently Mason had some lapses as indicated by newspaper notices begging borrowers to return books that appeared to be missing or were borrowed "some time since."[28]

Military training and drill were required of every able man at this time in the country's history, and Mason participated in two military organizations in Savannah. One was the Third Company of the Sixth Battalion, a group that fined him five dollars at one point because he defaulted on a parade appearance. The other group was the Savannah Fencibles, identified by a scholar of military history as one of the independent military companies to which the more prominent men of the city belonged. Some notices of the Fencibles' activities appeared with Lowell's signature as sergeant.[29]

Mason also served on the board of health after appointment as the Brown Ward representative on April 9, 1823. Called for jury duty in 1824, he defaulted and was fined three dollars unless he could file "sufficient excuse, on oath, on or before the next term." It is not known whether he filed his excuse or paid the fine.[30]

Near the end of his years in Savannah, Mason ventured in yet another direction: the establishment of a new, independent church. He and three other petitioners from the Independent Presbyterian Church were dismissed in good standing and, with thirteen other people, became charter members of the First Presbyterian Church in Savannah. Mason was one of the first three elders, and he assumed charge of the music for both the Sunday school and the church.

His close friend Joseph C. Cumming (1790-1846) was made Sunday school superintendent. Cumming, "a commission merchant from about 1817," had been an elder in the Independent Presbyterian Church,[31] where he and Mason had met. The Mason-Cumming friendship lasted for years. Indeed, friendships formed in Savannah held a special place in Mason's affection ever after as shown by references in his journals and letters.

Mason's affiliation with the new church lasted only a few weeks, for in July 1827, he moved to Boston. That move marked the end of eking out an existence by working at miscellaneous odd jobs. His involvement with charitable organizations had passed its peak, and understandably so, for his music career was then well under way.

Lowell Mason in His Early Years, c. 1815
(Used by courtesy of Elizabeth Mason Ginnel, a great-
granddaughter of Lowell Mason)

2

Early Manhood

Lowell and Abigail

Lowell Mason was not only able and hard-working; he was also personable. Stocky and just below average height, he carried himself with poise and dignity. His thick brown hair fell loosely backward from his brow; even in his old age, he had thick, heavy hair. His blue eyes were wide set; he wore a short beard during part of his adult life. By all accounts, he was a handsome man.

Soft-spoken by nature, Lowell rarely laughed loudly but often laughed heartily. He had firm opinions and made them known. Sometimes he became irritated over trifles, in the manner peculiar to those who demand much from themselves and will settle for little less than perfection from others. He based his views upon the highest ideals he knew, then persisted wholeheartedly with little or no question as to his "rightness" in procedures, tastes, and attitudes. He was sometimes viewed as supremely self-confident, other times as blindly pigheaded. Fortunately his strong will was tempered with sound judgment and personal charm.

This charm or personal magnetism helped him make friends easily and keep them. Combined with a genuine devotion to children, this personal attractiveness made him one of the great teachers of his time. It enabled him to influence his contemporaries so as to leave a lasting stamp on American music for generations.

In early manhood, Lowell's charm served more immediate ends. He developed close associations in Savannah even though he arrived with no intention of remaining there long. In a letter written to his family on June 8, 1814, after mentioning that he had not intended to stay so long in the South, he added, "Little did I realize that in the short space of two years, my whole acquaintance would be changed. . . . My situation here is very pleasing—much more so than it could be in Medfield—except I would be with my relatives."

Among his pleasing relationships was his friendship with Mr. and Mrs. Phineas Miller, themselves native New Englanders. When or where they met

Mason is not known, but they offered him a much-needed escape from the summer heat of Savannah that first summer (1813).

On July 3, 1813, Lowell began a fourteen-day voyage down the Georgia coast to St. Mary's in the southeastern corner of the state. He remained there a full month at Dungeness House on Cumberland Island with the Millers. Mrs. Miller (1756–1814), born Catherine Littlefield of New Shoreham, Rhode Island, had married Nathanael Greene, a distinguished general in the Revolutionary Army. Widowed in 1786, she subsequently married Phineas Miller, copartner with Eli Whitney, who invented the cotton gin in 1793. After a month with the Millers, Lowell returned to Savannah, according to his diary "fully restored to health."

Throughout his life, when Mason wrote about his health, he was vague. Apparently he suffered a serious illness that first summer in Savannah. Though the nature of the illness cannot be determined, it seems to have been linked with his religious conversion experience. By the summer of 1814, he assured his family that "I do not feel that fear of the climate that many do," but remembering the ordeal of the previous year, he added, "This summer may terminate my existence here." He concluded by affirming his faith in Providence and the prospect of heaven.

The charm that helped him win friends like the Millers and establish solid business connections in Georgia also helped him win an extraordinary bride. The courtship must have been carried on largely by correspondence, since Lowell seems not to have returned to Massachusetts until 1817. Then, in that year, he spent an undetermined amount of time in Medfield and the town of Westborough about twenty miles away.

On September 3, 1817, in Westborough, Lowell married Abigail Gregory, daughter of Daniel and Hannah Buckminster Gregory. Abigail (Abby), born July 21, 1797, had grown up as an only child after her younger sister Harriet (born in 1801) died at the age of three. Little is known of Abby's early life, but her life as Mrs. Mason is sufficiently recorded to indicate that she shared many of her husband's interests, including music. Lowell and Abby enjoyed a long, happy marriage broken only by his death almost fifty-five years after their wedding.

A descendant of a long line of New Englanders, Abigail could trace her ancestry back to 1640 in Massachusetts. Her father, Daniel Gregory, was a captain in the state militia, but he earned his living as a tavern keeper, as did his father-in-law Thomas Buckminster. The village innkeeper around 1800 was an important person because the inn was both a shelter for travelers and a community social center. No better training ground for a hostess could have been found for Abby than her father's inn; she grew up welcoming all kinds of guests and treating them hospitably.

Lowell remarked years later that in his youth he was as interested in dancing as in music. The Gregory Inn probably attracted him for that reason, as well as for Abby's sake. He may have met her there at one of the dances or dinner parties, or they may have met through his friend, Joseph Stevens Buckminster, Abby's cousin, while Lowell was in Boston the winter of 1810–11. It is also possible that the Buckminsters and the Gregorys were Mason family friends of long standing.

Immediately after the wedding, Lowell and Abby left Westborough for a brief visit in Medfield and then for Georgia. They moved into an apartment at Chatham Academy, a coeducational private school in Savannah with an enrollment of about 800 students. The new, attractive building had one wing that was maintained as a hotel-apartment building. The Masons knew the instructors and administrators at the school, some of whom also lived in the academy building.

Mason picked up ideas on teaching from these associations. He and William Russell, who became the Chatham principal in 1821, learned a great deal from one another during their long friendship. After a short time in the South, Russell moved to Massachusetts to continue his career there. Years later he and Mason collaborated on several projects.

One especially memorable event that occurred at the Mason's Chatham Academy residence was described by Lowell himself years later in a letter to his eldest son:

May 8, 1865

Dear Son,
Well do I remember when on the morning of May 8, 1820, Doctor Lemuel Kollock met me in the hall as he came from the room of your mother in Chatham Academy saying, "You have a fine boy." I soon was admitted to look at a little red infant and to kiss the suffering mother. . . . Beloved son . . . while you live you shall have . . . the unchanging affection of your father.

This child, named Daniel Gregory Mason, held a special place in Lowell's affection for many reasons, and their close relationship was reflected in many ways over the years.

Abby's father died unexpectedly on August 11, 1822. So far as can be determined, she never saw her father again after her wedding and move to Georgia. The death had practical as well as emotional consequences for Lowell, Abby, and their infant son: it occasioned some trips to Massachusetts to help the widowed Hannah Gregory; and it placed another financial responsibility on Lowell, for from that time until her death in 1860, he supported his mother-in-law. According to family records, he also supported Hannah's sister until her death.

Within a month after her father's death, Abby wrote her mother a detailed letter revealing thoughts she and Lowell had concerning their future. She began by speaking of their "natural affection" for the North and their "natural inclination to move there." Then she mentioned their "supreme concern" that Daniel Gregory be given the best possible education, something that "cannot be done here." The crux of the letter is her forthright admission that "the moment we can see any reasonable prospect of obtaining a decent and comfortable support at the North... we will give up the pecuniary advantages of the South—and return with gladness and thankfulness to the hills . . . of Massachusetts."

So far as the "pecuniary advantages" of staying in Savannah were concerned, Abby also commented that money is a "trifling consideration, but it is our duty to exert ourselves for a support and to make use of such means as Providence places in our power for this purpose." No better statement of the Masons' attitudes about money and their sense of vocation could be found than this statement of Abby's. Her letter concluded with an invitation to her mother to join them in Savannah, an invitation that was not accepted.

The following spring Abby went to Westborough to spend a few months with her mother. She took Daniel Gregory (almost three years old) along. There on June 17 (1823) she gave birth to her second son, Lowell Mason, Jr. She remained in Massachusetts until fall, then returned to Savannah with the children.

The Masons shared common attitudes and interests. Like Lowell, Abby was a pioneer in the Sunday school movement. Before her marriage, she and five of her friends set up one of the first such schools in Massachusetts.[1] She taught in Savannah under Lowell's superintendence. She sang soprano in his choirs even while their sons were growing up. Lacking any evidence of Abby's being a soloist, it is assumed that hers was a supportive, not a solo voice. Nevertheless, her assistance with the choirs was important, musically and otherwise. When Lowell opened their home to the choir as a group or to individual members, Abby was a gracious hostess.

Later, after they had left Savannah and settled in Boston, Lowell and Abby had two more sons. When their third son was born January 24, 1829, Abby wanted to name him William Henry because they were so fond of William Henry Cumming, the son of their friend Joseph C. Cumming in Savannah. Lowell objected to the use of a double name, but Abby persisted in her preference. Finally, Lowell "good naturedly but resolutely" said, "Patience, my dear, patience; we'll name *this* son William."[2] Henry Mason was born October 10, 1831, completing the family.

During the busy years that followed, Abby relied on the sound judgment, amiability, and fairness she had learned from her father and on the efficient household management she had learned from her mother. Her cheerful disposition carried her through the long hours when Lowell was occupied with his work and through the weeks and months when he was traveling.

In the rearing of her children, Abby had two important advantages: Lowell's devotion to his family and his ability to provide them a comfortable living. His love of children in general prompted his years of teaching, and his love for his own children (and later, grandchildren) prompted an outpouring of emotion in letters, some of which still exist as a testimony. Abby sometimes chided him for indulging their boys. She told a friend that if she sent one of her sons to bed without supper to discipline him, she was likely to find Lowell later, sitting on the child's bedside, feeding him pieces of pie. She told this story with a smile and gesture as if to say, "Not much use disciplining the boy with Lowell present."[3]

From their first home in a Chatham Academy apartment, the Masons moved through many residences until they reached the quiet elegance of their retirement home at Silver Spring estate, Orange, New Jersey. By any standard, they were prosperous; by the standards of many of their contemporaries, they were wealthy. The family enjoyed better health, more travel, and a wider circle of acquaintances than most people of their time. All these factors added to the satisfactions Lowell and Abigail found in their long, devoted married life together.

Musical Apprenticeship in Georgia

Though Lowell Mason had no intention of becoming a professional musician during his Savannah years, music was a serious avocation and one means of support. From the time of his arrival in that city, Mason participated in its musical life. Johnson Mason's hopes that Lowell would outgrow his musical inclinations were dashed in Savannah. Instead the young man continued his previous music activities and ventured into new ones. In fact, in one of the rare solo performances of his lifetime, he played the cello while singing a second, independent part at a program in one of the local churches, an impressive performance for his audience.

In Savannah, Mason continued studying, composing, and arranging music; he became a church organist and choir director; he organized and led singing schools and concerts; he built lasting friendships with leading musicians; he saw the publication of his first music composition; he compiled and published one of his most successful music collections; he wrote and lectured on music. In all these ways, he laid a firm foundation for the work ahead.

Mason studied figured bass through correspondence with S. P. Taylor, an organist in Boston, but his chief instruction came from Frederick L. Abel whom he hired as a private tutor. A highly skilled German musician, Abel was a nephew of the celebrated Carl Frederick Abel (1722-1787), noted composer and viola da gamba player who had studied under J. S. Bach. In 1817 twenty-two-year-old Frederick Abel emigrated to Savannah where he quickly attained his reputation as a superb musician.

Under Abel's direction, Lowell composed hymn tunes and anthems, many of which were published later. He also began to compile his first music anthology, a book published in 1822 under the sponsorship of the Boston Handel and Haydn Society. Abel never saw his pupil's success, for he died September 23, 1820, at age twenty-six, a victim of yellow fever.[4]

That music anthology grew directly from Mason's work as organist-choir director at the Independent Presbyterian Church. On January 1, 1815, he was hired as choir director. Beginning February 2, 1820, he was officially appointed organist, though he had unofficially held that position for more than five years prior to that date. His salary for those jobs cannot be determined because existing figures conflict. It is known that the church ran into financial difficulties soon after undertaking a building program in 1817. By 1820 the church owed Lowell $650, but he continued without salary, assuming (correctly, as it turned out) that the financial crisis would soon pass. He led the music program there until he left to form a new church in mid-1827.

Through his church work, Mason met a major organ builder, William M. Goodrich of Boston. With his brother Eben and his brother-in-law Thomas Appleton, Goodrich had a virtual monopoly on organ building in Boston from 1805 to 1827. During his career, Goodrich built about 135 organs. By 1817, he was already widely known as a builder. It is not surprising, therefore, that the Savannah congregation turned to him for the $3,500 organ for the new building.

As May 9, 1819, the dedication day, approached, Mason worried that the new organ might not be installed in time for dedication ceremonies. These worries were expressed in a personal letter to John R. Parker in Boston, editor of the music journal *The Euterpeiad:* "The organ loft has long been completed and is waiting. . . . I hope he [Goodrich] will be here this month—if he is not he will hardly get it [the organ] up in April."[5] These worries were well founded, for records of the dedication ceremonies show that only a cappella music was used.

Even so, the ceremonies were extraordinary. By coincidence, the president of the United States, James Monroe, was present. He had come to Savannah to inspect the new steamship *Savannah* which was about to embark upon its twenty-nine day historic voyage to Liverpool, the first Atlantic crossing by a steamship. Contemporary reports of the ceremonies included references to the psalms, hymns, and vocal music, all "peculiarly well adapted to the solemnity of the occasion" and tending to "elevate the soul to sublime and heavenly musings."[6] The long-awaited organ was finally installed in 1820.

Mason's reputation as a church musician grew steadily during these years. As early as 1817, his choir presented public concerts of works by European masters, often arranged by Mason himself. The group's repertoire indicates above-average abilities. Newspapers carried announcements and program notes Mason had written. This program, run in the *Savannah Georgian,* is an example:

A CONCERT OF SACRED MUSIC given this evening May 16, 1826, in the Presbyterian Church, for the benefit of the Savannah Female Asylum. To commence at 8 o'clock.

Part First
> Selections from Haydn's *Creation.*
> [Words and comments about each selection take up almost two columns.]

Part Second
> Psalm Tune London, Dr. Croft. [Words to Psalm 95] This tune which is one of the finest specimens of Metrical Psalmody is introduced on the present occasion, with a view to show what our church music *ought to be,* and what it *might be* did it receive that attention which it deserves as an important part of public worship.
> Recitation and song from Oratorio of the Intercession by M. P. King. Eve's lamentation when driven from Paradise.
> Chorus from Oratorio of Judah by Wm. Gardiner
> Chorus Thou Art Our God—Haydn
> Recitative and Song from Oratorio of Jephtha—Handel
> Quartette from Masses of Mozart
> Chorus—Gloria in excelsis—Mozart.[7]

This particular concert was especially well reviewed. According to an editorial in *The Georgian* on May 18, 1826, "The execution of the difficult pieces . . . was very creditable to the taste and musical acquirements" of the choir and its director.[8]

On another occasion, a similar concert prompted a letter to the editor of *The Georgian,* specifically praising the choir's director:

To Mr. Lowell Mason, under whose superintendence the entertainment was prepared, the community owes many thanks. His distinguished talents in sacred music have been exerted with virtuous zeal and an honorable liberality, to correct the taste and improve the knowledge of all classes of Society . . . and I hope I may not derogate from . . . others when I say that the improved psalmody observable in our churches is chiefly attributable to him.[9]

The concert to which the writer referred was presented on May 21, 1824, and included selections by Chappel, Mozart, Shaw, Kent, Arne, Haydn, Pucitta, and Mason himself. The comment about improved psalmody in the churches referred to more than just the choir's concert work; psalm singing involved congregational and choir participation.

With improved church music in mind and with his earlier experiences as a guide, Mason organized singing schools in Savannah beginning February 8, 1813, less than three weeks after his arrival. At first his main goal may well have been earning part of his living, but after he found steady employment elsewhere, he taught for other reasons. His first class, consisting of thirty members, met at a building owned by Solomon's Lodge, one of America's oldest Masonic fraternities. That was only the start.

Mason continued to organize and lead singing schools in Savannah as late as 1824. This advertisement outlines his procedure:

SACRED MUSIC

A school for the instruction of this delightful and useful accomplishment will commence at Chatham Academy under the direction of L. Mason, on Tuesday evening next.... Particular attention will be paid to the selection of the best music, and to taste and manner of performance. The terms will be $5.00 per quarter, payable in advance. The school is to be open two evenings a week.... Tickets of admission may be had of Mr. Mason at the Academy.[10]

Five years later, his ideas ran along the same lines. In an announcement for a singing school, he asserted that a main objective was "to encourage and cultivate this pleasing accomplishment [vocal music] and to improve an interesting and important part of public worship."[11]

Indeed, Mason's ideas about music crystallized during the Savannah years through his practice, observation, and study of music. By 1819 he had confidence enough to write an article on music that was published March 22, 1819 in the *Columbian Museum and Savannah Daily Gazette*. In this, his first published statement on music, Mason said:

As an art, music depends upon the powers, abilities, and genius of the writer; it cannot be limited, or restricted with any particular rules. The genius, the feelings, and the improved taste of mankind, must regulate every good writer. Like the painter, the sculptor, the architect, and the poet, nature and propriety must direct the effusions of his mind. As a science, it is regulated by measure, harmony, cadence, accent, mode, etc. Science may invent good harmony, agreeable measure, flowing and easy cadence, but genius only can give force and energy to the music.[12]

Nothing new appears in this pronouncement, just as nothing new appears in the few musical compositions Mason published in books and journals during the Savannah years. These compositions included the hymn tunes Andover and Bridgeport first published in *The Euterpeiad* whose editor, John R. Parker, was an early confidant of Mason's. It is not known how Mason and Parker met. Merchant John Rowe Parker has been described as "a wide-ranging observer of the arts of his city, an amateur musician and zealous laborer for the cause of classical music."[13] The full title of Parker's journal reflects that description: *The Euterpeiad: or Musical Intelligencer. Devoted to the Diffusion of Musical Information and Belles Lettres.* The journal, a pioneer publication of its type, served Boston readers from 1820 to 1822.

Mason's association with Thomas Hastings (1784–1872) also dates from the Savannah years, an association especially significant because Hastings' ideas powerfully affected Mason's developing concepts of church music. Hastings, working chiefly in the state of New York, became the leading Presbyterian musician of his day. During the 1820s he edited *The Western Recorder,* a weekly religious journal in which he referred to Lowell Mason as "the distinguished musician in Savannah." He mentioned that he and Mason had corresponded for years. Later Hastings spoke of their relationship in terms of "regular and friendly correspondence on... uniformity in the revised harmonies of our plainest standard tunes," adding that they had also met and discussed these matters.[14] There is no indication of the time or place of the meeting.

During the Savannah years, Lowell thoroughly absorbed Hastings' book, *Dissertation on Musical Taste: Or General Principles of Taste Applied to the Art of Music* (1822). Hastings' aesthetic ideas stimulated Mason's thinking on sacred music, particularly in these respects: that religious music should be distinctly for religious purposes, not concert purposes; that church music should be simple and unaffected, yet impressive; that congregational singing and choir music should be backed up with organ music; that teaching children music is a means of improving church music, and that they should be taught early at home, in church, and in school.

Two major musical accomplishments highlighted Mason's Savannah years: the publication of his first collection of music and the delivery of his first major address on church music. These achievements grew from his desire to improve church music, a desire that sprang from his religious fervor and his musical inclinations. Both the book and the address were issued in Boston with the result that his musicianship was brought sharply to the attention of Bostonians, leading to his return to Massachusetts in 1827. When the time came for that move, he was prepared for the music career ahead.

Title page of the Ninth Edition of *The Boston Handel and Haydn Society Collection of Church Music*, 1830
(Copy owned by the author)

THE

BOSTON HANDEL AND HAYDN SOCIETY

COLLECTION OF CHURCH MUSIC;

BEING A SELECTION OF THE MOST APPROVED

PSALM AND HYMN TUNES, ANTHEMS, SENTENCES, CHANTS, &c.

TOGETHER WITH MANY BEAUTIFUL EXTRACTS FROM THE WORKS OF

HAYDN, MOZART, BEETHOVEN, AND OTHER EMINENT COMPOSERS.

HARMONIZED FOR THREE AND FOUR VOICES, WITH A FIGURED BASE FOR THE ORGAN AND PIANO FORTE

"The long-resounding voice, oft breaking clear,
At solemn pauses, through the swelling Base;
And, as each mingling flame increases each,
In one united ardour rise to Heaven."—*Thomson.*

EDITED BY

LOWELL MASON.

NINTH EDITION, WITH ADDITIONS AND IMPROVEMENTS.

Boston:

PUBLISHED BY RICHARDSON, LORD, AND HOLBROOK, NO. 133, WASHINGTON-STREET.

1830.

3

Commitment to Improved Church Music

The Boston Handel and Haydn Society Collection of Church Music

For about 150 years, the American tunebook served the unique needs and traditions of our expanding musical life. These books, distinctive artifacts of American culture, first appeared in the early 1700s, then multiplied after 1760 as singing schools became widespread. During the first half of the 1800s, tunebooks were manufactured by the thousands.

Lowell Mason's tunebooks followed a pattern that had become traditional by the time of his youth:

1. A lengthy title, detailing the book's contents and purposes.
2. A preface or advertisement setting forth the editor's or publisher's ideas concerning the contents of the book or its music in a broader context.
3. A step-by-step primer in music reading, often with specific instructions on singing. Vocal exercises and practice pieces were sometimes included.
4. Psalm and hymn tunes, partly original and partly borrowed, newly arranged from works of the compiler's favorite composers. Sources were sometimes credited, but often they were not. By modern standards, plagiarism ran rampant.
5. A few, longer, more complex compositions, again, partly original and partly borrowed. These were intended for choir use in worship services or concerts.
6. An index or indices.
7. Advertisements for other tunebooks, placed on the inside jackets of the book.

These books were oblong, generally using fine, hard-to-read print in the prose sections and mostly vocal scoring without keyboard or other accompaniment, but (until well into the 1800s) including figured bass. In the latter respect,

American tunebooks were old-fashioned by comparison with contemporary European music books of the time.

Tunebooks were meant for students to use privately or in singing classes, for church choirs and congregations, for music societies, and for family use in homes. Because the books got hard use, just like school textbooks, nearly all the copies were utterly worn out, then discarded. Today, surviving tunebooks are rare.

Lowell Mason described his first tunebook in a letter to his friend, John R. Parker, in Boston. He delineated his methods and attitudes and appealed for promotional assistance:

June 20, 1821

In addition to the two pieces published in "Old Collony" I have since sent several others which have not appeared in "The Handel & H. Collection.". . . For several years past I have been constantly importing from Europe the best publications of Sacred Music and have at the same time been attending to the principles of Thoro' bass and Composition under the direction of an eminent German master [presumably Abel]—from all the mass thus *collected* I have been constantly *Selecting*—and my work is now nearly ready for the press—my plan is a Book about the size and price of Bridgewater Collection—containing a sufficient number of psalm and hymn tunes for the common purposes of public worship and a small number of longer pieces for Country Choirs.[1] My book will contain all the best music published in the Bridgewater, omitting a large quantity of the music of Leach [?], Dixon and several other inferior authors—these however will all appear in a different dress—harmonized according to the modern principles of thorough bass—and I trust every false relation, and every forbidden progression will be avoided—in general this will be four parts—but in some few instances but three. The principal European publications to which I am indebted are Dr. Callcott's and Dr. Arnold, Coll.—Costellows Coll.—and Weyman's do. 4 vol.—the Seraph by Whittaker—Gardiner's Sacred Melodies—from the latter work (which is truly classified) I have selected many pieces from Haydn, Mozart, Beethoven and other celebrated German composers—My object is to have the book become popular and supplement the Bridgewater which really does not deserve public patronage any longer. Two things I principally fear—1st—that my collection will be too classical—that is—too much of Mozart, Beethoven, etc. and of consequence too much chromatic—I fear musical taste is not sufficiently advanced to appreciate these authors—again—2nd—I fear that there will be objection to the harmonizing of the old established church tunes—as Old Hundred, Angel's Hymn, St. Ann's, London, etc. etc. altho' it is done by such masters as Stevenson, Weyman, Whitaker, Webb &c. . . . Several pieces have appeared in the Euterpeiad which has much encouraged me. It will be desirable to get the recommendation of Doc. Jackson also a warm recommendation from Handel and Haydn Soc.—Doc. Jackson has seen some samples of the manuscript and speaks very highly of them—now Sir, can you do anything to prepare the way for this work—by the Euterpeiad or otherwise—I would not urge you to do this from personal consideration—but by doing so you will perhaps exert your influence for a work meriting patronage and calculated to improve in a high degree the taste for Sacred Music. Shall be happy to hear from you on this subject provided you can write so as to reach me by 1st Aug. about which time I expect to leave Savannah for Massachusetts where I hope to see you and publish my book.

Yrs.,
   L. Mason

Mason's promoting of correctness (as he understood it) and the latest "modern" or "scientific" principles is a motif of his life's work. Though it is characteristic of him, he was not the only one who promulgated these objectives. In part, Mason and his associates reflected the temper of their times; in part, they shaped the temper of their times. This letter of 1821 also illustrates Mason's business sense: he could always be counted on to figure out the promotional angles. In this respect, he surpassed his associates.

From the English hymnal compiler William Gardiner (1770-1853), Mason adopted both materials and procedures. Gardiner's *Sacred Melodies from Haydn, Mozart and Beethoven, Adapted to the Best English Poets and Appropriated to the Use of the British Church* was a two-volume set dated 1812 and 1815. Gardiner had traveled across Europe gathering instrumental works. He then arranged them for three or four voices with figured bass for keyboard accompaniment. It was his intention to replace the English hymnals then in use with better music.

Gardiner's books attained immense popularity in the United States. When the first volume was reprinted here in 1818, the tide of imported European and British music was running high. Appeals for improved sacred music were ubiquitous—in lectures and pamphlets, in editorials and letters to editors, in sermons and essays of all sorts.

In 1820 *The Euterpeiad* published a striking commentary on music books that, according to the editorializer, ought to be superseded by correctly written ones. This passage was part of a review of the first music anthology issued by the Boston Handel and Haydn Society. Lowell Mason, who was working on the manuscript of his first book at the time, would have agreed entirely with this view:

> In some of the musical publications lately brought before the public, are contained many bold and impressive flights of fancy in the Melodies, that do honour to first rate talents, but at the same time many of them are encumbered with *false harmony, forbidden progressions and injudicious and fruitless attempts at counterpoint.* Psalmody generally, being thus defective, it has been the endeavour of the compilers of this work, to remove those defects; and to introduce to the notice of the pious, many fine specimens of compositions from the works of *Handel, Haydn, Mozart, Pleyel, Beethoven,* and other eminent Foreign and English composers.[2]

This reviewer was referring to a work issued by the society in three stages: volume 1, 1821; volume 2, 1823; volume 3, 1827. In 1827 the three volumes were published together and titled *The Boston Handel and Haydn Society Collection of Sacred Music, Consisting of Songs, Duetts, Trios, Choruses, Anthems, &c. Arranged for the Organ and Piano Forte.* Though Lowell Mason had no part in this book, he attempted some of the same reforms in his work.

When William Goodrich arrived in Savannah in 1820 to install the new organ at the Independent Presbyterian Church, he brought along Colonel Newhall, a Boston singing-school teacher who apparently had business of his own in Savannah. When Mason became acquainted with Goodrich and Newhall, both of them advised him to seek help in Boston in getting his music anthology published. Because Savannah printers were not equipped to handle such a work, Mason had already tried to interest publishers in Philadelphia and Boston in his work. These efforts had failed even though he had asked no royalties. He had become discouraged, but Goodrich and Newhall renewed his hopes by urging him to go to Boston in person and contact specific people whom they recommended.

Persuaded to do just that, Mason set off with a companion, S. Jubal Howe, on a sailing ship in 1821, probably about August 1. They landed in Falmouth, Massachusetts, where they hired a boy with a horse and a "carryall." This conveyance took them the approximately thirty-five miles to Plymouth (Massachusetts) where they stayed overnight.

The following day they visited the publisher of the *Old Colony Collection,* a man named Hobart. Produced by the local music society, Hobart's book was a collection of works by Handel, Purcell, Boyce, and others. He had produced two volumes, one in 1818, the other in 1819. The collection was endorsed by the Boston Handel and Haydn Society, and after the second volume appeared, the society obtained the copyright.

The *Old Colony Collection* held special importance for Lowell Mason. His first musical compositions were published in revised editions of this work. According to his own account, he adapted a Kyrie of Mozart, added an English text, and submitted it to the society through a friend in Waltham, Massachusetts. About 1820 he did the same thing with a Gloria by Mozart. The society was preparing a new edition of the *Old Colony Collection,* and Mason's adaptations came along at the right moment for inclusion.

Mason and Howe soon went on to Boston, having determined that Hobart could be of no help on this occasion. Hobart lacked the musicianship to evaluate Mason's manuscript, and his contacts were no better than Mason's so far as Boston music leaders were concerned. Arrival dates are not known, but Mason attended the September 18 meeting of the Handel and Haydn Society. Apparently his reputation had preceded him, for the group immediately voted him an honorary member. He declined because he wanted to be an active member. The following month (October 1821) he joined this group, and he maintained his membership continuously for the next fifty-one years—for as long as he lived.

Newhall introduced Lowell to Dr. George K. Jackson, organist of the society. Mason's interview with Jackson was memorable, but then, Jackson was memorable. A flamboyant man, he had arrived in 1812 in Boston where he was "hailed with delight—he always was—but the combined weight of his knowledge and vanity, undermined by the slenderness of his patience, frustrated fullest employment of his undoubted talents."[3] By all accounts, his musicianship commanded respect; his personality commanded, at the very least, a spot in the memories of those he met. At Mason's meeting with him, the 300-pound Jackson sat "sipping a bottle of gin and listening to individual selections . . . sometimes interrupting with comments which the young man soon found he might adopt or not according to his own judgment, since at the next meeting they were all forgotten by Jackson."[4]

His eccentricities notwithstanding, Jackson was a decisive man. He liked Lowell's collection, added a few pieces, and approved the manuscript on October 5, 1821. Five days later the contract between the society and Mason was signed. Amasa Winchester, the society's president, arranged the copyright and made an agreement with Mason to publish the book without mention of Mason's name. This move was in Mason's best interests. As a relative unknown, he was able to offer his ideas under the aegis of a known, respected organization. Before long, however, he did become known as the compiler, and by then, having his name associated with the society boosted his reputation that much more.

The contract included these provisions: no compositions could be added to subsequent editions without the consent of both parties; the society was to superintend publication of all editions and could sell copies at the price it deemed appropriate; the society could not dispose of the copyright without Mason's consent; Mason was to select and arrange music for subsequent editions; profits were to be divided equally between the two parties. Mason was immediately given five hundred dollars as an advance payment.

The new tunebook (published late in 1821 but dated 1822) was heralded by the leading music journal of the day, Parker's *The Euterpeiad.* This enthusiastic announcement conveyed the editorial position of that journal and provided a summary of the contents of the book:

> The Handel and Haydn Society, desirous of diffusing more generally a correct taste for scientific Music, would inform Teachers of Singing Schools, Choristers, and the Public generally, that they contemplate issuing from the press a Collection of Sacred Psalmody, selected from the most eminent composers, and adapted to the use of Singing Choirs and Schools. As it is the wish of many that this should be a standard work, no pains will be spared by the Publishers to render it worthy of patronage, by having it correct, not only in notation, but what is often deficient in similar productions now in use, harmony.

> A Figured Bass will accompany every piece throughout the work, inspected by a master, who, in the science of Music, it is presumed, is second to no one in this country [Dr. Jackson].[5]

The first advertisement of the collection was published in the same journal on April 13, 1822, indicating that the publisher was Richardson & Lord, No. 75, Cornhill, and giving the price as one dollar single, ten dollars per dozen.

In keeping with contemporary thinking, Dr. Jackson wrote an endorsement stressing that the music was "scientific" and "correct" according to modern principles. His endorsement, published in the volume itself, read as follows:

> I have been highly gratified with the examination of the manuscript of the Handel and Haydn Society Collection of Music. The selection of tunes is judicious; it contains all the old approved English melodies that have long been in use in the church, together with many compositions from modern English authors. The whole are harmonized with great accuracy, truth, and judgment, according to the acknowledged principles of musical science. I consider the book as a valuable acquisition to the church, as well as to every lover of devotional music. It is much the best book I have seen published in this country, and I do not hesitate to give it my unqualified approbation.
> Very respectfully,
> Gentlemen,
> Your obedient servant,
>   G. K. Jackson

Another recommendation, signed Frederick L. Abel, appeared in the *Savannah Museum* on May 14, 1822, under the heading "Music." This is remarkable, considering that Abel had died in 1820. Obviously if he had prepared a testimony to his pupil's work before his death, his statement had to have been altered for publication because in 1820, he could not have foreseen that the Mason collection would be published with this title. No proof can be found to substantiate or refute the claim that Abel left a statement praising Mason's work. The statement published in May 1822 again extols "science" and "correctness" in praising the book:

> Having critically examined the manuscript copy of the *Handel and Haydn Society Collection of Church Music,* I feel a pleasure in saying that the selection of the tunes is not only judiciously made, but the parts are properly arranged, the Bass is correctly figured, and in no instance are the laws of counterpoint and thorough Bass violated, as is the case in most American Musical Publications. To all the lovers of sacred music, I cheerfully recommend it as a work in which taste, science, and judgment are happily combined.
> F. L. Abel
> Professor of Music[6]

Though Mason was not mentioned on the title page, his contribution was described in the preface as follows:

> The Society...consider themselves as peculiarly fortunate in having had, for the accomplishment of their purpose [preparation of the book], the assistance of Mr. Lowell

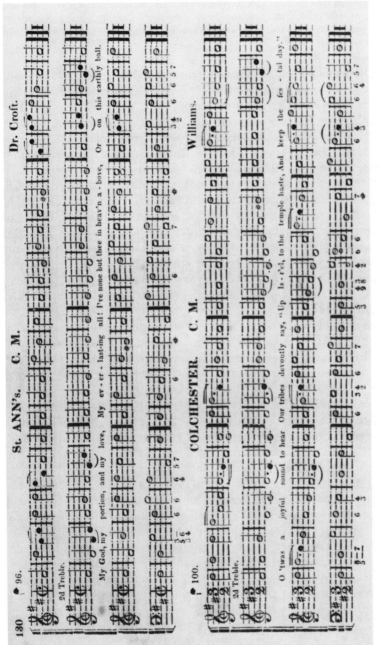

A Typical Page from a Mason Tunebook, *The Boston Handel and Haydn Society Collection of Church Music*, 9th ed., 1830
Note the melody in the tenor line and the figured bass
(Copy owned by the author)

> Mason, one of their members now residing in Savannah, whose taste and science have well
> fitted him for the employment, and whose zeal for the improvement of Church Music, has led
> him to undertake an important part of the labour in selecting, arranging and harmonizing
> the several compositions.

Mason's role in compiling the book was announced elsewhere at the same time. The newspaper account that carried Abel's recommendation stated flatly that the music had been compiled and arranged by Mr. L. Mason of Savannah. The May 11, 1822 issue of *The Euterpeiad* also carried that information, praising "the gentleman by whom the largest portion of this valuable book was compiled.... Mr. Lowell Mason... was several years engaged in collecting this truly erudite epitome of refined and tasteful melodies."[7]

The book itself was an oblong tunebook containing the usual sections: an Elements of Music or textbook section with vocal exercises; hymn and psalm tunes; choral sentences and anthems with and without solo passages; Anglican chants; and an index of tunes. In its first edition, the book was about 5-1/4" × 9", but it varied slightly in size with subsequent editions. A mixture of keyboard and choral scoring was used. Figured bass was included with nearly all of the compositions. Most of the music was four-part with three- and five-part pieces interspersed. The book contained approximately 360 pages, varying slightly from edition to edition.

Revisions from one edition to another ranged from minor adjustments to major changes. For instance, in the preface of the ninth edition (1830) Mason stated that he had added about a hundred new tunes and had altered others. He had also replaced longer anthems with shorter, easier ones, "more applicable...to public worship." These changes, he stated, were necessitated by "the improving state of psalmody and public taste." Adding that he avoided change based on "the excessive desire for novelty" in preference to his sole aim, "utility," Mason argued that changes should be made only when "imperiously demanded." New and additional music ought to be introduced in supplementary publications, according to his view.

As soon as the book appeared, it was a success. Dr. Jackson's endorsement helped, no doubt, because he was an accomplished and well-known musician. The book carried a flattering dedication to him, "not only as a tribute of gratitude for his great care and attention in revision and correction... but also as a testimony of the high estimation in which he is held for his exquisite taste, profound knowledge, and unrivalled skill, in the art and science of music." Another factor in the book's popularity may have been the favorable reviews it received. In fact, one reviewer, writing for *The Christian Advocate,* urged that the book be accepted as the standard for sacred music throughout New England.[8]

After returning to Georgia, Mason wrote to his friend, S. Jubal Howe, in Boston to inquire about the sale of the books. Howe visited Mr. Lord of the firm Richardson & Lord and learned that they had stocked 3,000 copies for $500 in their store and that these copies were moving quickly. Upon hearing this report, Mason began at once to select and prepare music for subsequent editions. By the end of the first five years, the book had yielded a total profit of $4,033.32, an amount Mason and the society divided equally.[9]

The first five-year contract was succeeded by a new contract, negotiations for which began in August 1827. The committee appointed by the Handel and Haydn Society to consider the new contract readily agreed to a supplementary clause providing that if Mason should die, his share of the book profits would go to his heirs. The new contract retained the original term that Mason was not to publish any other works, but this provision was apparently waived. By April 4, 1832, a formal agreement was reached allowing Mason to publish whatever works he wished, independent of the society.[10] Shortly before that, on March 1, 1832, the copyright was sold to Lord & Holbrook, Boston publishers, but Mason continued to receive one-half the profits of book sales.

The collection went through twenty-two editions, each one highly successful. The impact on the American public was significant, though the late nineteenth-century writer Theodore F. Seward probably exaggerated when he wrote that the book "took possession of churches, singing classes, and homes, purifying and elevating taste wherever it went. The absurd style of the previous generation [before Mason] was gradually supplanted and laid away among other curious relics of the past."[11] This oversimplification of changing tastes around 1830 reflects typical attitudes of many musicians of the middle and late 1800s regarding American compositions of earlier times. Mason himself did not say quite so bluntly what he thought of the styles of earlier American musicians, but his views were implicit in the "correct" music, English and European in origin, that he selected and promoted.

With the ninth edition, Mason's name appeared on the title page. His name had come to be associated with the book even before that, however. With or without his name on the title page, Mason had made a place for himself in the musical culture of Boston and anywhere else the book was used. Indeed, through the success of this one book, Lowell Mason had become a nationally known musician.

A Call for Reform in Church Music

While *The Boston Handel and Haydn Society Collection of Church Music* was introducing Lowell Mason's name far and wide, he continued to work quietly in Savannah, refining his ideas and occasionally stating them in public.

Steadily but carefully, he was building his reputation as a spokesman for improved church music.

On Saturday evening, October 7, 1826, Mason was a guest speaker at the Hanover Street Church in Boston. Using church music as his general topic, he outlined goals and means to attain them. Two days later, by request, he repeated the address at the Third Baptist Church. His proposals for improvement are summed up in this passage of the speech:

> When the church shall take this subject [music] into its own hands, when children shall be taught music, when choirs shall be composed of serious and proper persons who shall cultivate music as a religious duty, when singing shall be considered as much of a devotional exercise as prayer; then the evils which have been so long existing, will speedily be removed, and church music will be performed in some measure as it ought to be.[12]

Mason's philosophy of church music rested upon six basic points, not only in 1826 but throughout his career:

1. *Church music must be simple, chaste, correct, and free of ostentation.* It must lie within the performance abilities of those for whom it is intended, whether choir or congregation. In Mason's context, "correct" means in accord with standard contemporary European harmonic practices. In the address of 1826, he stated this ideal as follows:

> One of the most important characteristics of a good psalm [or hymn] tune is simplicity... with respect to both melody and harmony, as shall render the design intelligible, and the execution easy. Solemnity is no less important.... Correct harmony is undoubtedly important. .... Let there be... simple, easy, and solemn tunes selected for . . . worship.

2. *The text must be handled with as much care as the music; each must enhance the other.* As a minimum requirement for any singing, the text must be heard clearly; as a minimum requirement for any music arrangement, the music and the text must fit together to convey a single feeling, mood, or idea. Mason tackled the practical problems involved in achieving these musical, poetic, and spiritual goals. He weighed the moral implications of texts constantly because, like his contemporaries, he relentlessly sought "pure" texts for his books.

In this regard, Mason typified inclinations common at the time. The venerable Noah Webster (1758–1843), working in an altogether different context but with the same mind-set, sought to "clean up" the King James Bible. Said he, "The language of the Scriptures ought to be pure, chaste, simple, and perspicuous, free from any words or phrases which may excite observation by their singularity, and neither debased by vulgarism nor tricked out with ornaments of affected elegance."[13] (Like Mason, Webster had immense influence as an author and editor of many successful school textbooks.)

The address of 1826 alludes to Mason's thoughts on texts, in that he objected to singing school performances in which "the sentiment is wholly disregarded" and the words are used as a "mere accommodation to the music and are sung amidst unrestrained levity and folly." The consequences of that experience, Mason added, are that the pupils go into church, "not to assist in the worship, but to make an exhibition of their musical acquirements and to draw forth applause."

3. *Congregational singing must be promoted.* Though he was a choir director most of his life, Mason increasingly emphasized congregational singing as the years passed. As early as the 1826 address, he urged that members of the congregation take an interest in the singing, just as in other parts of the service. He admitted often hearing, "Oh! I can't sing. You must take care of that!" but rejected that argument: "Every Christian is, or ought to be, deeply interested in congregational singing."

4. *Capable choirs and judiciously used instruments, particularly the organ, are indispensable aids to services.* When addressing the Boston churches, Mason discussed the advantages of using instruments, especially the organ. He recognized abuses but concluded that ordinarily good church music is impossible without the support of instruments.

5. *A solid music education for all children is the only means of genuine reform in church music.* Though he had taught singing schools, Mason saw that they yielded little lasting benefit. His appeal for systematic music education resounded in the address:

> A thorough and permanent reformation in church music, however, cannot be effected, but by a gradual process. Children must be taught music as they are taught to read. Until something of this kind is done, it is vain to expect any great and lasting improvement.

6. *Musicianship per se is subordinate to facilitating worship.* Mason expressed this view repeatedly, whether in regard to singers or instrumentalists, soloists or ensemble musicians. This passage comes from the address of 1826:

> Mere *musical talent* will no more enable a man to *play* than to *sing* church music appropriately.... Execution ... is probably not more important to the organist, than studied elocution is to the preacher.... A minister must ... be able to speak

acceptably...and if he is eloquent...it is so much the better. So with the organist: he must be able to play in a plain and appropriate style...if he be a finished performer, it is all the better, provided he possesses the other more important qualifications.

Mason had previously argued that the undue ostentation of certain organists distracted from the central purposes of the organ in worship. Concerning choir directors, he said that every choir should have a competent leader, "if possible, a pious man; at least a man of intelligence, taste, judgment, and influence; one who is well acquainted with the whole subject of church music."

Mason's writings show that he did not change his mind on this last point despite critics' questions. Much later, in a lecture in 1860, he condemned "exhibitions of artistic music" in worship as "irreverent and out of place"; he compared them to "exhibitions of mere elocution in prayers," which he also regarded as out of place.[14]

A few days after the address was given for the second time, Mason received a letter from Lyman Beecher, minister of the Hanover Street Church, and four church members, requesting a copy of the address for publication. The writers argued that the address would awaken and promote "correct views" of church music.

This was Mason's reply:

Boston, October 11, 1826

Gentlemen,—The address on Church Music...was prepared on very short notice and amidst numerous engagements. Being about to leave the city, it is impossible for me to give it a thorough revision. The hope, however, that imperfect as it is, it may have some tendency to call the attention of Christians to a much neglected but pleasing and important part of public worship, induced me to yield to your request for a copy for publication.

Very respectfully,
   L. Mason

The address was published, and it became so popular that a second edition was soon issued. The effects of the address extended yet further, however, for soon after publication, a group of concerned Bostonians met to discuss the problems with respect to church music and Mason's proposed solutions. They formed a committee to devise ways to improve church music in their city. Representatives and their congregations were as follows:

Union Church	William Ropy, David Hale
Third Baptist	Ensign Lincoln, John B. Jones

Park Street	George Odiorne, George Denny
Methodist	Thomas Patten, John Templeton
Old South	David W. Child, I. S. Withington
Green Street	Elisha Hunt, Daniel Colby
Hanover	Rev. Mr. Rufus Anderson, Wm. G. Lambert
First Baptist	James Loring, Caleb H. Snow
Second Baptist	Herman Lincoln, Jonathan Carleton

This committee passed several resolutions, including one in December 1826 to the effect that it would be desirable to have Lowell Mason work in Boston. A committee of three was then selected to procure $1,500 to guarantee to Mason if he would devote a year to improving church music in Boston and its vicinity. Committee members were George Denny, John B. Jones, and Gilman Prichard.

By February 10, 1827, the $1,500 had been subscribed. Denny sent Mason a letter to that effect, enclosing with it a list of the subscribers.[15] These twenty-seven people agreed to pay the subscribed amounts or as much as necessary of those amounts to insure Mason an income of $1,500 provided that he did not obtain this amount otherwise by his professional services.

Mason declined the offer. Subsequently, in a second letter, Denny, writing for the committee, extended the offer to cover two years. Subscribers were principally from four congregational groups: Old South Church, Essex Street Church, Park Street Church, and Hanover Street Church. A separate two or three hundred dollars was assured by a group of Baptists. The exact amount of this second offer is not known because records have been lost.

Again, Mason declined, but again the group persisted. The next communication was a letter dated April 30, 1827 from Daniel Noyes, a trusted deacon at Lyman Beecher's church, a man upon whom Beecher depended because of his good judgment in many matters. Noyes referred to the first offers, and then mentioned a modification of the more recent offer: the terms would be the same, guaranteed income for two years at the specified amount of $1,500 per year, but with no strings attached. Mason would be "at liberty" to serve anyone else who would pay him for his services in the meantime.

Mason turned down this offer as well. Committee records of July 25, 1827 indicate that the group wanted to persist, but according to August records, subscribers (perhaps weary of the process) would not agree to any additional propositions.

All the while, Lowell Mason's actual work as a church musician (as distinct from his stated ideas on church music) was well known in Boston. The music of the Independent Presbyterian Church in Savannah had impressed visitors in both its musical and devotional aspects. Julius Palmer, another deacon at Lyman Beecher's church in Boston, was one of a number of Bostonians who observed firsthand and reported to others in Boston. Beecher, who had become discouraged with the efforts of his own church choir, eagerly campaigned for Mason's move to Boston in the hope that Mason's skills could be applied to the Hanover Street Church situation.

The fact that renowned clergyman Lyman Beecher sought his help must have pleased Mason. Beecher, a Yale graduate in 1797, was known as a dynamic preacher. He was a leader of the temperance movement and one of the founders of the American Bible Society. In 1826 he had moved to Boston to help establish the Hanover Street Society as a reaction to Unitarianism. After seven years there, he continued his preaching in Cincinnati. He called upon Timothy B. Mason (Lowell's youngest brother) to join him there. As a result the younger Mason built his music career in that state. Later Lyman Beecher's children became leaders, including Henry Ward Beecher, advocate of abolition, women's suffrage, and evolutionary theory; Harriet Beecher Stowe, author; Catharine, a champion of women's education; and Isabella, a campaigner for women's legal rights.

Though Lyman Beecher's encouragement did not change Mason's mind about accepting the Boston committee's offers, it must have weighed on his mind, as did other considerations, such as those Abby had expressed to her mother a few years earlier. The fact remained that the Masons had a comfortable life in Savannah. Lowell had business ties and professional work as a musician. He could not justify leaving that life until the right opportunity arose elsewhere. The fact that he embarked upon establishing a new church congregation in June 1827 suggests that he did not anticipate an imminent move.

The Move to Boston

And yet, suddenly, before the end of the summer of 1827, Lowell, Abigail, and their two sons moved to Boston to begin a residency that was to extend over the following twenty-four years. During those years (1827-1851), Boston grew in its cultural, religious, and educational leadership. Mason may have sensed Boston's cultural expansion and that it would, therefore, be to his advantage to relocate there.

. Such considerations, added to the natural attractions of the Masons' native area, probably played a part in the decision to move. But one key reason was personal and immediate: Mason knew he could become president of the Boston Handel and Haydn Society if he were to be a Boston resident by September 3, 1827, the date of the society's annual election. Evidently that presidency had been his dream for some time.

Many years later Theodore F. Seward related an anecdote from the Georgia years. According to the story, Mason had stood on the banks of the Savannah River, watching a ship pass on its way to Boston, and said to himself,

"How I wish I was going to Boston on that schooner to be made president of the Handel and Haydn Society."[16]

During the summer of 1827, Mason learned that Amasa Winchester, after seven years as president, had declined to continue in that role beyond September. Though no documents remain to prove that he had been contacted by society leaders before leaving Savannah, it is probable that Mason decided to move only after assurances that he would succeed Winchester.

It appears that Mason entered into serious negotiations with the Boston Church Committee only after he had decided to move to Boston to lead the Handel and Haydn Society. The agreement finally drawn up with the churches was a slight variation of the original proposals. He was guaranteed $2,000 salary for musical direction in three churches during successive periods of six months each: the Hanover Street Church, the Essex Street Church, and the Park Street Church under ministers Lyman Beecher, Samuel Green, and Edward Beecher, respectively.

The Handel and Haydn Society posed a challenge to the new president. After a promising beginning in 1815, membership had declined sharply in the 1820s. The original members, mostly musical amateurs, had set up two formidable goals for themselves. First, they intended to present concerts of the "best" sacred music, including anthems and oratorio excerpts. In this regard they succeeded, in that they presented, among other works, America's first complete performance of Handel's *Messiah* in 1818 and the complete *Creation* by Haydn in 1819. Second, they planned to produce sacred music tunebooks for their own use and for sale. Here, too, they succeeded with two good books even before the Mason collection of 1822. Then, with the spectacular success of the Mason book in its many editions, the society was financially secure and independent for decades to come.

Despite these successes, during the 1820s the organization lost much of its popular support. Concerts were so poorly attended that book sales accounted for most of the group's revenue. Trying to cope with diminishing public support, the society voted at one point that its concerts would thereafter be "for the improvement of its members and the amusement of their friends and that no season tickets would be issued."[17] Rather than induce support, this move only widened the gap between the group and the public, so public performances were soon reinstated.

It was hoped that the election of Lowell Mason, widely known for his anthology and his lecture of 1826, would spark new interest in the society. Whether this hope or his own popularity with the members led to his election cannot be determined, but he was elected unanimously. In accord with current practices, he became both the president and the music director; a separate conductor was not authorized until 1847.

Lowell Mason was very much in command from the start and soon proved to be a dynamic, resourceful leader. As one of his first official acts, he began training additional, more competent solo singers. He immediately requested a room with a piano where he could instruct those members who were likely to become soloists. The board of trustees acceded to this request, and with the newly acquired facilities, Mason began the first of his many music classes in Boston. By the second season, class members handled solo passages of Mozart's *Mass in C,* indicating the skill of their teacher.[18] The trustees did not, however, allow Mason full freedom in directing the group. He was not allowed to select performance repertoire until January 26, 1829.[19]

Mason first appeared in concert as conductor of the society on October 28, 1827, but unfortunately, for some reason, this program was not recorded in the major history of the organization. During the 1827-28 season the group performed several major works under Mason's direction: Haydn's *Creation,* Handel's *Messiah,* and the "Sanctus" and "Benedictus" from Mozart's *Requiem.*

In spite of their new leader and his efforts, the 1827-28 season was difficult for the society. The Tremont Theater opened in the fall of 1827 and thereafter competed for the services of skilled musicians. Because many fine musicians in Boston performed at the Tremont and at the rival Federal Street Theater, they were often weary when performing with the Handel and Haydn Society. Furthermore, the additional public performances competed with the society for audiences.

A highlight of the 1828-29 season occurred January 18, 1829, with the first American performance of Haydn's *Mass in B Flat.* So successful was the performance that it was repeated a week later. One critic praised the program as the most ambitious in the society's history to date, adding that the new president had improved the group considerably in the past year as shown by the solos, duets, trios, orchestra, and chorus.[20]

This occasion seems to have been a turning point for the society. It marked a departure from the 1827-28 season in which attendance had been mediocre and performances had been received with little enthusiasm. Mason's eighteen months of leadership had brought about some effective changes. Regarded as a strict disciplinarian, he drilled the group in a variety of styles so that members grew musically. The diligent preparation of solo singers through his classes and thorough choral training of the entire group had paid off. The success of this one performance may have led the board to empower Mason to select repertoire thereafter.

Mason's relationship with the society was enhanced by the continuing popularity of his anthology and the resultant financial gain for the group as well as for himself. But in addition his success stemmed in good measure from personal qualities: "a born teacher... but one of themselves," Mason related easily to those he led and they to him.[21] His position as president–music director for the society continued for five years. Though he resigned in 1831, the resignation was not accepted until 1832; he was elected for a fifth and final term on August 1, 1831.

When the 1832 book contract between Mason and the society expired in 1835, a new arrangement was worked out regarding book profits from the perennially successful *Boston Handel and Haydn Society Collection of Church Music*. On October 1, 1836, a new contract was signed stipulating that Mason, after paying the society $2,000, was entitled to all the profits for two years. After that, for the next two years, the society was to take two-thirds and the compiler one-third of the profits. Mason was free during the entire four-year term to publish anything else he wished. Subsequently, for a ten-year period (1840–1850), the society was to receive ninety percent and Mason ten percent of the profits. After that time the book profits were to go entirely to the society.[22]

Through the Handel and Haydn Society, Mason met many of the leading musicians of Boston. One example was an English immigrant who assumed great importance in Mason's life and career, namely, George James Webb (1803–1887). Webb was an accomplished pianist and violinist before he was twenty years old. In his late twenties he left his home near Salisbury, England, and in 1830 he settled in Boston as organist at the Old South Church. Soon he joined Mason in teaching, editing music books, and organizing teachers' conventions. Webb's compositions appeared in Mason's books and vice versa. Lifelong friendships developed between their families, culminating in the marriage of Mary Isabella Webb, daughter of the George Webbs, and William Mason, the pianist son of the Lowell Masons, on March 12, 1857.[23]

New Musical Leadership in Boston Churches

Concurrent with rebuilding the Boston Handel and Haydn Society, Mason was developing music programs in three Boston churches in accord with his agreement with the Boston Church Committee. His tenure at the three churches (all of them Congregational) can be summarized as follows.

Upon his arrival in 1827, he began six months' work at the Hanover Street Church under Dr. Lyman Beecher. Early in 1828 he undertook six months' leadership at the Essex Street Church under clergyman Samuel Green. He then served the Park Street Church under Edward Beecher for the six-month period agreed upon, but this stint was prolonged to two-and-a-half years.

After that (in 1831), Mason moved to the Bowdoin Street Church, to a new building that replaced the Hanover Street Church destroyed by fire February 1, 1830. At the Bowdoin Street Church he resumed working with Lyman Beecher until September 1832 when Beecher moved to Cincinnati.

Hubbard Winslow (1799–1864), Beecher's successor, remained twelve years. During most of that time Mason remained at that church.

Then on January 7, 1844, Mason moved to the Central (Winter Street) Church where he remained until his retirement from Boston's musical life in mid-1851. At Central Church, Lowell worked with the Reverend William M. Rogers (1806-1851) until Rogers was succeeded by Dr. George Richards (1816-1870), who remained fourteen years.

At the Hanover Street Church in 1827 Lowell found "an enterprising but incompetent choir." As has been indicated, Lyman Beecher was concerned about the music program of the church.[24] Mason took immediate steps to improve the situation. He tested singers individually to determine the quality and range of their voices and then assigned them to one of four sectional classes he convened for regular instruction. He also rehearsed the entire choir twice a week. Under such thorough, systematic training, the choir was sure to improve. Mason's popularity with the singers is shown by the fact that several of them followed him to the Essex Street Church. Again the building process was undertaken, only to be interrupted six months later with his move to the Park Street Church.

The choir at the Park Street Church was second to none in Boston at the time. Indeed, it had a long-standing reputation for excellence. Even before the completion of the church building dedicated January 10, 1810, nineteen members had organized the Park Street Singing Society to promote sacred music. Out of this organization and the church choir, the Boston Handel and Haydn Society had emerged. The choir had been capably led in the early 1800s by Elnathan Duren, one of the society's founders. His son, Elnathan Duren, Jr., became a member of Mason's Bowdoin Street Church Choir. In his old age, he recalled that Mason had described his father as a man with "a fine voice, a poetic soul, and quick perception ... whose musical taste was much in advance of the age."[25]

A few months after Mason began work at the Park Street Church, he became the first organist in its history. The congregation had just authorized the purchase of its first organ, and after $2,000 was raised, William Goodrich was hired to build and install the instrument in 1829. This was but one of several "firsts" involving the Park Street Church and Lowell Mason.

Another "first" occurred on July 4, 1830, as part of a celebration of Independence Day. A children's chorus sang one of Mason's anthems, "Suffer the Little Children to Come Unto Me," a composition later published in his *Juvenile Lyre* (1831). But of greater significance is the fact that this occasion was one of the first, if not *the* first, in which children sang as a group in public in the United States.

A more famous event occurred at the Independence Day celebration in 1831. That celebration featured a new Mason arrangement of music set to words by a Boston minister named Samuel Francis Smith (1808–1895), a friend of Lowell Mason's. Several months earlier, Mason had loaned Smith some music books gathered by William Woodbridge during a European trip. Mason thought highly of the music selections, but could not read the German texts himself. Knowing that Smith read German well, Mason thought he was a likely person to examine the material, then translate or compose new texts for the music.

In looking through the books, Smith had found a tune he liked and, in one sitting in February 1831, wrote the text beginning "My country, 'tis of thee" for a tune that he claimed he did not recognize as the British national anthem. When it was first sung at the Park Street Church as part of that year's July 4 celebration, no one could have predicted its lasting popularity. The church building, dating from 1809, still stands on the edge of the Boston Common, is used by its congregation, and is a revered historical site on Boston's Freedom Trail.

Although he was a part of that historic celebration in July 1831, at that time Mason was no longer working at the Park Street Church. Dissatisfied with dividing his efforts among three churches, Mason had sought a stable position. Several churches had vied for his services. The Park Street congregation, in a letter dated September 24, 1830, had asked him to continue beyond the current agreement and had offered assistance to promote "the object that occupies so much of your time," namely, improving church music. Nothing specific was said about salary; there remain no records of amounts paid him at that church.

A few months later, Mason received the following invitation from another congregation:

January 24, 1831

Dear Sir,
We are authorized by unanimous vote of the Stockholders of Bowdoin St. Church to request you to officiate as organist and chorister of said church, for the term of one year at a salary of $400 per year.

Geo. E. Head, Wm. W. Stone, Julius A. Palmer

William G. Lambert, a member of the Bowdoin Street Church who had known Mason while he worked at the Hanover Street building, wrote him a lengthy, confidential letter the following day. In this letter, Lambert listed twelve advantages the Bowdoin congregation could offer. Chief among these were the new $4,500 organ under construction by Thomas Appleton (an organ that was to be "*decidedly* the *best* in the city"), Lyman Beecher's growing reputation that drew many visitors to his services, and the probable adoption of Mason's new book for church hymnals, inasmuch as their former hymnals had been lost in the fire. Lambert also mentioned the congregation's desire to have Mason return to their service, stressing the interest members of the congregation took in his various activities and their need for his leadership.[26]

Mason accepted the offer, but it is impossible to determine which of these factors led him to his decision. Lambert's prediction about the choice of hymnal was accurate; *Church Psalmody: A Collection of Psalms and Hymns, Adapted to Public Worship* (1831) by Mason and David Greene was selected.

The new Bowdoin Street Church building was extraordinary. "Of primitive Gothic design, it presented an exterior of dignity and strength, while the spacious interior, notable for its symmetrical proportions, chasteness of decorative detail, and suitability to its purpose was at once impressive and signally pleasant."[27] In this new brown stone edifice, Mason did have fine facilities, just as Lambert had anticipated. The new organ consisted of about 1,400 pipes with thirty-three stops. The choir, Mason's first large group, had about seventy members. Mason and Lyman Beecher participated together in the dedicatory services for the new building on June 15, 1831.

When Hubbard Winslow succeeded Beecher in 1832, the music program and the church maintained their eminence among "evangelical communions of the time," prospering with members "representative of liberal orthodoxy, wealth, and social distinction."[28] Concurrently, the choir grew in prominence and musical abilities. Members were drawn from many sources, for Mason always watched for the chance to add new, capable singers.

For example, when his friend George William Gordon told Mason about a gifted young singer in Exeter, New Hampshire, he traveled there to visit her and her parents. After hearing her sing, he invited her to move to Boston, live in his household, and attend the Mt. Vernon School (a private school where he taught at the time) if she would sing in his choir. The year was 1832. The young lady was Anne Rowland Folsom, then twenty-one years old. She gladly accepted the offer, moved to Boston, and lived with the Masons for a time. Abby Mason undoubtedly welcomed her help; among other things, Anne assisted in serving refreshments to choir members after the small sectional meetings held in the Mason house.

Anne Folsom became one of Lowell's two soprano soloists; the other was Hannah C. Woodman. In 1833 Anne married Asher C. Palmer, a bass in the choir. Their first child was a son whom they named after Lowell Mason; the second, a daughter, was named Helen Augusta. Abby Mason gave the Palmers the cradle in which she had rocked her sons. This cradle was later passed along to Helen Augusta Palmer Mason (1836–1905), who married Lowell and Abby's youngest son, Henry, in 1857. The cradle was used by Mason and Palmer descendants until at least the 1940s.[29]

The Mason-Woodman association was a long-standing one also. Hannah Woodman sang in the Bowdoin Street Church choir as long as Mason remained there, then moved to Central Church with him. Her brother, Jonathan Call Woodman (1813–1894) became Mason's assistant organist. In 1832 Mason named hymn tunes in honor of his two soloists: Folsom for Anne Folsom Palmer; Oliphant for Hannah Woodman, who married Henry D. Oliphant in that year.[30]

All evidence indicates that Mason was an effective choir director. According to Elnathan Duren, Jr., Mason's remarks as director were "pertinent and impressive," and he gave "illustrations on the organ. The organist and choir rendered their part of the service devout and impressive."[31] This firsthand assessment coincides with Mason's determination to mesh the musical and devotional effects of the service.

At the same time, Mason showed a sense of humor with his singers. An account in *The Boston Courier,* 1848, describes his relationships with his singers:

> Lowell Mason possessed a rich fund of humor and was very popular with young people, and the rehearsals of his large choir of nearly a hundred singers he always made attractive by his apt illustrations and pleasant talk. In my younger days I was a member of his Winter Street Choir. One evening the . . . gentleman appeared unusually serious and announced that he had a grievance to relate. Said he, "I have lately missed from rehearsal several of my best female voices. Upon personal inquiry I have ascertained that they have kept away because they had to go home alone after rehearsals. Now I have to say, Shame on you, young men! What's the matter with you? Haven't you the manliness to step up and offer your company? Remember you are not popping the question, but doing a dutiful action. Don't forget to be gentlemen! This is all I have to say." It is almost needless to add that the girls did not go home beauless after that. He was a jolly soul, as many Boston boys will attest.[32]

During these years, Mason's reputation grew constantly. In 1838, a young man from North Reading, Massachusetts, newly arrived in Boston to study music with A. N. Johnson, heard from his teacher that the Boston Academy of Music choir was advertising for new members. Encouraged by his teacher, he tried out, even though at the very suggestion, "I shook in my shoes." Webb did the actual testing while Mason watched. The young man, whose name was George Frederick Root, not only passed the singing test, but was soon invited to join Mason's Bowdoin Street Church choir, "the like of which has rarely been equaled . . . in this or any other country." This invitation convinced Root to pursue music professionally: "Lowell Mason had wanted me in his choir, and that was as good as a warranty that I could succeed."[33] Of course, he did succeed, becoming a major educator and song writer.

By 1841, the Bowdoin Street Church was declining as some members died, others moved away, and still others withdrew. Of those who left, sixty-two left as a group to join the Central Congregational Church, a congregation organized in May 1835 as the Franklin Street Church. By 1841 the Central Church was the fastest growing and most popular Trinitarian Society in Boston.

In December 1841, the Central Church dedicated a new building in Winter Street. Soon after that, Mason was invited to direct the music at this church, but he declined. Having close musical, social, and spiritual ties with the Bowdoin Street Church, he much preferred to remain there, provided its position of leadership could be restored. Determined to do all he could to that end, he composed a special anthem for the services of August 21, 1842. Because on that Sunday the church reopened after a brief summer intermission, Mason composed an anthem on the text "I was glad when they said unto me, Let us go into the house of the Lord" from Psalm 122. His eighty-voice choir sang the anthem under his direction. The anthem was soon published in various books, his own and others. But this effort (and indeed all other efforts to improve the situation) failed, and as 1842 passed, still more members transferred to the Central Street Church.

During 1843, as attendance continued to decline, Mason came to doubt the desirability of remaining. He confided these doubts to a friend, William A. Brewer, a member of the Bowdoin Street Church. Brewer responded, first summarizing Lowell's point of view:

Sept. 28, 1843

If I understood your proposition [Mason's] it was in substance this: If I can do any good in the world, it is by promoting the cultivation of Sacred Music. To do this to the greatest possible advantage, it is necessary that I should be connected with the religious society where the greatest number of strangers congregate on the Sabbath; in other words, a society that is attractive and popular. Heretofore Bowdoin St. Church has furnished these requisite facilities; but from some causes (be they what they may) it does not now possess them, and if it should lose as much for a year and a half to come, as it has the last year and a half, it will be so crippled that its influence will be exceedingly limited and its condition... not dissimilar from Dr. Jenks' society [referring to Dr. William Jenks, pastor of the Green St. Church]. I wish to be governed strictly by a Christian sense of duty in regard to a continuance of my connection with Bowdoin Street. . . . I ask advice of you, what shall I do?

Brewer's answer was, in essence, have patience and faith that the spiritual power which had once been in that group would return. Mason was not entirely persuaded. Within a few months, he received the following letter:

Boston, December 8, 1843

Mr. Lowell Mason

Dear Sir,
The subscribers being the Committee on Singing in the Central Cong. Society propose to you to take charge of their music, as organist and leader and instructor of the choir for five years from the 1st January next, at compensation of one thousand Dollars per annum, with use of vestry and Lecture room for teaching. We shall be glad of an early answer accepting this proposal.

The letter was signed by three committee members, Daniel Noyes, F. A. Benson, and R. E. Bates.

No record of Lowell's response exists, but it is clear enough from this letter that he received a few days later:

Boston, Dec. 16, 1843

Mr. Mason Sir

Having received your answer accepting our proposal with the condition that your removal from New England should terminate the engagement we hereby assent to the condition.

This letter was signed by the same three committee members. No further comment was made concerning Mason's request for this change in the condition. It is interesting to note that he made the request in 1843, evidently with thoughts of leaving New England already in mind.

In preparation for his new position, Mason invited a number of persons to join the Central Church choir. One invitation, to Mary E. Beck and her sister Lucy M. Beck, read as follows:

Misses Beck

Being about to take charge of the music in the Central Church, it is with pleasure that I hereby invite you to become members of the choir.

Very respectfully,
    Lowell Mason

Boston, Dec. 25, 1843[34]

When Mason began his work at Central Church on January 7, 1844, many choir members from the Bowdoin Street Church went with him. With these additions, the Central Church choir had approximately a hundred singers. F. A. Benson, who had once been the principal bass at Bowdoin Street, had already assumed that role in the Central choir. Hannah Woodman Oliphant moved with Lowell to the new position and continued as the leading soprano in his group. Rehearsals were frequent and rigorous; the entire choir met on Saturday evenings and often on other evenings or afternoons during the week. Sectional rehearsals were held also; for example, the women met one afternoon each week for solfeggio practice.[35]

Heavy though his choir responsibilities were, Mason did other work at Central Church as well. He played a recently installed three-manual Appleton organ with two octaves of pedals and numerous couplers. The instrument was placed so that the organist sat in the midst of the choir where the singers could hear and be heard distinctly. As music director, Lowell selected the hymns after conferring with the minister about the text of the day. At this church, he was able to introduce Anglican chant, often substituting a chant for a hymn tune. This innovation pleased the congregation, and it put into practice ideas that Mason had been expressing in his various books containing chants.

At the time of his retirement in 1851, members of Mason's various church choirs gave him a farewell party and a gift as tokens of their respect and affection. The dramatic changes that occurred during the nearly twenty-five years of his church work in Boston owed much to his efforts as a writer, editor of music collections, and educator. In addition, his stature as a skillful organist-choir director added credibility to other aspects of his career.

In summary, Mason's church choirs were major performing groups. Their skill called attention to his musicianship and to the possibilities of enhancing worship through well-performed music. His church positions provided a testing ground for his musical ideas and compositions. All the while, he worked closely with outstanding religious leaders whose orthodox beliefs and evangelical zeal reinforced his own religious convictions. The music he composed, arranged, endorsed, and published reflected his opinions in that it was unpretentious, direct, and intended for the "average" worshipper, reflecting the standards Mason had articulated as early as his address of 1826.

Publication of Sacred Music

During the Boston years, Mason produced about seventy separate publications, approximately fifty of which contained sacred music. Over half of these publications were books, the rest individual anthems or other short works. Before his move to Boston, Mason did not anticipate such a volume of work, just as he did not anticipate that *The Boston Handel and Haydn Society Collection of Church Music* would sweep the country, giving him wide recognition. He issued a few other small items between 1822 and 1827, but only after settling into his new life in Boston did Mason plunge into publishing on a large scale.

One important reason for his extensive music publishing was simply need: music of various kinds was needed but not available. Mason saw the needs and sought to fill them. At the same time, though no one publication of the Boston years matched the impact of *The Boston Handel and Haydn Society Collection of Church Music* on his career, the cumulative effects of his publications were enormous.

First, the books built his national reputation, thereby boosting his local standing. This, in turn, was no doubt a factor in his Boston successes. Second, through the preparation of his books, Mason made many friends, some of whom were influential in fields he himself did not enter. For example, in 1828 he met Sarah Josepha Hale (1788–1879), for forty years editor of *Godey's Lady's Book,* the most widely circulated magazine of the time. She supplied texts for some of Mason's songs for children, and her association with Mason may have inspired her to write *Poems for Our Children* and *School Song Book* (1834).

Third, the music books directly underwrote Mason's other work. Their commercial success enabled him to teach with little or no salary in private schools and later in the public schools. And at the same time, the successful young singers in those classes were developing appetites for more music books, as were the better-trained church choirs and other adult musical groups.

Well aware of his family's financial needs, soon after arriving in Boston Mason took a part-time job at a local bank (reports differ as to which one). This work occupied him only in the mornings, leaving afternoons and evenings free for music activities. But his music commitments soon became so demanding that he resigned his position at the bank. Through the sale of music books, part-time work outside of music became unnecessary from then on. Indeed, he went on to earn a great deal of money through his music career.

How did Mason manage such prolific writing and editing while handling his other responsibilities? A partial explanation of his extraordinary capacity for work is his robust health, combined with an ability to concentrate and apply himself assiduously to his work. Even during his meals, his mind was occupied with his work. It was not unusual for him to get up abruptly from the table, go to the desk, and jot down a musical theme or memo to himself. This practice continued throughout most of his active life.[36]

Mason's typical work day during his Boston years followed this approximate schedule: rising about eight and correcting music proofs during breakfast; from nine to noon, teaching and "other public labors"; afternoon, again teaching or lecturing; at tea time, more proof correcting; after tea, choir or class teaching, unless "otherwise engaged"; return home and after dinner, correcting more proof, often working until midnight or as late as two in the morning. Yet, in twenty years in Boston, he was never known to spend even half a day in "mere amusement."[37] He appeared never to know fatigue or disinclination to work; he never let music be published hastily, but rather corrected "final" proofs repeatedly.[38]

Mason's passion for improving church music pervaded his public work and his private contacts throughout the Boston years. In a letter to a friend, Austin Willey, he expressed that concern:

Boston, 27th June, 1838

Dear Sir:

I am fully convinced that we need a reformation in the music of the Church. I am satisfied that it does not answer the needs of the institution, and indeed it may be doubted whether it is not often so managed as to be directly injurious to religious effect and impression. But how shall this reformation be brought about? Musical knowledge must be extended, and attention of the people must be called to the subject, and especially must churches and ministers be enlightened. If we could have a man well qualified who would act as a missionary, and who would go about the country and preach on the subject and who could always do something practical in the way of enlightening and leading taste great good might be expected to result. [someone like himself perhaps?]

The great thing as it appears to me that is to be done is this—to convince the people and make them feel that the music of the church should be a devotional act and not a mere concert or exhibition.... This is the great thing for unless I am mistaken in almost all cases now throughout the country music in the churches is conducted on the latter principle. Almost all the ministers with whom I am acquainted who have made some little progress in music and who wish to do all they can to promote it make this fatal mistake and encourage concert music rather than church music, and this through ignorance—their own musical education has been all wrong, and therefore their efforts in the cause are all wrong.

Works through which Mason advanced his ideas on sacred music were *Spiritual Songs for Social Worship* with Thomas Hastings (1832); *The Choir: or Union Collection* (1832); *The Boston Collection of Anthems* (1834); *Occasional Psalm and Hymn Tunes* (1836); *The Boston Anthem Book* (1839); *The Seraph* (1838-40); *Carmina Sacra* (1841); *The New Carmina Sacra* (1850); and *Cantica Laudis* with George J. Webb (1850).

In publishing *Spiritual Songs,* Mason and Hastings hoped to counter the vogue for revival tunes such as those found in a popular book called *The Christian Lyre.* That volume had sold at least two thousand copies in the first few months after its release in April 1831. Compiled by a Connecticut minister named Joshua Leavitt, this book was but one of a type that, in Leavitt's understatement, sought to supply "hymns and music of a different character from those ordinarily heard in church."[39] The music was meant for revivals or meetings of a similar nature. Leavitt freely admitted that he "possessed no musical skill beyond that of ordinary plain singers [and] that his book wasn't designed to please scientific musicians."[40]

Leavitt was right about that last part. His book didn't please "scientific musicians" like Mason and Hastings. But his book did publish tunes and texts on opposite pages, a big improvement over the standard church practice of having separate books for tunes and texts. That one feature alone simplified and improved singing. Mason and Hastings put tunes and texts together, too, in open competition with Leavitt, but they did not imitate Leavitt in the music selection. On the contrary, they indicated that they were appalled by the success of a book containing such "trivial melodies" as those in *The Christian Lyre.* In the preface to *Spiritual Songs,* the editors wrote disparagingly of the "multitude of insipid, frivolous, vulgar, and profane melodies [that] have been forced into general circulation." They set forth their ideas about proper types of devotional music, types that "call forth the right emotions."

Mason and Hastings had originally intended to issue their book in periodical form. No copies have been located, but *The Western Recorder* indicates that the first of the issues appeared between July 5, 1831 and August 16, 1831.[41] These dates suggest that the editors were rushing to compete immediately with Leavitt's April publication. The next two installments appeared in October and December 1831. It is not known how many separate issues were printed, but the entire volume, *Spiritual Songs,* appeared in 1832.

That small book contains 233 texts for which 83 tunes are provided. The simple musical settings use unison or two- or three-part arrangements, rarely four-part. The book was "an immediate success in evangelical circles but had surprisingly little influence on Presbyterians" (surprising considering Hastings' leadership).[42] The book failed to derail the growing enthusiasm for revival music; however, it is unlikely that any single book could have done so.

The informal approach of *Spiritual Songs* and its orientation toward use by families and "social religious meetings" contrasts sharply with the more formal, church-oriented approach of *The Choir* (1832), a book of psalm and hymn tunes, anthems and sentences, plus instructions for music students. The preface states that much new music was procured from German and English sources, including some manuscript works contributed to the editor personally for his use in the book. Mason arranged themes from Haydn, Mozart, and others especially for this book. Ever alert to a marketable item, he admits that many tunes were arranged in triple meter because such tunes have proved to be "easy and effective and universally popular."

Mason also watched for new possibilities in music publication. *The Boston Collection of Anthems* (1834) and *The Boston Anthem Book* (1839) provided church choirs and music societies with material. The advertisement section of *The Boston Anthem Book* claimed that the book drew together well-known and "decidedly popular" compositions that had previously been scattered about, causing inconvenience and extra expense for choral groups.

With *Occasional Psalm and Hymn Tunes* (1836), Mason experimented with publishing a series of volumes, the materials to supplement music books used in churches. This strategy assumed that church congregations (like choirs, school groups, and choral societies) would enjoy the variety and stimulation provided by a steady flow of new music. After this precedent came *The Seraph* (1838–40), a periodical with music for both congregations and choirs. An eight-page pamphlet, *The Seraph* was issued monthly from August 1838 to July 1840 and offered hymns, psalm settings, Anglican chants, and anthems— the same varied selection as in *Occasional Psalm and Hymn Tunes.* Subscribers to *The Seraph* received their copies by mail at the cost of a dollar per year.

In addition to regular revisions of *The Boston Handel and Haydn Society Collection of Church Music,* Mason issued *Sentences, or Short Anthems, Hymn Tunes and Chants* with the society in 1834. In this volume, he is identified not only as the compiler but also as a professor at the Boston Academy of Music.

Lyra Sacra (1832) was meant for church or home use by either trained or untrained singers, seemingly contradictory purposes. According to Mason's preface, the music should fill the gap between psalm and hymn tunes on the one hand and anthems and other sacred music which, on the other hand, "in the present state of music education . . . [are] too difficult for . . . choirs to perform, or for audiences to comprehend." He became fairly specific on this point, citing music of Handel, Haydn, and "other celebrated Masters," plus most of the anthems of the English church as belonging to that latter category. All these works he ruled out as too long for practical use in worship, too theatrical in their origins, and often too dependent upon difficult accompaniments to be practical for most American congregations.

Filling that gap was hard, Mason admitted, because of the scarcity of appropriate music. To achieve the goal, he drew heavily on the compositions of his colleagues among Boston church musicians, especially his associate George Webb and organist Charles Zeuner (1795-1857), then working at St. Paul's Church. Zeuner, a native of Saxony, emigrated to Boston in 1830 and became organist for the Boston Handel and Haydn Society from 1830 to 1837, then its president in 1838-39. By contemporary accounts, Zeuner was an eccentric man who made enemies easily. He moved to Philadelphia in 1839 where he lived until committing suicide in 1857. Zeuner issued a number of music books himself, and Mason used many of Zeuner's compositions in his books.

Mason was sensitive to critics' charges that he adapted too freely from other works, particularly from the European masters. In *Cantica Laudis* (1850) he defends the practice of borrowing and adapting music. He contends that new compositions are often highly disappointing when compared to the standard works of major composers. The extraordinary themes of the leading composers, he says, can be highly effective *if* they are arranged with taste, with feeling for the original music, and with a realistic understanding of the needs of American churches. He adds that he reviewed many materials to find suitable choir music and to provide the best possible tunes for congregational use.

According to published statements of some of his contemporaries, Mason selected music wisely and arranged it well ("well" meaning in a manner compatible with their own tastes). For example, *The Musical World and New York Musical Times* of September 17, 1853 carried these endorsements of *Cantica Laudis* (1850):

From John Zundel, organist, Plymouth Church, Brooklyn, New York, this statement: "I have been astonished at the fidelity and skill with which many of the sublimest strains of the greatest composers are here brought into tune form. . . ." And from F. Brooks, teacher of music in East Bethany, New York: "I have never before seen in a book of church music such a copious and choice selection from the great masters, rendered so practical and attractive, both to ordinary choirs and more advanced performers."

Endless debate is possible over whether adaptation should be done at all, and if so, what constitutes a good adaptation. The intent of Mason's adaptations was no secret: he argued repeatedly for practical material suited to the realistic limits of American church use. The verdict of his contemporaries was also clear: they bought his books by the thousands, edition after edition, volume after volume.

The New Carmina Sacra (1850) was not meant, the editor said, to replace *Carmina Sacra* (a popular book in its own right), but rather to complement it by providing additional and often completely new selections. He acknowledged Zeuner's *The American Harp,* a collection first published in 1832, as a source for many of the most useful works in his new book. *The New Carmina Sacra* sold at least 300,000 copies by November 1852. By October 1855, *Dwight's Journal of Music* reported that its sales were "unparalleled," a dramatic statement in view of the success of earlier books, including *Carmina Sacra.* The latter may ultimately have sold the greater number of copies, for it was published and sold simultaneously in ten different American cities, finally selling over a half-million copies. This may have been the book that William Mason later claimed earned a hundred thousand dollars for his father.[43] Through such successes as these, Mason amassed his fortune.

Yet Mason's work as an editor indicates more than a keen perception of the music market, important though that was. He exerted his influence forcefully as an editor, ever confident that the materials he approved were the most desirable and appropriate that could be found. Personal correspondence and published statements reveal his steady self-assurance regarding musical matters and an absence of self-consciousness about his views and practices.

Mason's musical tastes and preferences spread across the nation through the wide distribution of his publications. His ideas on sacred music, stated in prefatory portions of his books, were accessible to thousands of people who would otherwise have had few, if any, stated guidelines. Of course, the publications assured Mason's personal fame and prestige among those who were involved with church music. Then, as the years passed, he became recognized as a leading authority on musical matters in general. Mason's heightened prestige was to be an important factor in assuring that music would find a permanent place in the curriculum of American public schools.

4

Preparation for Public School Music

New Trends in Public Education

Increasing cultural and intellectual interest during the early 1800s prompted a broadly based drive for public education. For example, the New York Workingmen's Association, a predecessor of labor unions, called for free public schools in 1820. Similar demands arose in Rhode Island, Pennsylvania, and Massachusetts about the same time, but the path to free, universal public education was long and hard. John Adams' contention that "a child was better off never born than uneducated" stood curiously juxtaposed with the strident anti-intellectualism of the period.[1]

With the advent of the Jacksonian ideal of equality around 1830, anti-intellectualism developed a new dimension described as a "gravitating toward the common center" culturally. This "implied a leveling downward as one man sought to prove his taste as good as another's." As James Fenimore Cooper wrote to Horatio Greenough in 1836, "You are in a country in which every man swaggers and talks, knowledge or no knowledge; brains or no brains; taste or no taste. They are all *ex nato* connoisseurs."[2]

Education *did* develop even though few people in political authority promoted it. Only at the state level was much of anything done, and even there, beginning efforts were feeble. Before about 1810, the typical one-room district schoolhouse, established by taxes in New England states, struggled to teach as many as eighty pupils. School was noncompulsory, even for the few months it was held each year. Good teachers were rare. Girls were kept from school in some places and, when finally admitted, were allowed to attend for shorter terms, generally during the summer when the boys were out. Educational opportunities in the Middle states and the South were even skimpier.

In education, as in other respects, Boston was progressive. By 1818 the budget for the Boston primary schools was $5,000; by 1828 the amount had almost tripled. During the decade of the 1820s the city maintained eight public primary schools, including one at the Alms House. These schools reached 2,400 students while an additional 4,000 students attended the 162 private schools.

Children entered between the ages of four and seven to learn spelling and reading. Then they advanced to grammar schools where they remained until about age fourteen. The grammar schools leaned heavily upon the classical, college-preparatory studies of Latin, Greek, English, and mathematics.

Parallel schools arose to prepare the young for occupations in business and other specialized areas. These schools, called academies, offered such diverse courses as public speaking, logic, surveying, drafting, astronomy, bookkeeping, geography, navigation, and botany, among others, sometimes in combination with college-preparatory courses. By 1800 Massachusetts had seventeen academies, some of them diversified into training primary school teachers. "Female seminaries" for teenage girls developed as well, preparing the way for women's colleges in the latter part of the century.[3]

In 1821 the first publicly supported high schools were formed; these were completely open to the public. Classical School in Boston was one of the first of these schools. By 1824 Massachusetts required the establishment of a high school in every town having more than five hundred families. Every town with a population over 4,000 persons was required to offer a college-preparatory course in the school.[4] Concurrently, private schools continued, and in some of those, music became a part of the curriculum.

While schools were being built, educators were developing better educational practices. One group of pioneer educators formed an organization called the American Institute of Instruction. At an educators' meeting in Boston on March 15, 1830, a committee was formed to establish a permanent organization devoted to the betterment of public education. Specifically, the group wanted to alleviate conditions felt to impede education: the inexperience and incompetence of school teachers in general; the unsuitable locations and inadequacies of school buildings; the lack of regard for architectural beauty in school buildings; the lack of proper equipment for teaching; the resort to corporal punishment as a means of discipline; the curriculum being virtually limited to the three R's; and instruction consisting of memory recitations and "other unfavorable features."[5]

The committee issued an invitation to prospective members through the press in at least eleven states. About three hundred people responded and met in Boston August 19-22, 1830. The outcome was the American Institute of Instruction, destined to lead educational organizations in the nation. In 1831 it was incorporated through an act of the Massachusetts Legislature. Four years later, the legislature appropriated $300 per annum for five years for the institute's work. This appropriation was renewed again and again, and for seventy-eight years, the organization exerted a major influence on education. Meetings were held annually in various cities; hundreds attended the lectures.

At the same time, vital new educational concepts were reaching America. A key figure in this regard was the Reverend William Channing Woodbridge

(1794–1845). An 1811 Yale graduate, Woodbridge became a principal at Burlington Academy in New Jersey in 1812. Later he taught at Gallaudet's Institute for the deaf and dumb at Hartford, Connecticut. Before 1820 he developed health problems, and in the hope of restoring his health, Woodbridge traveled abroad in 1820 and again in 1825-29.[6] While there, he visited schools, talked with educators, and observed the latest practices. He became particularly interested in the ideas of Swiss reformers Johann Heinrich Pestalozzi (1746-1827), Philipp Emanuel von Fellenberg (1771-1844), and their followers, Michael Traugott Pfeiffer (1771-1850) and Johann Nägeli (1775-1836).

Pestalozzi and his associates had revolutionary ideas about education. They stressed direct rather than vicarious experiences, carefully planned, step-by-step instruction, and the development of individual abilities. They replaced much of the established rote recitation and memorization with group projects, creative writing, singing, drawing, physical exercises, and other activities appropriate to the age level of the pupils. Pestalozzi, who worked particularly with the poor and underprivileged, based his methods on a love of children as children. Here, too, he was revolutionary in that he challenged the rigid, authoritarian view of children as miniature adults.

Reports of Pestalozzi's work had reached America through the efforts of John Griscom (1774-1852) and Joseph Neef (1770-1854). Neef, once an associate of Pestalozzi, emigrated and taught in Philadelphia, then Louisville, and finally, in the communistic colony in New Harmony, Indiana.[7] However, when these men introduced Pestalozzian ideas, few people were receptive.

Woodbridge was more successful in promoting Pestalozzi's ideas, perhaps because he was a native American already familiar with the American educational system. Through statements published in the *American Journal of Education* and elsewhere, he attracted a broad audience for the new methods. With Emma Willard as coauthor, he published two popular geography textbooks (1824, 1833), applying the new principles.[8]

While promoting Pestalozzian principles and their application to music teaching, Woodbridge also worked to overcome public resistance to music in the public schools, resistance based on ideas widely held at the time: that music is impractical, hence, a waste of time; that a lifetime is needed to develop real musicianship, thus making limited instruction in school futile; that musical progress depends upon the natural gift of a "good ear," a gift possessed by too few to justify wholesale instruction; that music instruction would undermine discipline; and that teaching music would open the curriculum to other "frivolous" subjects, e.g., painting or dancing.

The work of Elam Ives, Jr. (1802-1864) of Hartford, Connecticut in 1830 put Pestalozzian ideas into practice with music students and into print with his textbook *American Elementary Singing Book*. Completed in 1830, the book was registered by the Hartford publisher F. J. Huntington in 1831 and published in 1832. It is not known precisely how Ives learned Pestalozzian principles, but he seems to have mastered them and applied them with much success to music teaching before any other American did so.[9] The results were reported in the *American Journal of Education,* 1830, as follows, in Ives' words:

> I entered upon the...system with some prejudices; but the more I examined it, the more I was convinced of its superiority . . . especially in the simple manner in which the principles of music are presented to the mind of the child. The pupils...after a short period of instruction...surpassed our ordinary choirs.[10]

Armed with his belief in Pestalozzian ideas and the practical evidence of Ives' success, Woodbridge was determined to persuade Lowell Mason (by then a Boston music leader with a reputation for excellent teaching) to adopt Pestalozzian principles. It is not known whether Mason had learned about them elsewhere—nor if he had heard of Ives' work—but even if he had, traditional methods had worked for him for eighteen years. Apparently he was not looking for new methods.

Mason's teaching in Boston had begun simply and quietly. In 1828, to bolster the alto section of his church choir, he tutored six or eight boys. Other children were soon attracted to the class. As months passed and the group grew too large to meet in the Mason home, classes were moved to the basement of whichever church he was serving, first the Park Street Church, later the Bowdoin Street Church.

Lowell taught these children free of charge. Soon the demand for instruction grew so dramatically that he had to have an assistant. It seems that George J. Webb, the English immigrant whom Mason had met through the Handel and Haydn Society, joined him in teaching children's classes by 1832, if not earlier. Mason assumed all the expenses for his classes, including not only music supplies, but also fuel and lighting. These efforts and expenses paid off in that his choir became the finest in Boston and the classes themselves became widely popular overnight.

By 1830 Mason was teaching 150 to 200 pupils. Though these children paid no tuition, they had to agree to remain in their classes for the entire year. Instruction included rudiments of music reading and elementary rules of singing, all with the goal of enhancing congregational and choir music. These classes were, in effect, singing schools, although (unlike singing schools in general) all the pupils were young and the sessions extended over a longer period of time. The one-hour lessons were held successively for separate groups with scheduling arranged to avoid conflicts with local schools. The classes gave concerts occasionally, sometimes as combined groups. Many of these concerts were free; others were for charity, but neither Mason nor Webb received any direct remuneration.

What did Mason gain from these classes? His original objective, improving his church choir, was readily achieved, but the teaching continued and, in fact, steadily expanded. One of Mason's gains was a large circle of admirers, some of whom later became his assistants. His teaching ability attracted attention and a following throughout his life.

Another gain was public support for his ultimate objective: the inclusion of vocal music in the public school curriculum. Through his classes Mason showed that all children can learn to read music and that all children can sing, allowing, of course, for individual differences in ability. The children's accomplishments in Mason's classes far exceeded public expectations. Because these accomplishments were displayed in public concerts, people began to realize that music training for all children was at least possible, perhaps even desirable.

Woodbridge brought this possibility into focus for educators in an address before the first meeting of the American Institute of Instruction, August 19, 1830, in Boston. Speaking on "Vocal Music as a Branch of Instruction in the Common Schools," Woodbridge refuted common objections to music education. He argued that music is a gift of the Creator, not just to a talented few, but, by implication, to all:

> The immediate object to be accomplished by making vocal music...a branch of common education...is to cultivate one of the faculties which our Creator...has seen fit to bestow upon us. To neglect it, is to imply that it was unnecessary.... It is to treat a noble gift in a manner which in any other case would be considered as disrespectful and ungrateful. ...

He also argued that music would improve discipline rather than impair it:

> The study of music from its very nature, cultivates the habits of order, and obedience and union.... We were struck with the superior order and kindlier aspect of the German schools in comparison with our own; and ascribe it not a little to the cultivation of music among them. ...[11]

Finally, whether by accident or by shrewd design, Woodbridge made one point that clinched his argument: music instruction would enhance religious training and experience. As exponents of music education, Woodbridge and Mason grasped, exposed, and indeed, belabored connections between music and religion or music and morality. Making this connection helped their cause tremendously. In fact, it may be that music was admitted to the public school curriculum because the public had been persuaded of the morally uplifting nature of music and musical participation. Practical considerations, especially the prospect of improving church music, also played a major part.[12]

In speaking before the American Institute of Education, Woodbridge underscored his points by using a children's choir to illustrate what could be achieved through music education. At Woodbridge's request, Mason had brought a group of boys he had been teaching. These children sang three songs for their audience: "The Morning Call," "The Garden," and "The Rising Sun," all of which were published the following year (1831) in Mason's *Juvenile Lyre,* coedited by Elam Ives, Jr.

By contemporary accounts, the beauty of their singing cast a spell upon the group. Added to Woodbridge's persuasive arguments, the choir carried quite an impact. This event in Boston stimulated scattered instances of school music teaching in New York, Ohio, Pennsylvania, and Connecticut.[13] The institute immediately asked Mason to address the group at his earliest opportunity, but he was not able to do so until their third annual meeting on August 27, 1832.

Meanwhile, Mason had been impressed with Woodbridge and his address. The men had become well acquainted through their work on this presentation of August 19, 1830. Soon afterwards, Woodbridge gave Mason a treatise in German, the title of which could be translated "Instruction in Singing According to Pestalozzian Principles," by Pestalozzi disciples Nägeli and Pfeiffer. Woodbridge offered his help in translating the material for Mason, but got no encouragement. Despite growing admiration for Woodbridge, Mason went on with his own teaching methods and had the usual good results.

Undaunted, Woodbridge assembled Pestalozzian materials appropriate to music teaching and approached Mason saying, "If you will call together a class, I will translate and write out each lesson for you as you want it, and you can try the method; it will take about twenty-four evenings."[14] Mason agreed. He invited children to join a class at the Park Street Church, and, in accord with Woodbridge's offer, he taught the class literally with the music book in one hand and Woodbridge's lesson plan in the other.

Mason began to understand that Pestalozzi's approach was natural, rational, and effective. The concept of gradual learning, going from the known to the unknown, contradicted the time-worn, virtually universal practices of memorization and recitation. In musical terms, the old method started a student with rules, memorization, and performance, then corrected errors as they occurred. The Pestalozzian method did the opposite: students were led gradually to the point of performing an entire composition. In other words, the Pestalozzian method "built up rather than patched up."[15]

Another novel aspect of the Pestalozzian approach was its emphasis on the child. This was one of the first times in history, if not *the* first time, that education focused on the child rather than on the subject matter. This "first" fit perfectly with Mason's love of children.

Mason and Woodbridge found that the experimental class learned more easily and more thoroughly than had any previous Mason class. Though amazed, Mason remained skeptical. To test the Pestalozzian methods under different circumstances, he invited interested adults to join a tuition-free class, advising them that he would try a new teaching method. Five hundred people enrolled. Remarkably, this group learned just as happily and as thoroughly as had the children's class, if not more so. The class members were so delighted with the results that, at the last session, they voluntarily presented their teacher with a bonus. Asked about this episode years later, Mason confirmed the story with a smile, adding that the group had agreed to pay him five dollars per person, making a total of $2,500—a generous bonus indeed![16]

Mason's Emergence as a Leader in Music Education

Through successful application of Pestalozzian ideas to music teaching, William Woodbridge and Elam Ives, Jr. had provided Mason with another essential element for public school music, namely, a coherent, reliable pedagogical system. Mason's interpretation of Pestalozzian principles is summarized here because he followed and advocated them consistently after 1830. But their significance goes far beyond his own career, for through his influence these ideas spread across the country with lasting impact on later generations of music educators.

Only a summary is needed here because detailed analyses are readily available in many sources. The most complete offering of Mason's ideas appears in his *Manual of the Boston Academy,* 1834. In that work, he applied specific concepts to specific though hypothetical classroom situations. He also summarized his ideas in short works published years later, such as *The Pestalozzian Music Teacher* (1871) and *A Glance at Pestalozzianism* (1863). In addition, many scholars have discussed Mason's ideas in articles, books, theses, and dissertations.

The principles of Mason's philosophy are as follows:

1. *Things (experiences) come first; then come the signs (symbols).* Teachers should withhold technical terms until they are needed or convenient. That time comes only after the students clearly understand what the signs designate. No other idea of Mason's is so frequently repeated in his writings. This passage conveys his thinking on the matter while acknowledging his indebtedness to Woodbridge:

> We would not commence with book rules, not attempt to lead from general laws to particular facts, but rather from particular facts to general laws; not from theory to practice, but from practice to theory.... We attempt...that form...of

teaching which is called Pestalozzian, or inductive. The writer has followed this [system] for many years. It was hard for him at first to receive it; and had it not been for the patient and persevering efforts of a most excellent friend... Rev. Wm. C. Woodbridge... he might still have continued in ignorance. . . .[17]

The motto "Things Before Signs" ignited a controversy over rote learning. Mason obviously favored rote singing as a means to introduce musical experience. After knowing the pleasure of singing, children undertook learning to read music. Mason often compared reading music after singing to reading words after speaking. To arrive at this approach, he had to reverse his ideas, inasmuch as the singing schools taught music reading first, then singing.

2. *Teaching is based on understanding the child.* A teacher's methods and materials must appeal to children through their senses, using also their experience and intelligence. In Mason's words, thorough musical knowledge "must find its way to the mind through the avenue of the ear. . . . Music does not consist in things seen, but in things heard."[18]

3. *Teaching should promote natural, pleasant, and wholesome growth.* The Pestalozzian teacher analyzes and simplifies the material to help his students learn. He proceeds from the simple to the complex. He subordinates rules to underlying principles. Thus, for example, in "giving moral and righteous instruction, religion itself is to be sought rather than its formulas (dogmas) only." To achieve natural, pleasant growth, Mason said that the teacher needs to cultivate "a child-like spirit, or humble state of mind."[19]

When approached in this spirit, music will awaken and promote the best in the pupils. In a letter to his son William on April 12, 1855, Lowell summed up the influence of music as follows:

> He who views the subject [music] from the highest point, sees in it a most powerful instrument for the perfecting of man's emotional or moral nature. Thus we advance from the mere sensuous, through the intellectual and the aesthetic to the highest intuitional moral appreciation of the power of music.

4. *The teacher should remember that pupils must learn to think and act independently, to rely upon their own powers and to trust their own natural curiosity in investigating things.* Because the Pestalozzian teacher bases his lessons and his questions on the pupils' knowledge, they develop self-confidence in answering accurately the questions that arise in their own minds. This leads to freer, less inhibited decision making and usually to a higher proportion of "right conclusions."[20] This inclination toward "right conclusions" derives in part from personal acquaintance with objects and realities, not just words.

Knowledge thus attained will be "deeply impressed on the mind, and therefore durable."[21]

5. *The Pestalozzian system relates directly to religious and philosophical values.* Mason compares the two ways of learning, direct and vicarious, to the "two ways that man is taught by his Maker":

> Does the Divine Teacher design to communicate that which, by our own powers, we could never attain? [These matters] He teaches us by direct revelation... when He would have us to know of the wonderful works by which He has surrounded us.... He requires of us the exercise of those powers [of our own].... Here then we have the two grand forms of teaching; the first *immediate*, by positive affirmation;—the second *mediate*, through our own powers of observation and action. This latter is the Pestalozzian, or inductive method.[22]

The correlation between religion and Pestalozzianism is a common theme in Mason's writings. He concludes *A Glance at Pestalozzianism* saying that the method "is no other than the spirit of the gospel, applied to the work of education in all its details."

These ideas were revolutionary in 1830. It took professional courage for an already successful teacher to embrace this strikingly different approach to education. All through his life, at every opportunity, Mason reminded others of the lofty purposes behind music instruction: music was to "exalt, ennoble, purify thoughts, feelings and associations of the young" with the result that our children will be "better and happier" (*The Song-Book of the School-Room,* 1847).

In addition to espousing the bold, new Pestalozzian approach, Mason dared to teach at the Perkins Institute for the Blind in Boston in 1832-36. This school, the first of its kind in America, was a pacesetter in many ways, including music training for its students. The school was the idea of Dr. John D. Fisher, who had visited the Royal Institution for the Blind in Paris. Two benefactors who helped establish the American school were Dr. Samuel Gridley Howe, the school's director, and Thomas Handasyd Perkins, the Boston merchant-philanthropist who endowed the New England Institute for the Blind, which then changed its name in his honor.[23]

Dr. Howe had studied European methods of education during a trip abroad in 1831. The following year Perkins supplied the funding for the program Howe developed, and the school opened in 1832 with six pupils, ages six through twenty. Seeing the need for such a program and the progress being made, the state legislature appropriated $6,000 for 1833. From then on, the school's existence was assured.

While organizing the program, Dr. Howe decided that music would make his wards' lives more pleasant. Having heard of Lowell Mason's work, Howe contacted Mason, who readily agreed to teach at the School for the Blind. So far as Mason could determine, no music teacher had undertaken such a task before, at least not in the United States. Therefore, he had to devise a system suited to the unique circumstances. The method he settled upon was chiefly a rote system, but included vocal music, piano, and organ. The program continued after he himself had left the position.

Mason's abilities as an educator became well known. Having built a distinguished career, he found himself a leading promoter of music education. His various activities in Boston added up to impressive credentials, and his music books had spread his fame far beyond that city. Yet, despite growing public recognition and personal prestige, Mason had not moved the Boston public school officials to include music as part of the regular school curriculum. That one goal eluded him and others who believed as he did in the importance of music training for all children. Mason seemed to have exhausted his resources. What more could he do to convince the Boston School Committee?

Mason himself answered that question in two ways. First, he intensified the promotion of his ideas through his books. Using his prefaces as a platform, Mason widely circulated his educational goals and ideals. Second, he joined others with similar beliefs in forming an organization through which mutually agreed-upon objectives could be pursued. Thus was born the Boston Academy of Music on January 8, 1833, coincidentally Mason's forty-first birthday.

The idea of a music academy in Boston had been considered as early as 1826. In fact, the possibility was a minor consideration in efforts to bring Mason to Massachusetts from Georgia. But before such a venture could succeed, public support was essential, and support probably would not have been forthcoming in 1826 or even in 1830. Perhaps the experience of another community is noteworthy. A music academy was opened in Philadelphia in 1825 as an adjunct of the Musical Fund Society. Though it had a "complete corps of instructors, even the orchestral instruments being represented," the school lost money for six consecutive years, after which it closed.[24]

Mason and his closest associate, George J. Webb, made certain that they had firm public support before trying anything comparable. The chief means to that support were their tuition-free music classes and their students' public concerts. Contemporary accounts indicate that these performances had electrifying effects upon the audiences. Here is one account:

> The public were surprised and delighted by the exhibition of the musical attainments of a class of very juvenile performers. . . . Never shall we forget the mingled emotions of wonder, delight, vanquished incredulity, and pleased hope, with which these juvenile concerts were attended. The coldest heart was touched, and glistening eyes and quivering lips attested the depth . . . of the feelings excited in the bosoms of parents and teachers; while the happy little pupils . . . seemed to have acquired a new sense. . . . Their excitement was so great as to make frequent repetition dangerous, and the concerts were soon discontinued, notwithstanding

the urgent solicitation of many to whom they were equally new and delightful. But it was manifest that the object had been gained; a deep and lasting impression had been made on the public mind and the public heart.[25]

Lowell Mason did not allow this "deep and lasting impression on the public mind and heart" to dissipate; rather, he rallied supporters and established an organization to advance his educational concepts and goals.

The Boston Academy of Music

The Boston Academy of Music began as an association of about fifty Bostonians dedicated to offering musical opportunities to more people than ever before. Most of the founders were businessmen, civic leaders, clergy, or educators, not musicians. Organized on January 8, 1833, the academy was incorporated March 22 with its first annual report dated July 3 of that year.

Though he was the key figure in the academy, Lowell Mason deliberately kept his name in the background. This was politically astute: the prestige of the academy and its leaders stood in the foreground while Mason worked steadily in the background. There, under his watchful promotion, the right conditions developed for attaining his goals (identical with the academy's goals). In the first annual report, Mason is recognized only as a "professor." Understating his role, the report adds that the academy's first step was "to engage Mr. Mason to relinquish a lucrative situation [unspecified, but perhaps his part-time bank job] for the purpose of devoting his whole time to the instruction of classes" under the auspices of the academy.

These classes continued the music teaching Mason had done in Boston in the preceding five years. Because the academy had no facilities of its own until 1835, he went on teaching in community facilities, including churches. As before, he conducted classes for both children and adults. In March 1833, the academy hired George J. Webb as an "associate professor" because the demand for instruction was more than Mason could handle alone. Webb taught instrumental and secular music; both men taught vocal music classes for children and adults.

The academy's objectives, fully outlined in the first annual report, were ambitious. They included extensive teaching (like that done by Mason and Webb) and the sponsoring of concerts to show pupils' accomplishments. The academy also planned to present lectures on music, to publish essays on music, and to form classes for training music teachers. Finally, the academy intended to "introduce vocal music into schools, by the aid of such teachers as the academy may be able to employ, each of whom shall instruct classes alternately in a number of schools."

The earliest extant membership list of the Boston Academy of Music is dated 1835. Though many of the sixty persons included were probably members earlier than that, a precise list of the actual founders cannot be formed. Within the early months these founders drew up a constitution that guided the academy well throughout its existence.[26]

That constitution placed responsibility on the officers "to devise and execute measures to accomplish the object of the institution," thus making the election of strong leaders important. During its first few months, the academy had a series of presidents, as indicated in *The Psaltery* (Mason and Webb, (1845): Bradford Sumner, William W. Stone, Jacob Abbott, Samuel A. Eliot. In the first annual report, Abbott was listed as president; Sumner and Stone apparently preceded him in those few months from January 8 to July 3, 1833.

Dr. Abbott was well qualified to be the academy president. A graduate of Bowdoin College and Andover Theological Seminary, he had founded Mt. Vernon School for "girls' higher education" in 1829. The first of its type in the United States, this school contributed to Abbott's reputation as a progressive educator. He was also an officer in the increasingly prestigious American Institute of Instruction. When he left his academy position in 1835, he became a pastor in Roxbury, Massachusetts.[27]

Other persons named in that first report as part of the governing board were David Greene, vice president; George William Gordon, recording secretary; William C. Woodbridge, corresponding secretary; Julius A. Palmer, treasurer; and George E. Head, Daniel Noyes, Bela Hunting, H. M. Willis, J. S. Withington, William J. Hubbard, George H. Snelling, Benjamin Perkins, Moses Grant, and William W. Stone as counselors. These men also served during the academy's second year.

The Reverend David Greene (1791-1866) was graduated from Yale in 1821. He taught for a year at a private girls' school in Boston before attending Andover Seminary. In 1826, as a graduate of the seminary, he became an assistant to the corresponding secretary of the American Board of Commissions for Foreign Missions, in which capacity he traveled over six thousand miles and visited thirty missions. Later he became secretary of the board. In 1831 he collaborated with Lowell Mason in the compilation of *Church Psalmody*, a volume containing seven hundred hymn and psalm texts without music. About 150,000 copies of the book were distributed over subsequent years.[28]

Julius A. Palmer (1802-1872), a deacon at Lyman Beecher's church, was a merchant and financier active in many state and city functions. His brother, the Reverend Ray Palmer (1808-1887), later contributed texts to Lowell Mason for hymn tunes. His most famous text, "My Faith Looks Up to Thee," has (as Mason predicted) been remembered long after his other work has been forgotten.[29]

George William Gordon was a senior member in a prosperous firm of importers and from 1831 to 1836 a member of the Boston city council. Because he actively supported William Henry Harrison for president in 1840, Boston citizens got up a petition of nine hundred signers (mostly from among Boston's elite) and sent it to President Harrison, requesting that Gordon be appointed Boston's postmaster. This request was granted, and Gordon served until President Tyler replaced him in 1844. Gordon was reinstated by President Fillmore on the recommendation of Daniel Webster.[30]

One of the shrewdest moves of the organizers was the selection of William C. Woodbridge, editor of the *American Annals of Education,* as corresponding secretary. This one move insured that the academy's every act was promptly reported across the nation in that widely circulated publication.

The academy attracted the support of other leaders as well. Samuel A. Eliot (1798–1862), the mayor of Boston from 1836 to 1840, was involved with the organization from the very beginning. After his 1820 graduation from Harvard Divinity School, Eliot had studied abroad, concentrating on languages, literature, and music. When he returned, he became active in civic affairs. In December 1833 he was elected to the Boston School Committee. The following two years he served on the board of aldermen, the city council that appropriated funds.

Upon Abbott's resignation from the academy presidency in 1835, Eliot began his twelve-year tenure in that position. The academy had been firmly established by that time and was widely recognized for musical leadership. Eliot, an articulate spokesman for the causes espoused by the organization, delivered a powerful speech extolling those causes at ceremonies for the opening of the Odeon (the academy's first home) on August 5, 1835. Mason and Webb immediately published the speech in their magazine, *The Musical Library,* in the August and October 1835 issues. Other journals also printed Eliot's remarks.

Lowell Mason forfeited personal attention by being designated as only a professor at the academy, yet he could undertake in the name of the academy more than would have been possible as an individual. Theodore F. Seward, who knew Mason well, said that official reports were carefully worded to convey the impression that the academy was first and that Mason was subordinate.[31] But such was not actually the case. Mason was a man who wanted to be the leader in any undertaking. In this situation, however, he kept deliberately behind the scenes so that his objectives (and the academy's) could better be achieved.

Officially, Mason had two assignments at the academy: to improve church music and to establish music in the public school curriculum. The academy classes fit perfectly with both those goals, and they were popular as well. As indicated in the annual reports, the classes drew large numbers of students. At the beginning of its operation, the academy enrolled nearly 1,200 children and

500 adults. By the close of the first six months, the children's classes had grown to over 1,500 pupils with some as young as five years old. During the second year of its operation, the total number of students reached about 3,000. Classes were held in various places in Boston, Salem, Lynn, and Cambridge. During that second year, about 500 additional students were reached in private schools in Cambridgeport, Charlestown, and Boston.

After more than two years of operation, the academy leased the Federal (or "Boston") Theater at the corner of Franklin and Federal Streets, then remodeled to provide a large hall for public concerts and smaller rooms for offices and classes. The concert hall accommodated 3,000 people and featured one of the finest organs in the nation, an instrument built by Thomas Appleton, an associate of William Goodrich.[32] The name of the building was changed to the Odeon, derived from the Greek word, *oideion,* meaning a small, roofed theater in ancient Greece or Rome, hence a hall for musical or dramatic performances.

The academy sponsored many public lectures and concerts at the Odeon and elsewhere each year, all the while gaining public support for music and music education. Concert programs, announcements, and reviews of these functions appeared in almost every music journal. In 1835 the academy had a trained choir of about two hundred members and a fledgling orchestra composed mostly of amateurs. In that year, Joseph A. Keller, teacher and violinist, was hired to direct the orchestra. In the annual report of the following year, five public concerts by the choir are mentioned, and in each instance, the orchestra assisted the choir.

One of the earliest performances of the choir (May 13, 1835) featured portions of Sigismund Neukomm's oratorio, *David.* Because the Odeon had not yet opened, this program was presented in the Bowdoin Street Church, one of several sites for academy concerts in the first years. A typical program offered a wider variety of selections, as was the case for a May 30, 1838 program. A copy of the printed program for the occasion is preserved at the Newberry Library in Chicago. An eight-page pamphlet, it lists selections, but without credits given to performers or directors:

BOSTON ACADEMY OF MUSIC ANNIVERSARY CONCERT
by the CHOIR with Organ
Accompaniment
Wednesday, May 30, 1838

Part I
1. Handel Chorus "How Excellent is Thy Name, O Lord"
2. G. J. Webb Song "When From the Sacred Garden Driven"
3. Recitative and Chorus by Haydn
     Recitative: "The Host of Midian Prevailed"
     Chorus: "The Arm of the Lord Was Upon Them"

4. Song, Novello: "The Infant's Prayer"
5. Chorus by Pergolesi: "Glory to God in the Highest"

---

5 minute interval

Part II
1. Chorus by Mozart "Glory be to God on High"
2. Duet "The Butterfly"
3. Chorus by Mozart:
     "Let us all with joyful mind,
     Praise the Lord, for He is kind;
     For His mercies shall endure,
     Ever faithful, ever sure."
4. Song by Dr. Callcott "The Seasons"
5. Chorus by Handel "Hallelujah"

By 1835 Mason had two adult mixed choirs of about two hundred voices each. One of these groups met at the Odeon, the other in Providence, Rhode Island. With these and other additions, his teaching and conducting duties expanded as the years passed. In 1837, about one hundred academy students organized the Musical Education Society. They wanted further musical training, and to that end, met weekly under Mason or Webb and sang glees, madrigals, oratorio choruses, and other works. Members of this group made so much improvement that, before long, they presented a concert at the Melodeon, a popular concert hall in Boston.

The Musical Education Society continued until 1857 when the members "became weary of courting fickle favor" and "retired into private sessions for their own improvement and enjoyment."[33] During the twenty years of its existence, the group grew in its abilities and as early as 1849 was considered a professional rather than an amateur agency. Its governing council included Jonas Chickering, Moses Kimball, Augustus Flagg, Oliver Ditson, B. F. Edmands, H. K. Oliver, and Lowell Mason. The group had its own constitution with bylaws stating that Lowell Mason was the leader of the organization.

Until 1838 the academy choir devoted itself almost exclusively to the cultivation of sacred music, but it then began to include glees and other secular music in its concerts. A representative program was reviewed in the *Boston Musical Gazette* in the November 28, 1838 issue:

Concert

At the Odeon, Wednesday evening, November 21, 1838

This was a very pleasant and rational entertainment, and met the approbation of a highly respectable auditory. Sacred music, almost entirely, has heretofore received the attention of the Academy, and their Oratorios have generally been very well attended. These Secular Concerts, of Glees, &c. which we understand are contemplated to be given occasionally by this Choir, will, no doubt, receive encouragement by our music-loving community, and will accord a very agreeable variety in this kind of amusement.

The Chorus:—"Awake, Aeolean Lyre"—was not given with the life and spirit that it is deserving of. But it is in the power of this Choir to do it justice, and we hope it will be performed again on another occasion.

Morning Song. This was very fine;—beautifully done. The coming-in exact in time was remarkable.

Glee—"The Fisherman"—Nothing pleased better;—it was repeated. We have heard it several times by the same FOUR; but never to so great acceptance. They are so well yoked that their performances of a certain character are extremely effective.

Glee—"Hail! smiling morn,"—This beautiful glee was excellent; —sung with spirit and expression.

Glee—"Here in cool grot"—It is a favorite piece, and was not *marred;* but given as we thought, agreeably to the distinguished author's design.

Chorus—"The sun's gay beam,"—gave much pleasure.

Chorus—"We are all noddin."—Never heard it performed so appropriately.

The organ and piano-forte were played by the talented Professor [Webb, presumably] with a taste and judgment, that we seldom witness. It is enough to say that this part was, what it ought to be,—an *accompaniment.*

The precision and exactness of the Conductor [Mason, presumably] we highly approved.

Further praise of the choir's abilities appeared in *The Musical Reporter,* which in February 1841 announced that the academy was to present a series of concerts including a portion of a Schiller poem set to music by Romberg. The writer adds that the choir "is well qualified to do ample justice to this or any other piece. . . . They are an able and powerful body competent to read the most difficult music and judge accurately of good musical expression and correct taste."[34] In 1838 the choir had forty sopranos, forty altos, fifty tenors, and sixty basses. An instrumental group of about thirty players, still mostly amateurs, performed with them.[35]

In the 1840s the academy devoted more attention to instrumental works. In 1841, the choir disbanded and a smaller one was organized. That group presented fewer concerts, while the orchestra presented more. At that time the academy orchestra concerts were the only such programs available to Bostonians.[36] Through the efforts of the academy, Boston developed its first large orchestra, a group that continued for seven years after the academy itself dissolved in 1847.[37]

Instrumental concerts entered the academy's series in 1841, though they were still interspersed with vocal solos and glees. A sample program, performed on February 13, 1841, included a Beethoven symphony, a song from *The Seasons* by Haydn, a Strauss waltz, the overture to the opera *Fidelio,* a duo for the organ by Mozart, a glee, and the overture to Rossini's opera *Gazza Ladra,* but development of a strong orchestra was slow and difficult.[38]

The popularity of the academy concerts was reflected in unusually good attendance and an occasional full house. This latter detail was often mentioned by contemporary reviewers, as for instance, in the account of a concert on October 25, 1845, in *The Boston Musical Review* of November 1 of that year. The reviewer also discussed the portion of Beethoven's Pastoral Symphony presented on that occasion by the academy orchestra. In addition, the academy brought in outstanding artists and groups to perform in some of the programs; for instance, in 1845 they engaged a large orchestra for a series of six concerts.

More important than the commercial success of the concerts was their offering of new works to the American public. A number of the Beethoven symphonies were introduced in this country by the academy. The very first American performance of a Beethoven symphony was heard on February 10, 1841, when the twenty-three member academy orchestra, directed by Henry Schmidt, performed the Fifth Symphony. Three days later the same group gave the American premiere of Beethoven's First Symphony[39] and on November 12, 1842, the first American performance of Beethoven's Second Symphony. Through these concerts A. W. Thayer (1817–1897), who became Beethoven's biographer, was first attracted to Beethoven.

As "agents of the public to procure good music . . . and [as] the stewards... to distribute [music],"[40] the academy provided various other services to the community. At least as early as 1834 it offered financial aid and tuition-free instruction to pupils who otherwise could not have afforded music training. To offset the scholarship students, the academy set up private classes for children whose parents were willing to pay for more thorough training than was provided in the classes.

Reports verify these arrangements, but the precise details are not spelled out. The second annual report of the academy (dated May 1834) states that the academy spent $600 to subsidize the free classes as well as $165 for concerts that year, but does not indicate the source of the funds. Apparently during its first year of operation, the academy collected money from class members though it did not pay its professors any salary. After that year, Mason and Webb apparently collected fees directly from their pupils, and the academy paid them for their other duties, such as choir directing. Mason was paid $2,286.88 in April 1834; he was paid $688.05 in April 1836, for "salary &c for 2 years." The probability that Mason collected money directly from his pupils after 1834 accounts for the difference in these amounts.

Although the academy offered lectures on the "nature, objects, and character of music," sometimes involving a choir "to give people an idea of what is to be attained for the churches,"[41] public school music education remained its goal as the chief means of church music reform. Little by little, the organization altered public opinion concerning music instruction for all children. According to the annual report of 1839, "In the present state of public opinion upon the subject of education in music, it is not easy to convey to others an idea of the apathy which formerly existed in relation to it, or the doubts and distrust which its friends had to encounter." The report states that people were accepting the idea of music education for all children and recognizing its potential for success.

By 1844 the annual report, referring to the orchestral programs and performances of Beethoven's symphonies, noted that the "taste of the public for this kind of music is now so decided, that we shall be able to do more for the encouragement of the artist and the pleasure of the audience [in the future]." But for the academy, the future was to be brief: it ceased operations in 1847. By that time, most of its objectives had been met and its leaders were committed to other endeavors, some of which had grown directly from their work in the academy. The academy had extended its influence across the state and nation through teachers' classes, conventions, music publications, and classes convened outside the immediate Boston area. Public support of music education grew from all these activities, and it came from many parts of the United States.

In 1851, in a farewell address to his choir members in Boston, Lowell Mason commented that the Boston Academy of Music survived through its descendants:

> The Academy is still living, though, since its children have grown up around it; as it never desired to exhibit itself, it has gradually retired from most of its active labors, leaving younger ones to carry on the work which it commenced. The Musical Education Society, the [American] Musical Fund Society, music in the schools, musical conventions, and teachers classes, are among its legitimate offspring, and are its heirs and representatives. The inheritance which they possess is not one of silver and gold, but it is a spirit of universal musical improvement. This they are bound to receive and cherish.[42]

The Outreach of the Boston Academy of Music

As early as 1835 the Boston Academy of Music received letters from Georgia, South Carolina, Virginia, Tennessee, Ohio, Maryland, New York, Connecticut, Vermont, New Hampshire, and Maine, plus several communities in Massachusetts. Most of these letters sought advice on means of introducing music in local public schools. This rapid, widespread recognition of the academy came through the *American Annals of Education,* as well as through

Lowell Mason's many activities. He was becoming ever more active as a teacher, a lecturer, and an editor of music books, thereby making the academy's objectives known far beyond Boston.

The *Essex Register* of May 2, 1833 announced the opening on May 15, 1833 of a singing school in Salem, Massachusetts:

> The subscribers, members of a committee appointed at a public meeting at the Lyceum Hall, respectfully give notice that they have engaged Mr. Lowell Mason, Professor of the Boston Academy of Music, to give instruction in the *Elementary Principles of Vocal Music* to a School organized on the following plan:-
>
> The school shall consist of two divisions, an Adult and a Juvenile Class. The Junior Class will assemble for instruction on the afternoon of Monday, at 5 o'clock, and continue until 6. It will re-assemble for instruction on Tuesday morning at a quarter before 6 o'clock, and continue for one hour. [These hours may have been chosen to accommodate Mason, who had to commute by stagecoach about 14 miles from Boston to Salem, or to accommodate the pupils' work hours.] This Class will consist of pupils of seven years and upwards. The Adult Class will assemble on the evening of Monday at 8 o'clock.
>
> The school will continue during one term of 6 months, commencing on the 2nd Monday of May. Tickets for admission for the term, at Five Dollars for the Adult Class, and Four Dollars for the Juvenile Class, may be found at the Bookstores of Messrs Whipple & Lawrence, J. M. Ives, W. & S. B. Ives, and Samuel West. . . .

Subscribers were then listed. One of them was Henry Kemble Oliver (1800-1885), a Harvard graduate who spent his life in teaching, politics, and church music. During a lesson of the adult class thus advertised, Oliver's tune, named Federal Street, was discovered. Mason had asked his pupils whether any of them had ever composed a tune. The question jogged Oliver's memory. He had written a short hymn tune, then cast it into a dresser drawer and forgotten it. He had named it for the street he lived on in Salem, Massachusetts. When Mason saw the tune, he was impressed; with Oliver's permission, he published it in 1835 in *The Boston Academy Collection of Church Music*. The tune, still widely used, has been set to various texts, including "Jesus, and shall it ever be."

Shortly after accepting this teaching engagement in Salem, Mason was invited to address the Essex County Teachers' Association at nearby Topsfield, Massachusetts. At this semiannual meeting (May 25-26, 1833) Mason was one of five speakers who addressed the 300-member audience.

A report in the *Salem Gazette* of June 21, 1833 described all the speeches as "highly interesting, generally extemporaneous, and of a more decidedly practical character than usually delivered on similar occasions." About Mason's speech, the reporter wrote:

Mr. Mason's lecture on teaching music to children was delivered in the meeting-house. He was attended by a select Juvenile Choir from Boston. Standing in front of the pulpit he gave to the audience, by means of a blackboard, an outline of his method of teaching which, for some years past, he has practiced with so much success.

The proficiency of his pupils was truly astonishing. They would read, at sight, lessons in music written on the blackboard, with the greatest apparent facility. Their singing, too, was characterized by a precision, richness, and perfection, utterly incredible to those who have not had the pleasure of listening to their performances. It will doubtless be gratifying to teachers to learn that Mr. Mason is preparing for publication a Manual of Instruction, embracing his whole system of teaching, and that it will probably be issued from the press in about four months.

The Salem school was so well received that Mason was asked to repeat it and double the length of sessions. He agreed, then invited his friend Joseph A. Keller to assist him. Keller, who had settled in Salem in 1830 to teach piano, flute, violin, and vocal music, taught one of the two children's classes set up for the 1834–35 season. Mason continued to teach the adult class and one children's class, necessitating continued travel to Salem weekly in 1834–35. He and Keller worked together later as well, for in 1836, Keller became a full-time teacher at the Boston Academy.

The printed program of the December 30, 1833 concert (concluding the first series of lessons), carried this announcement:

JUVENILE SINGING SCHOOL

Mr. Mason and Mr. Keller will commence on Monday, 14th January, a Class for children and youth to be continued twice a week (with the exception of the usual vacations) for one year, or, until the close of December, 1834. Tickets of admission for the whole term may be had at the bookstores, for $6 each.

A Class for Adults will also commence on the 4th Monday in January, and be continued through the year, once a week. Tickets at $6 for the whole term.
L. Mason, Professor, Boston
  Academy of Music
J. A. Keller,
  Salem[43]

By 1835 Mason managed heavy responsibilities as a teacher and a busy itinerary as a lecturer. The lecture engagements often involved tiring, time-consuming travel to cities that (by the standards of the 1830s) were at a considerable distance from Boston. For instance, to speak to the third annual meeting of the American Lyceum in New York City on May 4, 1833, Mason rode in a stagecoach over forty miles of rough road to Providence, Rhode Island, then spent about twenty-three hours on a steamboat to New York City. On this and other trips, he carried a notebook for jotting down ideas as they came to him, thus using the time as best he could.[44] Despite the time and inconveniences involved, in a typical year (1835) he spoke to groups in churches, schools, private clubs, and music organizations in Boston, Newton, New Bedford, and Bradford, Massachusetts; New York City; Hartford and New Haven, Connecticut; Brunswick and Portland, Maine; Portsmouth and Exeter, New Hampshire.[45] (For an overview of his lecture schedule during the Boston years, see the listing of Mason's activities in appendix A.)

Mason's speech before the Boston Brattle Square Church on January 13, 1835 was especially memorable. In this church he and Joseph Stevens Buckminster had been friends twenty-five years earlier. Immediately after speaking, Mason motioned his assistants, the academy choir, to rise. The group then demonstrated several musical styles under his direction with Webb accompanying them at the organ. The speech, plus the performance, made such an impression that a repeat of the evening's presentation was requested. Academy leaders agreed, suggesting that a children's choir might be of interest the next time. This idea having been approved, on February 25, Mason directed his children's choir in a concert of twenty-two songs, some of Swiss origin and some of his own composition. Many of these were later published in the *Juvenile Lyre* and similar books.[46]

The close links between teaching and lecturing were also apparent in Mason's work at Andover Theological Seminary in Andover, Massachusetts. This school was founded in 1807 by Congregationalists as one reaction to the Unitarian movement at Harvard. In 1832 Mason was invited to speak before the Lockhart Society for Improvement in Sacred Music, a voluntary student group at the seminary. Unable to appear because of other commitments, he sent a complimentary copy of his latest book, *The Choir, or Union Collection of Church Music*. Then in 1836, he set up a music class at Andover, reputedly the first of its kind in any Protestant seminary in the United States. For the first time the seminary fulfilled this objective in its constitution:

> As it is proper for those, who are to preside in the assemblies of God's people, to possess themselves of much skill and taste in this sublime art [music], as at least to distinguish between those solemn movements, which are congenial to pious minds, and those unhallowed, trifling, medley pieces which chill devotion; it is expected, that serious attention will be paid to the culture of a true taste for genuine Church Music in this Seminary; and that all students therein . . . will be duly instructed in the theory and practice of this celestial art.[47]

Members of the Bowdoin Street Church choir often went along to Andover to illustrate points Mason made in his class there. Though his course was extracurricular, nearly all the seminary students enrolled. The Boston Academy Report of 1837 recognized the class as "very large" and "most interesting." Mason continued these classes annually—apparently with no pay—until 1844, when he had to give them up because of the pressure of his other work.

In recognition of his efforts, upon his resignation the Andover students presented him a copy of the Holy Bible, bound in full black morocco, tooled in gilt and lettered with his name and the date on the front cover.[48] Mason made deep, long-lasting friendships at Andover, and also at Phillips Andover Academy, a closely aligned institution nearby. He often composed music for the annual academy "exhibitions," events similar to modern commencement exercises. He was as warmly received at Phillips as at the seminary. It was not unusual for him to linger after classes to talk informally with the students.

One of Mason's most important lectures during the 1830s was his address to the American Institute of Instruction in August 1834. He spoke on "Music, as a branch of school instruction, and the Pestalozzian Method of teaching it," with his children's choir providing illustrations. After the lecture, a well-established Boston educator, Gideon F. Thayer, offered a resolution supporting music instruction in the schools. Thayer, founder of Chauncey Hall School in Boston in 1828, had employed Mason to teach music at Chauncey Hall during 1833-34 and was impressed with Mason's teaching before this address. It is therefore not surprising that he offered a resolution which read in part:

> *Resolved,* that the introduction of Vocal Music into our schools is an object of high importance to the community, and the American Institute of Instruction do hereby most cordially recommend it to public favor.[49]

The group unanimously adopted this resolution, but it is not clear what effect, if any, the passing of this or any other resolution had upon the Boston School Committee or upon officials of any public school. Indirect effects, such as swaying public opinion, cannot be weighed precisely either.

The Boston Academy of Music also encouraged others to lecture on behalf of the causes it endorsed. According to the tenth annual report of the academy, July 1842, a circular was sent to clergy in Massachusetts and surrounding states, asking for their help. It suggested that if clergymen exerted their influence in favor of music, both public school music programs and church music programs (congregational and choir) would improve. The circular was sent in October 1841, and by the following summer many of the recipients had responded favorably. Indeed, some of them had spoken out concerning musical needs of their communities and had subscribed to singing schools to improve music locally.

Deliberate seeking of public assistance typified the academy's operations. At the same time, however, personal contacts were always maintained. In the midst of his other activities, Lowell Mason took time to correspond with those who sought his advice through letters. A few from the 1830s are extant, including one dated July 6, 1833. Simply addressed to "Dear Sir," there is no identification of the addressee. It is clear from the content, however, that Mason was answering specific questions raised by a church musician–singing school teacher:

> In performance of music in *Church* it often has a good effect to dwell a little upon the last note of each line. But in a singing school I always require them to sing in exact time and obtain the pause at the end of the line by making the last note of the line shorter. I always urge it upon a school to make all notes which are followed by rests shorter by considerable than they otherwise would be—also to make the last note of the tune and the last note of each line shorter than the same kind of notes in other places. There is always a disposition to drawl out the last notes of lines and I try to correct it early in a School.

Mason also maintained contacts with other musicians through publications during the years of his work at the academy. Those years marked the publication of a number of important books, many of which sold widely across the country. The first of these was also one of the most important publications of his career, namely, *Manual of the Boston Academy of Music, for Instruction in the Elements of Vocal Music, on the System of Pestalozzi* (Boston: Carter, Hendee & Co., 1834). This 252-page book was intended to help teachers apply a specific pedagogical system in their classrooms and to help parents teach music in their homes.

The book begins with general observations on the Pestalozzian system as Mason understood it, a statement about his sources of information, and a summary of the advantages of cultivating vocal music. He then discusses appropriate classroom equipment for music teaching, qualifications for teachers, and—at the heart of the book—methods of teaching individual elements of music, e.g., rhythm, tempo, melody, intervals, transposition, dynamics, and articulation. Dozens of music examples are included. Explicit instructions are provided for the teacher, along with material to demonstrate or write on the chalkboard and questions to ask the students.

The intentions of the academy and of Mason himself were announced in the preface:

> One of the objects originally contemplated by this institution, was to furnish facilities for teachers of music, and thereby diminish the obstacles which impede the progress of those who wish to acquire a correct knowledge of the art. In conformity with this design, the Academy now present to the public the following Manual... prepared by one of their professors.[50] The method of teaching music here proposed having been applied to various classes of learners with great success under the auspices of the Academy, they feel prepared to recommend it to teachers of music, instructors of common schools, heads of families, and to all who desire to acquire and to communicate a thorough knowledge of the elementary principles of vocal music.... This treatise is essentially different from that of any other... which has been published in this country.... We cannot but hope that this Manual will prepare the way for, and be the means of introducing a greatly improved method of teaching vocal music; and that this study so deeply interesting, especially when its connexion

with the public and social worship of God is considered, will receive a far more general and thorough attention from all classes of the community, than it has received heretofore, and will, at no distant day, take rank among the branches of common school education.

The novelty of this book was recognized by William Gardiner, the English compiler whose *Sacred Melodies* had been a model for Mason in his earlier years. Gardiner was sent a complimentary copy of the *Manual*. In response, he wrote an American friend, James A. Dickson, on February 26, 1835 from Leicester, England, as follows:

I have duly received your letter, also the parcel, for which I am truly obligated to you. I beg of you to make my acknowledgments to the author, Mr. Mason, and to thank him for the very ingenious little book he has sent me. . . . It is remarkable that, in this country, though we have books upon music as far back as Thomas Morley, certainly we have not a book as yet, comparable with the manual, printed at Boston. It is highly creditable to the new world, to set us such a pattern.

The *Manual* became so popular that it went through eight editions, the last one in 1861. In all editions Mason makes the following statement:

SOURCES OF INFORMATION. These are various, but always derived from personal experience, or the written experience of others, and never from mere theory. The system must be traced to Pestalozzi. . . . He obtained the services of Pfeiffer and Nägeli, who . . . drew up a very extensive work on elementary instruction in vocal music [the *Gesangbildungslehre nach Pestalozzischen Grundsätzen,* or *Instruction in Singing According to Pestalozzian Principles,* Leipzig, 1810]. Other works on the same general principles, were afterwards published by Kübler, and other distinguished German teachers, in which much improvement was made on the original treatise of Pfeiffer and Nägeli. These German works have been introduced into this country by Wm. C. Woodbridge . . . and these have been made the basis of the following work.

Mason was more precise in a footnote in *Carmina Sacra: or Boston Collection of Church Music* (1841). There he referred to a work by the Stuttgart music teacher G. F. Kübler, a work which "was mostly followed, so much so, indeed, that to a great extent the *Manual* may be called a translation of that work." Kübler's work, *Anleitung Zum Gesang-Unterrichte in Schulen,* or *Guide to the Study of Singing in Schools,* was published in 1826 in Stuttgart. The translation of the work was evidently commissioned by Mason; the translator is believed to have been James F. Warner.[51]

Analysis, such as that done by Howard E. Ellis, has shown that Mason followed the text and music of the *Anleitung* very closely. Of the hundreds of examples and exercises included by Kübler, all but ten appear in the *Manual*. It is of special interest that much of the Kübler material deviates from the psychological bases that Pestalozzi used, so Mason was in fact less "Pestalozzian" than he apparently believed himself to be. Whether or not

Mason followed Pestalozzi's theories or Kübler's interpretations is not the real issue, since neither Mason nor his followers claimed that he adhered to anyone's precepts rigidly. On the contrary, as Mason himself said repeatedly, he drew on many sources, including his own teaching experiences, in developing his ideas.[52]

As a matter of principle, Mason should have acknowledged his indebtedness to the Kübler work in the *Manual* itself. Such an acknowledgment would not have detracted from him; he had arranged to get the translation, had analyzed and tested its contents, and then presented the results coherently to the public. His name and that of the academy hastened (and probably assured) the volume's acceptance. Because the *Manual* filled a definite need and enhanced music teaching and learning, Mason could have been proud of the book even while acknowledging the Kübler work as its basis. Then why didn't he do so? One explanation is that standards of borrowing, assimilating, and giving credit were far looser in the 1830s than is true today (a fact that applies to the handling of music in Mason's many anthologies as well). Another explanation may be that he felt he had acknowledged Kübler's work sufficiently in his opening "Sources of Information" statement in the *Manual.*

According to its stated objectives, the academy sought "improved" musical taste. To this end, it underwrote publication of a magazine, *The Musical Library,* from July 1835 to June 1836, with Mason and Webb the official editors (and unofficial driving forces behind it). The magazine consisted of sixteen super royal quarto pages of music and four pages of printed matter in each monthly issue. Subscription was four dollars annually, though anyone who procured six subscribers and sent the twenty-four dollars got a free subscription. *The Musical Library* published a total of sixty-three vocal pieces, eleven organ and twenty-five piano pieces, representing such diverse composers as von Weber, Neukomm, Himmel, Broaderip, Mozart, Oliver Shaw, Sir John Stevenson, Pleyel, and Boston Academy of Music professors.

Though publication ceased after one year, those twelve issues disseminated ideas from the academy (and Mason in particular). On page one of the first issue, the editors announced that they would endeavor to provide information that would be "interesting and useful" to singing school teachers and to give "instructions as to the formation and conducting of choral societies and choirs of singers," based on their own experience and that of others.

The twelve issues included subjective articles on the value of music for all children, on music in the schools, and on the desirability of certain teaching methods. The editorial stance was further revealed by the choice of more objective reports concerning music education activities and full reprints of annual reports of the academy. Some articles of a more general nature were also included, e.g., analyses of selected music and discussions about the execution of certain musical passages.

In addition to the publications already mentioned, Mason issued a number of other works under the auspices of the academy, two of which demonstrate his simultaneous efforts in different areas.

The Boston Academy's Collection of Church Music (1835) lists in its full title the musical types it includes and its sources: Haydn, Mozart, Romberg, Nägeli, Kübler, and "other distinguished composers," identified as German, English, and American. The music includes "psalm and hymn tunes, anthems, sentences, and chants," some using the music of the "celebrated composers" only as a point of departure for a new arrangement (almost invariably meaning a simplified one). Mason's part as an arranger is openly stated in the preface.

In 1836 a more uniform collection of sacred music, *The Boston Academy Collection of Choruses,* was published. This volume consisted of twenty-nine choir selections drawn chiefly from Handel, Haydn, and Mozart, with Beethoven, Rossini, Righini, Pergolesi, Graun, and Naumann also represented. According to objectives stated in the book itself, Mason intended to draw into one volume many "useful compositions" and to introduce some "beautiful and effective pieces from German sources which had not been published in the United States previously." This collection of oratorio recitatives and choruses, as well as cantata and mass excerpts, was meant for public concerts by church choirs or music societies rather than for use in church services.

In these and other publications of the 1830s, Mason revealed the spectrum of his interests and proved his dedication to each one. Because he directed his work toward various age levels and many interest groups, he reached millions of Americans. The success of his books added to his reputation as well as to the prestige of the Boston Academy of Music. The net result was that Lowell Mason became a figure of national prominence.

5

Teacher Training Programs

Lowell Mason knew that the success of music education lay in teachers' hands: if the teachers were good, music education could thrive; if the teachers were poor, music education would falter. He could look at singing schools for evidence: inadequately prepared singing school masters limited what those schools accomplished.

Forming a teachers' class was one of the original objectives of the Boston Academy of Music because improved teaching was expected to improve church music. Almost immediately the academy's teachers' class led to conventions, and out of those came instructors capable of making music a valuable curricular addition rather than a short-lived experiment in the public schools.

The teachers' conventions that grew out of the academy's pedagogy classes offered instruction in teaching methods and practice in group singing. These conventions generally extended over a week or ten days, and closed with a public performance of the choral music that had been rehearsed. Because most of those who attended were also church choir directors, the repertoire was mostly sacred choral works. These meetings were well publicized and widely reviewed in music journals from about 1830 to 1900, long after Lowell Mason's participation.

The idea of gathering music teachers for pedagogical purposes was not original with Mason. One earlier convention, specifically for singing school masters, was organized by Henry E. Moore in 1829 under the auspices of the Central Musical Society in Concord, New York. Though there is no evidence that Mason knew about this particular event, he and his associates probably had heard of similar meetings.

In 1834 Mason set up a class in Boston to examine and interpret the *Manual of the Boston Academy*. Twelve teachers attended the ten-day session with lectures by Mason and Webb. They were so impressed with all they learned that they requested a similar meeting the following year, a request that was granted. From that beginning, Mason came to lead a great number of teachers' meetings, thus advancing the music education movement by propagating workable theories and methods, by broadening music repertoire for teachers, and by creating personal rapport among the music teachers who attended. Many of those who attended became, quite naturally, Mason enthusiasts.

These meetings also served to disseminate Mason's books because he based his programs on his own materials. All of the books could be purchased at the convention for use "back home" in whatever quantities were needed. This commercial aspect, definitely a money-maker for Mason, aroused jealousy on the part of some of his less successful rivals.

In August 1836, a teachers' class with an enrollment of twenty-eight members created an organization designed to deal with music education, church music, and music performance. The new organization came to be called the "Musical Convention." The group unanimously adopted three resolutions reflecting the purposes of the conventions from that time on. Printed two years later in a fifty-page booklet entitled "Proceedings of the Musical Convention Assembled in Boston August 16, 1838; Together with a Brief View of the Origin of the Same," the three resolutions read as follows:

> *Resolved,* That the introduction and application of the Pestalozzian System of teaching music form a new era in the science of musical education in this country; and, that in pursuing our labors as teachers, we will conform ourselves as far as circumstances will admit, to that system, as published in the *Manual of the Boston Academy of Music.*

> *Resolved,* That, in order to diffuse a knowledge of music through the community, it is necessary to teach it to our youth; and that it is desirable, and practicable, to introduce it into all our schools, as a branch of elementary education.

> *Resolved,* That it is a source of deep regret to this Convention, that, in so many instances, Religious Societies and Parishes, instead of exerting a fostering care and influence over the cause of Sacred Music, neglect it, suffer it to fall into unskilled hands, and thus, not only wound the cause itself, but make it a detriment, rather than a help, to the best interests of the Church.

These resolutions are Lowell Mason's ideas exactly. From the teacher-training standpoint, forming the convention was a major step. In subsequent years the convention was convened regularly, usually in August, in Boston. The 1838 gathering was especially memorable, in part because of the publication of the proceedings and in part because of innovations in the program. Mason incorporated a lecture on chant that year, while his associate, George Webb, added a lecture on thorough bass. Also included were secular works, such as glees and madrigals, in the choral program.

When the question of music in the public schools came up, the debate was stimulated by one of the members playing the devil's advocate. That member was George Hood (1807-1882), later known for his *History of Music in New*

England (1846). Despite the negative points Hood raised—or perhaps because of skillful countering of those points—the members voted unanimously in favor of music in the public schools, thus affirming the resolution of the 1836 convention. Because the members attending in 1838 represented ten different states, the Boston Academy of Music's ideas were immediately spread far beyond Boston. Indeed, inquiries started to come to the academy from distant points, asking that the professors give short courses in their cities. The academy agreed, and Mason traveled even more extensively, taking his philosophy, methods, and books with him.

For several reasons, Mason's conventions grew faster than those led by his rivals. Without a doubt, he was a masterful organizer and a charismatic leader. Annually he convened regular enrollees and newcomers. He applied his organizational skills to keeping things moving and moving smoothly at the meetings. He demanded top-quality teaching on the part of those who led the sessions. All these factors contributed to remarkable growth in enrollment: in 1838, 134 attended; in 1840, 344; in 1849, about 1,000; in 1851, about 1,500.[1]

By 1840, the convention agendas had settled into a standard pattern to include lectures on the principles in the *Manual of the Boston Academy;* exercises in singing chants, choruses, glees, psalms, and hymns; lectures in harmony; and informal discussion and sharing of problems and experiences. Figured bass was sometimes added as an optional course, offered at a special fee for enrollees. Essentially, though, the conventions focused on pedagogical training and choral participation.

This duality of purpose ultimately led to two specialized organizations. The pedagogical aspect led to teachers' institutes, often called "normal institutes"; the choral participation led to choral societies and choral festivals. Some early participants came with only one of the two purposes in mind and were perturbed about engaging in the other activity, thus causing division within the group.

In 1838 the split between the two factions came into the open. Understanding that jealousies, rivalries, and wounded feelings were involved, Mason tried—not successfully, as it turned out—to smooth over the breach. One of the most outspoken members was a long-time friend and convention member, George Washington Lucas. For at least the previous ten years, Lucas and Mason had been congenial allies as spokesmen for public school music. Lucas had urged ministers to support singing schools and had pleaded for more tastefully selected and better performed church music. Indeed, he had advocated the same reforms as Mason.

Nonetheless, when writing about Mason's music conventions, Lucas' admiration for Mason turned to bitterness. His pique may have been stimulated by H. W. Day, another of Mason's rivals. Day and Lucas, personal friends themselves, apparently encouraged one another's attacks on Mason. In

1844 Lucas aired his resentments in a publication specifically dealing with the conventions. In that essay, "Remarks on the Musical Conventions in Boston," he stated that "the venerable Bartholomew Brown [1772-1854, compiler of the popular *Bridgewater Collection*, 1810], the lamented [Henry W.] Moore [who had died in 1841] and many other persons did not consider the Professors at the Boston Academy of Music to be the *ne plus ultra* of all musical light and excellency."[2]

In addition, Lucas charged Mason with backstage machinations to keep control of the conventions, with planting questions in order to steer the discussion in ways he wished, with hand-picking members of the nominating committee, and with repeatedly backing the loyal but "inept" Colonel Asa Barr for presiding officer. According to Lucas, it was obvious to everyone in attendance that Barr was a puppet whom Mason manipulated at will while maintaining an illusion of a democratically run convention. In short, Lucas let it be known he did not share the "extravagent impressions the student-teachers had of [Mason's] infallibility."[3]

At the 1839 convention, a proposition was offered that would give subsequent meetings complete freedom from Mason's "teachers' classes." Committees were formed to draft a constitution for a new, independent convention. That new constitution, adopted at the 1840 convention, declared that the new "National Musical Convention" was a national agency, independent of the Boston Academy of Music. However, the constitution had little effect. That year, as before, Mason planned and controlled the meetings. Ratification of the constitution did, however, punctuate an otherwise routine convention.

Sometime after the 1839 convention, Mason and Webb had a "falling out," for reasons that are not explained in any remaining records. The eighth annual academy report (issued in July 1840) states simply that Mr. Webb resigned late in 1839 "in consequence of a disagreement with Lowell Mason." The report expressed regret, but "they [the academy] saw, under the circumstances, no alternative preferable, on the whole, to accepting it [the resignation]. They therefore . . . thought it best to accede to his proposition, and to endeavor to supply his place as well as they were able."[4] F. F. Müller was appointed organist for the academy to replace Webb so that, as of July 1840, the staff consisted of Mason, Müller, Joseph Keller, and Henry Schmidt.

Sometime during 1841 the rift was mended, though during that year Webb formed his own teachers' class under the auspices of the Boston Handel and Haydn Society. This deliberate rivalry constituted only one of Mason's problems that year. A more vexing problem was that the convention over which he presided split into two groups midway through its meeting. When Mason and Webb reconciled, Webb resumed his duties at the academy and remained there until the institution dissolved. Some writers believe that because of this estrangement, Mason subsequently consigned Webb to a lower position at the academy than Webb's talents warranted. Whether or not this was the case, the two men remained professional associates and close friends for the rest of their lives.

Meanwhile, Day and Lucas continued their attacks on Mason. Day was a singing school teacher, a publisher, and a compiler of music books, none of which equaled Mason's books in commercial success. There is evidence that Day was intensely jealous of Mason's successes, both in the sale of books and in his position in the Boston Public Schools. As will be discussed in chapter 7, Day was apparently responsible in part for Mason's removal from his school position in 1845.

The climax to the bitterness between Mason and the Day-Lucas duo came in 1846–47. At the 1846 Musical Convention, Day showed up unexpectedly. According to the account of James C. Johnson, who was present at the time, Mason was on the platform when Day appeared. When Mason saw Day, he took a Bible and read, "Now there was a day when the sons of God came together, and Satan also came among them." Then he shut the book, marched down the aisle, and walked Day out of the hall.[5]

Within a year of this episode, Lucas poured out his bitterness in a letter to Day. The letter was printed, but distribution seems to have been limited. A lengthy letter, it sought to cover the full spectrum of grievances Lucas had felt himself or heard expressed, one way or another, by Mason critics over the years. Because it is so comprehensive in reflecting criticisms of Mason and his views and in reflecting tensions between schools of thought in America at the time, much of the letter is quoted here. Other portions are summarized and enclosed in brackets.

Boston, August 23, 1847

To H. W. Day

Dear Sir,—It is amusing to see with what industry and adroitness Mr. Lowell Mason turns every little scrap and thing in the musical world—nay, almost everything in the universal nature, to his own private advantage.... His magic wand has suddenly inspired many a dunce with a superabundance of musical genius and sent him forth a professor, too profound for the tasteless trash of Handel, Haydn and other great masters. So long, then, as Mr. Mason can convert sounds utterly...incompatible with the very nature of melody into strains most enchanting, and so long as he can annually in Boston and other places manufacture hundreds and thousands of illiterate voices into competent teachers of church music...all of whom more highly appreciate the beautiful, airy and *original* productions of their *revered* master, so much better suited to their skill and love of display than the *dull* and *massy* compositions which so inspired...our forefathers.... And, moreover...in almost every church, especially in New England, a choir of some...graduates from that climax of all musical quackery, "the Boston Academy of Music," may be had, who are ready to perform the most difficult music in sight, and who can by frequent use of new tunes prevent all in the congregation but themselves from an active participation in this [musical part of the services].

[Lucas then accuses Mason of having no other purposes in setting up the academy than monopolizing the production of books and promoting sales of his own books. He says that the academy was needed to inspire public confidence in the sale of books. The graduates of the teachers' classes, he says, were "subject to his will to sell them—a splendid scheme and well worthy of the man."]

As a general thing, the graduates of the "Boston Academy of Music" have been found utterly incompetent to teach church music and this has led many to disregard the whole subject. More pernicious to the stability and character of the music in many churches has been the almost constant change in their singing books and tunes, the last fifteen or twenty years. [He then denounces the taste for glees and other secular music which he says was only a "decoy or allurement to the class" at the Academy.]

Why has Lowell Mason recently taken such an interest in congregational singing? An interest so adverse to all his former plans of monopoly and self-aggrandizement? The answer is plain, the great dissatisfaction with the present character of Church Music is too general and strong to be longer concealed or resisted. A time-serving policy therefore, than which no man better understands, now induces Mr. Mason to advocate Congregational Singing—doubtless a prelude to a new book. [Lucas says that many persons still prefer the music of Billings.]

. . . In all his Choirs, Teachers' Classes, and Musical Conventions, he has ever been in my opinion the centre and radiation of the most consummate cant, quackery and self-display. He speaks of "emotion." Cool, cunning, and selfish, what music ever moistened his eye, or except the clinking of silver and gold, ever touched his heart? He is not, however, incapable of "emotion," especially when in a furious rage he ejected a gentleman from last year's class in Boston [see above]. In this kind of "emotion," especially at the presence of his superiors he is not a stranger. . . . [Lucas then accused Mason of repeating entries in his music collections.] . . . The same tune in almost every new book and edition has appeared in a new dress.

[He claims that Mason ridiculed the idea of congregational singing when it was attempted by one or two Baptist churches in Boston "a few years since."] Had Congregational Singing prevailed in our Churches generally as it ever has in Scotland and Germany, the sale of books in which Mr. Mason has been concerned would have been restricted to at least one copy in a hundred which have been sold. Nay, there would have been no "Boston Academy of Music," Teachers Classes, diplomatic professors of music, and no glee Concerts, fashionable singing, etc. in the churches. . . .

Lowell Mason's response to this tirade is unrecorded, but it is certain he knew about it. He had heard similar criticisms before, though probably not at such length and in such vituperative tone and rarely from a friend. Lucas, who was intemperate in more ways than one (as will be shown in chapter 12), revealed more of himself than of Mason in this letter. Ignoring Mason's dedication to teaching, his devotion to the church and its mission, and his desire to bring music to all children (and adults) through whichever organization seemed appropriate, Lucas based his criticism on the common complaint that Mason was an opportunist. The charge was an easy one for any critic who saw how much money and prestige Mason drew from his books and his associations. Judging Mason's motives on that evidence is as one-sided as ignoring the business and political savvy that Mason surely did possess.

More moderate journalists, while observing that the conventions could be used for peddling books (and indeed were used for that purpose), concluded that overall they still did more good than harm. At the very least, teachers who attended had their appetites stimulated for various types of music, at least some of which was better than they had known earlier. This, in turn, led to demands for better music books. Of course, in the thinking of the most capable critic of the period, John Sullivan Dwight (1813–1893), founder and editor of *Dwight's Journal of Music,* "better" music meant European music. He said at one point, "The person who can comprehend, appreciate, feel Mendelssohn, has already won admission to the finer spheres of life."[6]

Mason's conventions reached their full maturity in Boston in the late 1840s and their climax with the five-day meeting that began August 25, 1851. By 1848 his convention attracted about 1,000 people. In both 1847 and 1848, he was assisted by Webb, by his old friend William Russell and Russell's son Francis T. Russell, by Silas Bancroft and L. P. Homer, by George F. Root, and by his son William Mason. The 1849 convention, held in October because of the cholera epidemic in Boston that summer, brought about 1,000 people together. In 1851 Mason knew that his convention was meeting for the last time in Boston. He himself had decided to leave Boston permanently. With Webb as his closest assistant again, he presided over the group. He gave an address recapping the seventeen years since beginning his teachers' class with twelve members. The meeting closed with a performance of Handel's *Messiah* by the Musical Education Society with the orchestra of the Musical Fund Society.

Neither the complex problems nor the complaints of critics slowed the spread of Mason's reputation to every geographic area from which participants were drawn to his meetings, and, in addition, to every point to which he traveled over the years to lead conventions and institutes. Throughout New England, south into New York State and west as far as Cincinnati and Chicago he traveled, annually in some cases, to preside over such meetings. He formed lasting friendships with many of the outstanding musicians and educators of his day, who, in turn, perpetuated his theories, books, and personal acclaim. He became well acquainted with those leaders because he arranged their appearances as guest lecturers and teachers and worked closely with them during their tenure. These teachers included (among others in the loosely knit "Mason circle") George Frederick Root (1820–1895), Luther O. Emerson (1820–1915), Isaac B. Woodbury (1819–1858), and Benjamin F. Baker (1811–1889), all of whom Mason profoundly influenced.

Benjamin F. Baker had an illustrious career as a singer, editor of the *Boston Musical Journal* and several song books, composer of part songs, officer of the Boston Handel and Haydn Society, and educator. He attended

Mason's classes in 1842, 1844, and 1845. In 1845 when Mason was dismissed from the Boston Public Schools, Baker was appointed to take his position. Later, when Mason was reinstated, the two worked together closely. In 1851, when Mason left Boston, Baker assumed full charge of the school position.

Another of Mason's close associates, Isaac B. Woodbury, was similarly involved in a wide range of musical activities: conducting and concertizing with a glee club, editing the *New York Musical Review,* compiling music anthologies, teaching, and composing. Some of his music was used at the conventions and in the anthologies of Mason and others; though it has since fallen into oblivion, at the time of his death, Woodbury's music was sung by more American worshippers than that of anyone else.[7] One of his more original accomplishments was a do-it-yourself book entitled *Woodbury's Self-Instructor in Musical Composition and Thorough Base* [*sic*], a revision of his *Elements of Musical Composition* (1844).

Because of the exceptionally close association that developed between Mason and Root, it is fitting to examine their long friendship somewhat more closely. Root had studied with Baker and Webb, the latter described years later in Root's autobiography as a "delightful teacher."[8] Root also described the incident that led to his appointment to Mason's convention staff. While attending a convention, Root informally gathered a group of about twenty singers from his section of the chorus to help them learn their parts. These singers were so impressed with Root's musical and pedagogical abilities that they went to Mason and requested that Root be allowed to teach singing as an addition to the curriculum. Mason agreed at once and allocated the last hour of each morning for that purpose.

Root instigated the New York Normal Musical Institute, the epitome of the teachers' class-convention concept. The initiation of that institution opened a new dimension in the lives of both Root and Mason (see chapter 10). Root also edited many music books and composed both sacred and secular music.

When Root returned from his European trip of 1850-51 and noticed the great vogue for Stephen Foster's songs, he entered the field of popular song writing. He became one of the Union's most popular composers of Civil War songs, some of them still known and enjoyed: "The Battle Cry of Freedom" and "Tramp, Tramp, Tramp," for example. After 1859 Root settled in Chicago and joined Root and Cady, music publishers and retailers. This firm, established in 1858 by George's older brother, E. Towner Root, and C. M. Cady, prospered until 1871 when destroyed by the famous Chicago fire.

Root described one small incident that indicates Mason's immense popularity and the wide use of his books. While the men were riding on the train toward Auburn, New York to conduct a convention, a group of young ladies in their car began to sing a selection from *The Boston Glee Book* (1838). The men listened attentively, although without revealing their recognition of the music. Meanwhile they thought ahead to a solo bass passage and wondered what the girls would do when they came to that section. Root and another member of the party (identified only as Mr. Johnson), without a word to one another, spontaneously sang the bass passage from memory at the proper time. The girls were astonished. Then Mr. Johnson introduced himself and the others, including Mason. This pleased the young ladies, though, as Root pointed out, it caused that special embarrassment which occurs when one unexpectedly meets a prominent person.[9]

Rochester, New York proved to be an especially successful location for conventions. Mason appeared there frequently, beginning at least as early as 1842. When announcing the convention program to be held in Boston during August 1846, the leaders stated that the entire meeting would be duplicated in Rochester the following month. This procedure was not unusual. That same year lecturers from Boston went as far west as Cleveland for conventions; in fact, Mason himself went there in 1851, if not before.

Concurrently, other musicians were opening successful conventions in other parts of the country. New York City, for instance, seems to have had its first such meeting in 1846. The *Boston Musical Gazette* announced in that year a four-day session to be led by Thomas Hastings, Ed Howe, Jr., and William B. Bradbury. This group called itself the American Musical Convention. Its work constituted the first step toward the leadership that New York City subsequently attained in music teachers' conventions.

During the summer of 1837 Lowell Mason had no part in the classes and conventions that were otherwise so important in the work of his Boston years. That summer he was making his first tour of Europe and England. It was during that tour that he put the finishing touches on his educational philosophy, a fitting climax to the long preparation for that climactic event in his career: the inauguration of music as a part of the public school curriculum.

6

The European Trip of 1837

Lowell Mason's trip to Europe in 1837 has been described vaguely in other studies because his personal diaries of those months (the richest source of information) have not been published; nor have they been edited, quoted, or summarized (as of this writing) except in Henry Lowell Mason's manuscript. These diaries were kept in the family until 1970 when the estate of Henry Lowell Mason donated them to the Lowell Mason Papers at Yale University. During the preparation of this biography, the diaries were read and portions were recorded for inclusion here. This chapter differs from others in that Mason himself tells much of the story, thus letting the reader know him better while learning about his travel experiences.

The 1837 diaries are interesting in several ways. First, they reveal Mason's feelings as a relatively unsophisticated American traveling alone in countries entirely new to him, his ease in meeting people, and his modest amazement that he is received as a distinguished visitor. Second, they describe his contacts with many important musicians and educators along the way, contacts sometimes facilitated through letters of introduction by William C. Woodbridge and others. Third, the diaries chronicle his tireless searching of stores and publishing houses for music to buy and send home. Last, they document his observations of music teaching in Europe.

It has been widely supposed that observing European music teaching methods was his chief (or sole) purpose for the trip. The diaries do not support that supposition. Fairly extensive periods of time pass during which he visited no schools. Furthermore, when recording his visits to schools, Mason is rarely specific about what he noticed; on the contrary, he seems almost casual at times. The most specific observation in his diary concerning music education appears in the July 24 entry where he wrote, "It is by constant practice—and by learning from childhood upward that they [European children] acquire such proficiency in music. The singing I heard satisfied me that there is no native capacity in the children superior to that which we have in America." Thus, while the importance of Mason's visits to European schools ought not be minimized, it is worth remembering that his trip had other purposes at least as important to him as visiting schools.

Beginning just ahead of the May 2 entry below and continuing for the rest of this chapter, Mason's exact words as found in the diaries are presented in italics. Other statements are paraphrases of diary material. Because he often wrote sentence fragments in his diary, paraphrases and other explanatory materials often follow that pattern. No page numbers are used in the diaries, so dates alone must be used to identify passages. A question mark in brackets means that the preceding word was illegible and may not be accurately quoted. Mason's long letter to Boston book publisher-retailer Melvin Lord is quoted in full for its summary of Mason's reactions to London—and vice versa.

For the reader's convenience, the following chart, prepared by Henry Lowell Mason, is provided as a guide to the trip:

Lowell Mason's European Trip in 1837

Left		Arrived	
New York	April 25	Liverpool	May 15
Liverpool	May 16	Manchester	May 16
Manchester	May 17	London	May 18
London	June 28	Hamburg	June 30
Hamburg	July 5	Berlin	July 5
Berlin	July 8	Dresden	July 9
Dresden	July 12	Leipzig	July 13
Leipzig	July 13	Frankfurt	July 15
Frankfurt	July 19	Mainz	July 19
Mainz	July 21	Carlsruhe	July 21
Carlsruhe	July 25	Stuttgart	July 25
Stuttgart	July 28	St. Gallen	July 29
St. Gallen	Aug. 1	Zürich	Aug. 1
Zürich	Aug. 3	Berne	Aug. 3
Berne	Aug. 5	Freiburg	Aug. 5
Freiburg	Aug. 7	Vevay	Aug. 7
Vevay	Aug. 10	Geneva	Aug. 10
Geneva	Aug. 15	Paris	Aug. 18
Paris	Aug. 31	Boulogne	Sept. 1
Boulogne	Sept. 2	Dover	Sept. 2
Dover	Sept. 4	London	Sept. 4
London	Sept. 14	Oxford	Sept. 14
Oxford	Sept. 16	Birmingham	Sept. 16
Birmingham	Sept. 22	Liverpool	Sept. 22
Liverpool	Oct. 1	New York	Oct. 28
New York	Nov. 1	Boston	Nov. 1

In summary, Mason's ocean voyage took about one month each way. He spent about seven weeks in London, about a month in Germany, two to three weeks in Switzerland, about two weeks in France (Paris almost entirely), then another month in England before his voyage home. On the ship *Virginian* which left New York on that April 25, he departed with *15 passengers and 49 in the steerage.* By the sixth day out, several were seasick, but Mason reported

> *I do not feel it in the least. I ate a hearty breakfast and feel perfectly well.... Felt disposed to chant a psalm of praise—read and sung over "Praise the Lord O my Soul" & also "O Sing unto the Lord a new Song." I have read... Biddolph on conformity to the world—It condemns me. In mus'l matters especially I have been too much conformed to this world. The Bos. Ac of Mus. is the cause of my associating much with merely worldly people—& I need more Christian influence... as I had in Savannah.*

May 2:

Had tea and toast for breakfast and did not feel as well.

May 3:

Eighth day out—rather rough weather—*hard to keep warm, esp. my feet. Decks are damp.*

May 5:

Not really seasick but *head ache & cold feet almost constantly.*

May 8:

This day I remember the birthday of my eldest son now in college—Daniel Gregory Mason—17 yrs. old. [Daniel Gregory was then a freshman at Yale; he spent only that one year at Yale.]

May 15:

20th day. Left the ship by steamboat and landed in Liverpool where he went first to the King's Arms Hotel. Then called on music publisher Vincent Novello and also his sister Clara, the singer.

May 20:

London. *What a wonderful place this is—What New York is to a country village London is to New York.* Vincent Novello provided Mason the tickets he needed for the Philharmonic Society program of the 27th. Mason felt highly favored because only 150 tickets had been issued and none were for sale. Novello also gave him a ticket to a concert of the Royal Society of Musicians June 5 when the *Messiah* was to be performed.

May 21:

(Sunday) To church with Novello. On the way they visited Westminster Abbey and Handel's monument. Later they heard a program there. *The harsh tone of the Boy's Soprano was disagreeable.* Later to St. Mary's where Isaac Watts had preached. They sang there *miserable tunes from Rippons Collection.*

May 22:

To Greens Folio Square and selected some music—to Novello's from 1:00 to 5:00 P.M. and selected from his music collection.

May 26:

At Novello's he met William Gardiner. *I was sorry to hear profane expressions from the compiler of Sacred Melodies.* In the afternoon heard *Messiah* performed by a group of about 400 with Clara Novello, Miss Birch, Mrs. A. Shaw, Mr. Hobbs as soloists. *I did not like the ad libitum ... cadenzas—so common. Choruses were good but not better than our Boston churches often do. Generally slower than I have been accustomed to hear. ... The effect of this performance was far enough from any thing devotional.*

There are many customs here strange to one accustomed like myself to the plain and simple manner of doing things in America—the pomp and splendor and parade—even servants and those who perform the office of sexton— doorkeeper, etc. are draped up in such a style that a simple American might take them for lords and great ones!

May 30:

To St. Paul's to hear the "Charity Children"—about six thousand of them and four thousand spectators. *The singing of so many children with the powerful organ was quite sublime. This was what so affected Haydn. They sang the same chant today that he heard.* Then to Ignaz Moscheles' (1794–1870) piano concert. (Moscheles was a famous pianist and teacher; he was associated with Beethoven, Mendelssohn, and other leading composers throughout his career.)

May 31:

Met William Ayrton and talked about American music. Ayrton (1777–1858) was a distinguished organist and composer, editor of the *Harmonicon* and *Sacred Minstrelsy . . . quite a literary and musical man.* Spent one-and-a-half hours with Ayrton and gave him a copy of the *Manual of the Boston Academy.* Visited two music stores. In the evening attended the "Concert of Ancient Music" at the King's Concert Rooms in Hanover Square, a concert attended mostly by nobility. The music was *splendid—tho' not so good as the Philharmonic on some accounts. They did Haydn & Handel selections. "Horse and his rider" was slower than I have heard it. . . . Braham sung. Had fine view of Lord Wellington and heard him converse for some time . . . very superior concert—but too long—from 8-12 P.M.*

June 4:

(Sunday) To foundling Hospital, had a letter of introduction to the organist. The organ was *powerful and played very loud. The organ was presented by Handel—but has since been enlarged.*

June 6:

Wrote to his friend Melvin Lord as follows:

My Dear Sir,
I have now been in this great city . . . nearly three weeks. I have had time to look around a little among the musical people—to become acquainted—etc.

I have been very cordially received by musical people, and have in general only found it necessary to announce my name and residence, and I am on intimate terms at once. Indeed, I am quite surprised that I am so well known among musical men of repute.

I have become acquainted amongst others with Misters Novello—the father and the son—with Mr. Gardiner,—Sir George Smart—Mr. Atwood—Purday—these are some of the principles. I am daily attending concerts, etc. twice have I heard Handel's Messiah—once the Mt. of Olives, once The Bell, etc. besides much secular music. Being known as professional I receive many tickets gratuitously to concerts. This is quite a matter of consequence here, where the lowest price is half a guinea—and often double that price. As to style of performance, I do not find that the Choruses are on the whole much better done than with us.

But the Orchestras here are much more complete—every instrument is well played and the part is sure—and the stringed instruments are far more numerous in all their Concerts—about 30 or 40 violins is not uncommon—but the very common orchestra would not have less than 12 to 18 violins.

The solos are also far better here—being all done by professional singers. I happened to come to London in a most favorable time for hearing music....I yesterday attended the performance of Handel's Messiah in the Hanover Square rooms at 12 o'clock....Braham sung and others of like character as vocalists. Among the great stars now in London [is]...Grisi—perhaps the greatest soprano in the world.

I have made some considerable purchases of music—say perhaps 200 or 300 dollars worth and find some things that I think will work up well. There remain many Music Shops and Publishers for me yet to visit. I stroll about and call in to them daily—make selections and then tell them I must have the music at professional price. "Have you a ticket?" they ask. "No," I reply. "What address?" I write my name—or hand out my card—and it is sufficient. Mr. Novello's is my packing place and whatever I purchase I have sent to him.

Novello will publish a book of Children's music [*The Juvenile Songster*] for me while I am here—and also a number of psalm tunes—probably a selection of a few from Occasionals. This will give us some hold on the people at home. What of the times? [referring to the financial panic of 1837] I suppose they are severe enough—I fear I shall lose by several failures of which I have already heard, and I fear more. Before this reaches you, you will have heard of the failure of the great American Houses here—Wilson and Co....besides others since of less note....I know not how soon I may leave London but probably in a few weeks more.

Church Music here is miserably low—I have not heard a tolerable choir altho' I have been to the Chapel Royal, Westminster Abbey, St. Paul's and other important churches.[1]

June 7:

Spent the entire day until 4 at Lordsdale's and at Chappell's selecting music.

June 10:

Mr. Banister called for me to go to rehearsal of Philharmonic. Very difficult to get into this—but got tickets. Pastoral by Beethoven, overtures by Cherubini and Weber were played, and a symphony by Spohr. Just before the music began, Miss Clara Novello introduced me to the Chevalier Neukomm who has just arrived in London. We were together during a great part of the performance. By appt. I am to meet him on Tues. morning next. . . . [The Philharmonic was] splendid indeed—6 double basses and other instruments in proportion—I should suppose about 30 vlns.

(Sigismund Ritter von Neukomm, 1778–1858, was one of the most celebrated musicians Mason met during his 1837 trip. Neukomm's compositions were especially popular in England. He wrote solo and ensemble instrumental works, operas and art songs, as well as sacred music. Besides his ambitious composing career, he conducted and performed as a pianist in many countries.)

June 12:

Heard the 1st Philharmonic Concert—Beethoven's Pastoral was the great piece. Thalberg's playing [of the piano] *far surpassed anything I have before heard.* Had visited the Zoological Gardens and was much impressed.

June 15:

Traveled to the Isle of Wight to see George Webb's family. Arrived there June 16 and was warmly received. Left the Webbs on the 17th.

June 18:

Recorded the names of persons to whom he had written—family members, George Webb, and his choir. [These are persons he wrote frequently, according to his diary.]

June 19:

Mentioned things he was sending to his family with a Mr. Slade who was leaving for America soon. To Mrs. Mason, a Bible recently purchased; to the boys, a book, gloves, a map, and nut cakes.

June 20:

The King [William IV] *died last night, or this morning, and as I came home by St. James I found a large collection of people expecting the proclamation of the new Queen Victoria—I waited some time and happened to meet Sir George Smart—he informed me that it would not take place today but tomorrow at 12. Sir George invited me to Chapel Royal next Sunday to hear the Funeral Anthem for the king.* (Sir George Smart, 1776–1867, was an organist, conductor, and composer of sacred music.)

June 21:

This morning at 1/2 past 10 went to Charing Cross to see the procession and proclamation of the new Queen—afterward went to St. Sepulcher's where

Neukomm was to play the organ. He played upwards of an hour without stopping and in a most beautiful and fitting style.

June 23:

Paid the bill at Novello's and ordered that music purchases be packed and sent home.

June 24:

Called on Neukomm and got a "circular" letter of introduction to various points in Germany. In the afternoon called on Dr. Crotch and presented a letter from Mr. Ayrton. *He played an overture by Handel on the organ for me.* (William Crotch, 1775-1847, was an eminent organist, music professor, and composer of oratorios, glees, and other works.)

June 25:

In the morning to the Chapel Royal where Sir George Smart had invited him to hear the funeral anthem. It turned out to be *better of the kind than any thing I have seen. Text Job 30:23.* Also visited Temple Church, then St. Paul's and Christ's Church to hear music at each place. On his way between two of these churches he passed *a poor woman with two children. . . . She held her face down but held up a card saying she had been deserted by her husband and had been driven into the street. I gave her all the pennies I had.*

June 26:

Attended a party at Moscheles' home in the company of Neukomm. Pieces played were as follows: (1) Beethoven's First Quartet; (2) concerto by J. S. Bach with the piano part by Moscheles and accompaniment by a quartet; (3) a violin solo ("Concerto") by a ten-year-old Master Moeser with Moscheles at the piano; (4) a quartet by Beethoven; (5) piano trio; (6) a piano "Fantasia" played by a Mr. Benedict; (7) a piano solo by Mr. Rosenhain from Germany; (8) a piano solo by Thalberg—"Fantasia." All the piano playing was *first rate—all wonderful—but Thalberg's was certainly the most astonishing. Met Mr. Horsley and was invited to visit him on the way back* [from Europe].

(Sigismond Thalberg, 1812–1871, was a piano virtuoso who concertized internationally. William Horsley, 1774–1858, was an organist and composer of vocal music and hymn tunes. He also edited works of John Callcott, 1766–

1821, his father-in-law. Mason used many works by Horsley and Callcott in his publications.)

June 27:

Spent all day getting ready to go to Hamburg. Had to leave some things behind. Visited the National Gallery of Fine Arts.

June 28:

Just after boarding the boat for the Continent he saw parents with their two boys. The boys seemed to be parting from the parents to go to school somewhere. This reminded Mason of his own children. *I could not avoid joining them in their tears. It would be very pleasant to me were I now commencing my voyage home.* Along the way he noticed the villages and the many women working in the fields. Found the passengers pleasant, English and German spoken.

June 30:

Recovered from seasickness of the previous day. Arrived in Hamburg and stayed at the Hotel Belvidore. *Everything here indicates that I am in a Foreign land—In London it always seemed only as though I was in another American City—the language being the same. But now it is all another language—and everything is different.* His first German meal was served at 4:00 P.M.: *Began with soup—then boiled beef, with potatoes, cabbage, new turnips in melted butter—this through, stewed pigeons and green peas, i.e., both stewed together. After these came some kind of fish with sauce of oil, catsup, and strewed over with parsley. Next came a fore quarter of . . . lamb with a piece of paper wrapped around the bone so the carver could take hold of it. He took it and cut the shoulder so as to lay it open. Then put in about 1/4 lb butter and herbs previously prepared and lemon. Then cut it up, into small pieces and the servants handed it around together with stewed strawberries . . . [which] appeared to have been stewed in something a little acid and were made very sweet with sugar. Also cucumber cut up and dressed in oil and vinegar. Next came pudding . . . very nice. After this bread and cheese and butter and oranges. It took little more than 1 and 1/2 hrs. While at dinner the landlord (seated next to me) took snuff frequently. He asked me, but I declined. He asked, "Do you not take snuff?" No. "Smoke?" No. "Why surely, you will go to heaven then if you commit no sin." I asked, "Do you think it sin to snuff and smoke?" He replied, "Yes, 'tis folly and folly is sin." Here the conversation dropped.*

July 1:

Called on Mr. Schröder and Mr. Schwenke, organists introduced through Neukomm.

July 2:

To St. Jacob's—everyone sang a chorale—*loud—solemn—devotional—* Could not understand the German in the sermon. Also called on the Rombergs. Went to various other church services. Saw the organ Schwenke played—a 4-manual organ with eighty registers and sixteen bellows. Two men worked the bellows. Mason went to the bellows room, found the men working the bellows with their feet—each man having to "blow" eight of them. Through the hotel he got a companion and interpreter for a dollar a day, a youth named John who helped him get around.

July 3:

Called on August Wilhelm Bach (1796–1869), who showed him some manuscripts of J. S. Bach, F. J. Haydn, and others and invited him to attend his school with him Friday morning and to hear him play the organ Friday afternoon. To a performance of Haydn's *Creation*.

July 7:

Went with Bach to the Institute for Church Music, where Bach taught. This institution was supported by the government so the young men enrolled were taught music tuition-free, having only to board and clothe themselves. Instruction included the practical and theoretical, vocal and instrumental. Three professors were on the staff, each one in attendance two days per week. Mason saw their thorough bass lesson. Bach wrote the lesson on the board. Also heard an hour's organ playing by five of the twenty organ students. Then an hour of singing with Bach at the piano. *Some of these pupils could now stand high in America,* so proficient were they. In the afternoon Bach played for him at the Marien Kirche, mostly of the music of J. S. Bach—three or four fugues—but also some of his own music.

Visited Spontini (1774-1851, opera composer and conductor) at home and was politely received. *He expressed regret that he had not met me before. He lives in very splendid style.* In the evening to the Gluck opera *Alceste*. The music of Gluck is *very popular and this is the first time in five years that this opera has been performed. Orchestra of about 80—largest that I have heard—very effective.*

July 12:

In Dresden. Visited Mr. Schneider's school, hoping to see the classes taught. But they only sang, first some hymns and then some difficult fugues. The boys class included fifty to sixty boys; they sang with great precision. Mason interviewed Schneider and found that the boys were taught one hour daily. Some had been there for six or seven years, others for three months. Schneider says he uses the same arrangement as Mason—sopranos in front of tenors, at the conductor's right.

Also heard Mr. Schneider play the organ—hardly knew who played better, he or Bach. *Both were excellent and by far surpassed any organ playing I ever heard in this style. Adams of London is a style so different that there is no comparison between them* (Thomas Adams, 1785–1858).

July 13:

Disappointed over not getting letters from home—two-and-a-half months away from home and had received only two letters. Called on Rochlitz, introduced through Neukomm, and on Mr. Fink, Editor of the *Musical Gazette*. The latter's daughter, Charlotte, *played the piano better than I ever heard a female perform.*

July 15:

Met with Johann August André (1817-1887, a music publisher), to whom he had a letter, and went with him to call on Mendelssohn, but *I was greatly disappointed to find that he is out of town.* Spent the afternoon in selecting music from Mr. André. *In the evening he took me to a men's singing group— about 40 were there. Singing was excellent. Some pieces accompanied by three horns and trombones. In a large hall, and all the singers were eating and drinking. The singers had (many of them) bottles of wine before them. Everyone who goes is expected to have something to eat or drink. I do not like this in musical performance.*

July 16:

Lamented that the Sabbath seems *only to be a holiday.* Schnyder von Wartensee (1786-1868, composer of cantatas, sacred and secular songs—some of which Mason included in his books) called on him. *He remained an hour conversing on Music very pleasantly—offers to introduce me to Switzerland of which . . . he is a native.*

July 17:

To André's store in the morning. In the afternoon with André, von Wartensee and John Barnett (1802-1890), an English compiler. Saw André's father, Johann André (also a composer) and some of his Mozart memorabilia and manuscripts.

July 18:

Called on a banker named Bethmann and drew thirty pounds, paid André a little over fourteen pounds. The banker extended Mason's credit to a bank in Switzerland. Had a package of music packed at André's. Later returned to the bank and drew twenty pounds more, for fear he would not have enough.

Visited Mr. Schott and went with him to hear fifty singers rehearse a Te deum by Neukomm. In the evening to a first rehearsal of a new oratorio on Gutenberg. *They drill something in our manner. Men's voices only—60 or 70 men. Most could sing at sight.*[2]

July 22:

Called on Professor Anton Gersbach (1803–1848) and went to his school. There he was introduced to a teacher who led him to Professor Horn. In all the schools of this dukedom music was taught. Mason taught a lesson to a class of twenty to twenty-four boys and girls. These students had been in the school for six months, and their music classes met twice weekly. The children examined the rhythm and melody, and then sang the music.

July 24:

Visited Gersbach and Sterne's School, a public school for boys. The five classes enrolled about two hundred and fifty students. Music was taught in all the classes, and only the youngest pupils were taught by rote—all others learned by "theory." Also visited a girls' school with four classes. The children were singing when he got there—about one hundred of them, singing in four parts. The music was by Kocher, who was also present.

July 25:

Upon arrival in Stuttgart, Mason sent a note to Kübler, asking him to meet him. He had a letter from Professor Horn to introduce himself. Kübler came and Mason found an interpreter there at the hotel. Mason was invited to attend Kübler's class.

July 26:

Visited the class which Kübler taught—not just music, but also geography, arithmetic, and other subjects.

July 27:

Visited a school in Statten with Kocher and Kübler—five classes of music, each meeting two hours weekly, were held. All the children were taught music. They had a separate music teacher for this. Mason saw a class taught and then wrote a lesson for them to do.

August 4:

Found Pestalozzi's disciple Philipp Emanuel von Fellenberg at his home about five miles outside Berne. He said that schools were on vacation now and would resume again August 25. Said Switzerland was behind the parts of Germany Mason had seen. Gave Mason a manuscript copy of a piece of music composed by Rinck at von Fellenberg's request. Visited churches and cathedrals. Reported on the music. Copied specification of the organ built by Aloys Mooser (1770–1839).[3]

August 18:

Arrived in Paris. Visited more music stores, packed items to send home, including some porcelain. Reported on churches, including famous ones. During stay in Paris he visited Notre Dame, Versailles, the Louvre, Palais de Luxembourg, the Panthéon, the Church St. Etienne, St. Stephen's, and other points of interest.

September 2:

Arrived in England. In preparation for going home purchased spoons, forks, cloth for both his wife and his mother, a silk dress for Abby, and for Lowell, Jr. and Daniel, pantaloons. *How beautiful England appears after the tour I have had—The moment I stepped on shore I felt the difference—in the appearance of the people—houses—and everything that strikes the eye. England is centuries before all other countries in the arts of life. I felt almost as if I had got home at Dover—and feel, now as if I should never want to go into France, Germany, any foreign land where habits, customs and language are so difficult again.*

September 8:

Evening attended a rehearsal of St. Paul at Exeter Hall—& was introduced to the author Felix Mendelssohn Bartholdy (1809-1847, celebrated German composer).

September 10:

Visited the Moravian Chapel in Fetter Lane, Nevils Court, Fleet Street. *The singing was by the congregation & very devotional. In some parts of the Liturgy the Minister sung the prayers & the congregation responded—It had a good effect—I like a liturgy to some extent, and should be glad to attend church where one is used.*

September 14:

Left for Oxford. At Windsor visited public areas of the castle. Purchased prints of West Windsor Castle at a nearby bookstore.

September 15:

Walked about the city.

September 16:

To Birmingham. A cold, rainy ride via coach. Caught a cold on the way.

September 18:

To a rehearsal for the festival. Saw Neukomm, Mendelssohn, Ayrton, Vaughn, Clara Novello, Mr. Hogarth (author of a history of music), a Mr. Vaughn and a Miss Vaughn.

September 19-22:

Attended festival performances. Mendelssohn conducted his oratorio *St. Paul,* but unfortunately Mason did not comment about it.

September 23:

In Liverpool, packing.

September 25:

Sent a package of gingerbread and toys to his children in care of Mr. Palmer who left by ship on September 27.

September 27:

Again buying music. Waiting for his baggage to arrive from London.

September 29:

Walked about; visited book stores. Still waiting in vain for luggage to arrive. *It is hard work to be idle—were I in London I could find enough to do—but here there is little to see—and the anxiety of this constant and protracted waiting unfits me for seeing that little.*

September 30:

This has been a day of anxiety to me. On inquiry I found that I cannot expect my luggage here until Tuesday next—and the Oxford sails tomorrow—the question was shall I wait—or shall I go without my things? I decided after reflection . . . to go . . . many things were then to be bought—shirts—stockings, etc. etc. all of which things I had provided myself with in London. I made all my purchases—took my passage—wrote some letters—bought trunks and packed my things, and am now at half past eight nearly ready. I cannot omit to notice the unspeakable goodness of God to me. . . .

October 28:

Arrived in New York.

October 31:

Took a steamboat to Massachusetts.

November 1:

Home, found all the family well. At 2:30 left Boston for Medfield, saw parents. Back to Boston by 6:00 P.M.

November 4:

Spent most of the forenoon with Mr. Webb—spent the day in making calls and received from all a kind welcome home. Evening meeting of the choirs. On my entering the room the choir rose and sang a hymn composed by Mr. Benson and set to music by Mr. Woodman [Mason's assistant organist] *welcoming me home.*

Music in the Boston Public Schools

Acceptance of Music in the Curriculum

Lowell Mason's musical leadership in Boston during the early and middle 1830s were well known to members of the Boston School Committee (the school board). So were his views on music in the schools, for he had repeatedly appealed for music as part of every child's education and, therefore, music as part of the public school curriculum.

Mason's ultimate success in getting music into the Boston public school curriculum derived in part from the climate of the times: the momentum behind public education in general and music activities specifically, including the rise of orchestras, the appearance of opera in some cities, the arrival and employment of talented immigrants, the continuing work of music societies, and the concertizing of European artists. Culturally and educationally, the stage was set for music education.

Beyond the circumstances of the times, however, were the circumstances of Mason's background and personality. He was equipped by experience and temperament to handle the political challenge of getting music into the school curriculum; he was equipped philosophically and pedagogically to make music teaching succeed. Others might have introduced music programs experimentally, but Mason went beyond that, succeeding so convincingly with the initial programs that music was assured a permanent place.

Another early proponent of music in the Boston schools was Mason's friend, George Henry Snelling (1801-1892), a lawyer who served on the primary school board and also as one of the first counselors of the Boston Academy of Music. In December 1831, Snelling presented to the Boston School Committee an elaborate, articulate report on the possibilities of music training for everyone. He offered the results of a study conducted by a subcommittee of which he was a part, a group set up by the School Committee to investigate music possibilities. In response to this report, the School Committee resolved that "one school from each district be selected for the introduction of systematic instruction in vocal music, under the direction of a committee."[1]

Despite this resolution, nothing changed. Music continued only in classrooms in which teachers, acting on their own, voluntarily included music. They taught according to their own tastes and methods just like singing school leaders. Some of these public school teachers who had tried music teaching for a few years were mentioned in a subsequent School Committee report as having agreed upon the value of music and upon keeping it in the curriculum.

During the years 1832 through 1836, Mason kept the music education issue alive through the Boston Academy of Music. He would have enlisted the Boston Handel and Haydn Society for that purpose as well, had not the directors of that society felt its work lay in the direction of classical concert music rather than in basic music education. The academy was the logical agency for making a strong case to the School Committee; the academy's lectures, children's concerts, and teaching in private schools of the community reinforced the arguments and left vivid impressions in many minds.

For example, Gideon F. Thayer of the Chauncey Hall School wrote a letter March 27, 1834 (addressee unknown), describing this one example of the academy's outreach:

> Mr. Lowell Mason ... has taught the pupils of Chauncey Hall School the elements of vocal music, during the past year, and to my perfect satisfaction. It was at first undertaken as an experiment, but has proved so popular among the children and parents, as to be now considered among the regular branches of instruction. Its influence I consider excellent, especially on the temper and affections of the children; nor do I find that its effect on discipline is, in the least prejudicial, although the exercises are highly exciting to the vivacity of young minds. It is not with us a required study, but four-fifths of our whole number engage in it.[2]

In 1836 the academy, moving boldly, petitioned the Boston School Committee to reconsider establishing music in the public schools. Two citizens' groups also presented petitions. One of the petitions led to a study by a three-member subcommittee composed of T. Kemper Davis, the Reverend Samuel K. Lathrop, and Justin Field. This group presented a highly favorable report on August 24, 1837.[3]

After discussing the merits of the question, the report concretely recommended that music be authorized as part of public school instruction and that the Boston Academy of Music take charge of the teaching under the supervision of a five-member committee appointed by the School Committee. This plan was accepted on September 19, 1837 with the stipulation that music be taught in four designated schools. The plan was then transferred to the Boston city council with a request for funding. However, that group failed to act, so the necessary money was not appropriated.

Success at last—so near, yet so far away! Rather than let the matter drop when success seemed within reach, Lowell Mason seized the opportunity: he proposed to teach for a year without salary, providing all the needed materials and equipment himself. In November 1837 the School Committee accepted his offer, specifying that he could teach at Hawes School in South Boston under the direction of that school's authorities and a Committee of Music appointed by the School Committee.

Journalists reported this arrangement at once. For instance, *The American Annals of Education and Instruction,* in January 1838, heralded the news in this report:

> We understand that the very general and very unreasonable public prejudice in this city against the introduction of vocal music into the public schools has so far subsided that the school committee have consented to permit gratuitous instruction, in one of the larger grammar schools, for a year, by way of experiment; and that in order to make a fair experiment, one of the professors in the Boston Academy of Music has volunteered his services for the purpose.[4]

Though the Hawes School was reputedly one of the most difficult teaching assignments in Boston, it was a fortunate choice for Mason in that the schoolmaster, Joseph Harrington, had formerly taught music himself. He could understand Mason's objectives and methods. Harrington had been appointed to his school position on January 14, 1834, at age twenty-one. A kind, progressive man, Harrington tried appealing to his students' sense of right and reasoning with them rather than using corporal punishment. He played games with them and planned excursions into the country to establish rapport with them. That he loved both music and children was demonstrated by the fact that, despite opposition, he placed a piano in the school at his own expense.

Hawes was a grammar school enrolling four hundred pupils of ages eight to fourteen. By his own account, Mason taught there two days a week, one hour each time with a half-hour for boys and another half-hour for girls. He had new music and additional teaching ideas gleaned from the European trip. By all reports, that year's work was highly successful. A detailed letter by Harrington and his assistant, John A. Harris, to the mayor of Boston described the effects of music teaching in detail. This letter—interesting partly for its quaint views— was published in the *Boston Musical Gazette* on July 25, 1838:

> Dear Sir,
> In reply to your communications, allow us briefly to state, that any very positive and splendid results, from the introduction of vocal music into the Hawes school, cannot yet be reasonably expected.... However, enough has ... been already accomplished, to warrant the belief of the great utility of vocal music, as a branch of public instruction. One thing has been made evident ... the musical ear is more common than has been generally supposed. There are but few in the school who make palpable discords when all are singing. Many who at the outset of the experiment believed they had neither ear nor voice, now sing with confidence

and considerable accuracy; and others who could hardly tell one sound from another, now sing the scale with ease; —sufficiently proving that the musical susceptibility is in a good degree improvable. The alacrity with which the lesson is entered upon, and the universal attention with which it is received, are among its great recommendations; they show that the children are *agreeably* employed; and we are certain that they are *innocently* employed. We have never known the time when, unless extraordinary engagements prevented, they were not glad to remain a half-hour, or more, to pursue the exercise after the regular hours of session. They prefer the *play* of a *hard musical* lesson to any outdoor sports, of course understanding that there are some exceptions. Of the great *moral* effect of vocal music, there can be no question. A song introduced in the middle of the session has invariably been followed with an excellent effect. It is a relief to the wearisomeness of constant study. It excites the listless, and calms the turbulent and uneasy. It seems to renerve the mind, and prepare all for more vigorous intellectual action.

It is delightful to see how spontaneously a chorus will spring up in any accidental collection of the pupils, about the school-house; and how soon the five will increase to ten, and the ten to twenty—all tranquil, yet intensely happy. How much such still, refined enjoyment, accompanied as it is with moderate physical exertion, is to be, occasionally, preferred to constant, boisterous, over heating, and sometimes dangerous play—with the girls more especially, is this to be desired; for although brisk out-door exercise is profitable and necessary, yet carried to excess it almost *unsexes* them, and does more harm than good. That the music is an *attraction,* is evident from the increased attendance of the pupils on the days of the lesson.

The advantages to be gained from instructing our children in vocal music, are of little consequence, when considered in connection with a *school,* compared with those which are more remote and far less perceptible—such as bear upon their *characters, employments* and *recreations* in after years—upon their condition as social and domestic beings; but with these we have nothing to do.

This brief notice of the results of so important a step in public education is...very insufficient—but we hardly know how to go into details; nor indeed have we time to enter upon an elaborate comment.... We have been equally delighted with the beautiful simplicity of the system upon which Mr. Mason instructs, and with his own personal skill in teaching; and we trust it will not be long before vocal music will be everywhere an essential branch of public instruction.[5]

Harrington echoes Mason here: music is desirable for moral benefits, for physical exercise, for enjoyment in later life—in short, practical applications are made in arguing for music in the schools. "Art for art's sake," a possible argument (not to mention the foremost argument for many musicians), is conspicuously absent in the records of those early years of music education. But the arguments that were raised on behalf of music were the very ones likely to sway the public in the 1830s.

Harrington's warm approval was not the only expression of satisfaction in Mason's work at Hawes School. According to the seventh annual report of the Boston Academy of Music (July 1839), the Boston School Committee sent a delegation to the school and the members visited...on the sixth of August [1838]...and heard the musical exercises with great satisfaction. The success of the experiment thus far has more than fulfilled the sanguine expectations which at first were entertained in regard to it. The Committee...request as many of the Board as can do so, to attend the annual exhibition of the Hawes School...Tuesday next . . . August 14. . . .[6]

That August 14 concert was the most dramatic demonstration of Mason's teaching during that year. The program, presented at the South Baptist Church, included eight songs sung in unison by the two hundred children. The most distinguished of the pieces was "Flowers, Wildwood Flowers," renowned as the first song ever sung in the public schools in Boston (and probably in any public school in the country, at least as part of an official program). The other songs were "Before all lands in east or west," "Children go, to and fro," "The sweet birds are singing," "Come and see the ripe fruit falling," "Of late so brightly glowing," "Come, seek the bow'r, the rosy bow'r," "Murmur, gentle lyre."[7] All of these except "Come, seek the bow'r" had been published in the *Juvenile Singing School,* compiled by Mason and Webb (1837); "Come, seek the bow'r" was later published in *The Boston School Song Book* (1841).

The concert proved to a large, skeptical audience that children—anyone's children, everyone's children—could learn music and could sing well, enjoying the experience and mastering the principles of music at the same time. The successful demonstration of children taught well at Hawes School also gave music education's long-time supporters further encouragement.

On August 28, 1838, the Boston School Committee passed a resolution which initiated music education in its full, modern sense. This "Magna Charta of Music Education in the United States" (a term first used in the 1839 annual report of the Boston Academy of Music) read in part as follows:

> *Resolved,* That the Committee on Music be instructed to contract with a teacher of vocal music in the several public schools of the city.
> *Resolved,* That the instruction...shall commence in the several public schools whenever the subcommittees of the several schools . . . shall determine. . . .

A maximum of $120 per annum was allowed for each school except for Lyman and Smith Schools which were each allowed only half that amount. These funds had to cover the teachers' salaries plus materials and equipment. The maximum time allowed for music instruction was two hours weekly. This instruction had to be presented at a fixed time throughout the city and, unless otherwise ordered, at the times stipulated in the resolution. During these instruction periods, school discipline remained the responsibility of the regular classroom teachers, all of whom were required to be present and to "organize the scholars" for the music class "as the teacher in music may desire."[8]

The vocal music teachers specified by this resolution were contracted to teach only music, specifically, singing and music reading. Nonetheless, regular classroom teachers could conduct singing if, when, and to whatever extent they desired, just as before, as an optional activity for their pupils. The practice of having a classroom instructor teach music reading did not come until many years later. Nor did the school authorities have in mind music supervisors in the modern sense. In actual practice, Lowell Mason began as a teacher under the new system but soon came to act as a twentieth-century music supervisor would. However, this development was unforeseen in 1838, and the rise of music supervisors in later years must be regarded as an unrelated development.

Mason's Career in the Boston Public Schools

The Boston School Committee immediately hired Lowell Mason to teach vocal music in accord with the resolution passed on August 28, 1838. He, in turn, was authorized to hire such assistants as he needed and to purchase the necessary books, equipment, and supplies for each school, keeping the costs within the specified funding. During the first year he had just one assistant, Jonathan Call Woodman, an organist and baritone soloist in the choir of the Boston Academy of Music. Instruction that year was offered to the two upper classes of the grammar schools. When music was adopted later in all the grammar school classes in ten of the city's schools, Mason had to hire additional assistants.

Among those assistants was James C. Johnson, a former Mason student at the academy. Johnson later recalled that Mason did as much of the teaching himself as possible, but had his assistants (Woodman, Johnson, Root, and others) assigned to various schools in the city. Mason occasionally visited their classes and even exchanged classes with them. Johnson described Mason's teaching from firsthand observation:

> The schoolhouses . . . each contained two large rooms, accommodating, each, about 200 scholars. Into one of these rooms 200 of the oldest pupils were gathered. Lowell Mason is at the piano. Every eye is upon him. He proceeds to drill the school in scale singing, in syllable skipping, and perhaps asks a few review questions. He sees everybody and any wandering of attention is met by some quaint observation or shrewd remark that at once secures the roving eye. Then comes a bright song, with all the life and all the expression put in it. Then follows the lesson on the board, with lucid Pestalozzian explanations; then more singing, and before any one is weary, the lesson is over. There was little or no practice between lessons but . . . the simple "elements of music" were pretty thoroughly gone over [in the course of a year]. As pupils usually attend the same schools for a series of years, three or four repetitions of the course were witnessed.[9]

Certain of the schools were for boys only, others for girls only, and still others for boys and girls. Notable among the latter was the Bowdoin School.

An alumna of that school wrote vividly of the pupils' reactions to the singing lessons:

> In 1839, the Bowdoin scholars were so fortunate as to have Lowell Mason as their first teacher of music. Two hours each week were given to music.... Mr. Mason was very fond of, and kind to, young people. His great enthusiasm in his work called out enthusiasms and interest in his pupils; they never seemed to tire of going over and over many times any particular passage, at his request. He was always ready with a word of praise and encouragement.... These lessons were recreations. What an honor, when we were called upon to move the piano and get the black-board ready!... One day he wondered how many could say that they had not thought of anything but the lesson during the hour, and I felt very virtuous because I had not.[10]

Other testimonials to Mason's teaching skill can be found in the memoirs of his students and contemporaries. For instance, William S. Tilden, at one time a student of Mason's, wrote that he had never seen any teacher hold the attention of a large class as well as Mason did. W.S.B. Mathews, who first met Mason in the early 1850s at a teachers' institute in Lee, Massachusetts, remarked on Mason's "commanding personality, dignity and simplicity of address and attractiveness to the public," all positive attributes for teaching.[11]

James C. Johnson's remembrances of Mason during the late 1830s include his description of the "square head, short iron-gray hair that seemed to stand up straight all over his head, and a shrewd, kindly teacher's face." He also recalled Mason's sense of humor. Together on an inspection tour of schools, the two men saw a schoolboy scratching on a gatepost with a pencil. Mason gently admonished him not to do that, adding, "If you were a gatepost, would you like to have boys scratch and write on you?" Johnson commented that this remark was as characteristic of Mason as his ordering baked beans in a restaurant.[12]

Just as important as Mason's personality and rapport with his students was his teaching technique. He began with rote singing, then moved to note reading. Next he introduced part singing through rounds and canons, and finally choral singing. He used solmization syllables, numbers, and selected vowel sounds in teaching reading, but taught the pitch names of notes as well. All the while he paid attention to the development of his students' voices. These methods, seemingly commonplace today, were revolutionary then. Because they got results then, they could survive to become commonplace today.

In the early 1840s Mason continued his private school teaching and also assumed responsibility for vocal music teaching in all the public grammar schools of the city. In 1841, for instance, he held one-hour lessons twice per week at Fowle's Monitorial School for Girls, a private school. At the same time, he was teaching half-hour lessons twice per week in the public schools. He and his assistants reached about three thousand students, about half of the students in all the Boston schools at that time.[13]

The Committee on Music (an arm of the Boston School Committee) visited the Mayhew, Wells, Eliot, Bowdoin, Hancock, Franklin, and Adams schools in 1842 to observe Mason's teaching. The group issued a detailed report describing what Mason was accomplishing:

> In general, the Committee were highly gratified, and are happy in being able to bear favorable testimony to the system of teaching adopted by Mr. Mason. It is eminently an inductive method, exercising actively the reasoning power of the mind . . . while at the same time, it tends to impart . . . a thorough knowledge of the rudiments of the science. In some of the schools, the scholars exhibited a very remarkable degree of knowledge of the principles of music, much to the surprise, and greatly to the delight, of the Committee. Examinations were made by Mr. Mason on the questions contained in . . . a book prepared by him, and used in the schools [*The Boston School Song Book*] especially those relating to the nature of the scale, and the transposition of it into all the major keys. Many of the schools seemed to understand perfectly the rules applicable, particularly those of the upper classes. Lessons, at sight, from the black-board, were readily and correctly sung. The intervals, natural and chromatic, were generally very firmly given.
>
> The exercises in singing were almost invariably good, and in some of the schools, they were very beautiful, affording much gratification . . . to the Committee. The scholars manifested a great interest in the study, and the Committee feel assured that it is not only a very useful, but also a very pleasing exercise to them. For the sake of illustration . . . a circumstance . . . at the visit of one of the Committee may be aptly mentioned. On his arrival . . . the exercises in music had been finished [for that day]. It was proposed to the scholars to remain, with the consent of the master, half an hour longer, that further exercises might be had in the presence of the Committee, with the *condition* that the time should be made up to them by omitting the singing exercises on another day. The condition was not accepted . . . [but] unanimously rejected. [But the students did remain and provide a demonstration of the lesson.][14]

Because the differences between Mason's practices and the European methods from which they were derived have been analyzed in detail elsewhere, only a few points need to be mentioned here. One of the significant differences was Mason's use of rote singing to introduce the pleasurable experience of making music. This approach reflects Mason's attitudes about children and about music, attitudes that shaped both his teaching and his editing of children's music books.

As important as pedagogy was, equally important were the underlying perspectives of Mason and other early music educators. They understood that Americans had values different from their European counterparts, values that precluded the transfer of the Continental system in which music was cultivated chiefly by the gifted and advantaged few. Mason and his associates based their work on the conception of music as a part of every person's life, one way or another, in homes, churches, and communities. This concept of music for all people was not exclusively theirs, any more than the concept of public school education was exclusively certain educators' conception. But it was Mason and his immediate associates who planned, promoted, and finally institutionalized curricular music in the public school system. Lowell Mason understood his countrymen: though he knew music's artistic side, publicly he emphasized its practical side, its place in American homes, churches, and communities.

By 1844–45 Mason was teaching without assistance in six of the Boston Public Schools and supervising ten teachers in ten other schools. Early in 1845 a "political revolution" struck the School Committee, and as a first indication of trouble ahead, Mason's work was suddenly placed under the control of a newly selected Committee on Music.[15] Just as the 1845-46 school year was getting under way, Mason received the following letter:

Boston, Sept. 11th, 1845

Lowell Mason, Esq.,

Dear Sir:
At a meeting of the Committee on Music, held this day, a majority of the committee voted to employ Mr. Baker for the ensuing year, to superintend the teaching of singing in the several grammar and writing schools.

It is my fault that the meeting of the committee was not called in August. So much school business has occupied my time for a month past, that I neglected to do so, but I presume that Mr. Mason will not be disposed to take advantage of my carelessness. I am sorry that the committee voted to make any change, and I did not suppose that it would do so. As they have done so, it is my duty to report to you this fact.

I wish to say that if Mr. Mason prefers, the Committee will give him three months from the 1st of September to resign the trust to the new superintendent.

Yours respectfully,
    Chas. Gordon[16]

There is no reason to question Gordon's sincerity in this letter, nor his loyalty to Mason. Mason and Gordon had been close associates in the Boston Academy of Music as well as personal friends. Therefore, Mason no doubt felt he would get a candid answer when he asked Gordon for details:

Boston, Sept. 13th, 1845

Dr. Chas. Gordon;—
I was not a little surprised at the receipt of your note informing me that the Committee had voted to employ another person to superintend the teaching of music in the Grammar Schools.

May I be permitted to ask the reason why I am not continued in the office? In particular, has there been any want of ability, faithfulness, fidelity, gentlemanly conduct towards committees or teachers, or kindness towards the pupils? Or have I in any instance failed to give satisfaction? Or is there any charge against me affecting my professional or moral character?

Respectfully yours,
    L. Mason

He did get a prompt and presumably candid answer, for Gordon responded that very day:

Boston, Sept. 13th, 1845

Lowell Mason, Esq.,—

Dear Sir:

In answer to your inquiry... I have to say, that the only reason given at the meeting of the Committee was, that as you had held the office for several years, and had enjoyed its benefits so long, it was proper to give to Mr. Baker, who was represented to be a distinguished and successful teacher of music, the encouragement of the office. The Committee do not charge you with want of ability or fidelity, or with ungentlemanly conduct toward the Committee or the teachers, or with any unkindness towards the pupils. The Committee are fully satisfied with the manner in which you have always discharged your duties. There was no charge made against you, affecting your professional or moral character.

Respectfully yours,
Chas. Gordon,
Chairman of Comm. on Music[17]

The school music committee consisted of three members: a Dr. Dale, the Reverend John T. Sargent, and Charles Gordon. Apparently Gordon supported Mason but had been unexpectedly outvoted by the other two members, neither of whom ever revealed much of his reasoning. Searching for a more meaningful explanation than the rotation-in-office theory, Mason wrote to Sargent on October 13, politely asking the reason for the committee's decision. The response yielded little because Sargent repeated Gordon's explanation. He did mention, however, a "suspicion of favoritism" in the selection of assistants.

This charge echoes journalist H. W. Day, who repeatedly published attacks on Mason, some of which alleged favoritism in the selection of assistants. It has been cogently argued that Day coveted Mason's job and that Day assumed if Mason could be dismissed, *he* would be appointed the music director of the Boston Public Schools. Though Day was mistaken about being next in line for the job, it appears that he pursued the prospect fervently.

Many criticisms of Mason and the music program had been articulated by Day, who was himself an editor of music magazines in the early 1840s, a singing-school teacher, and a compiler of music books (see chapter 5). Through such journals as his *Juvenile Minstral*[*sic*] (issued in 1840–41) and *The Musical Visitor* (begun in June 1840 and continued after the first two semimonthly issues under the new title *American Journal of Music*), Day launched some of his most vicious attacks on Lowell Mason.[18]

Day had complained that Mason was overpaid and that he tyrannized the music program by prescribing his own books and selecting his friends as assistants. These assistants, he continued, were persons whose ideas paralleled

Mason's, not only about teaching, but about other matters as well. Day questioned whether there were not Methodist and Baptist teachers as well qualified as Mason's Congregationalist associates. (Benjamin Baker was a Unitarian, however, and Mason had worked closely with him.) Day belittled Mason's part in getting music programs instituted in the public schools. He denounced the *Manual of the Boston Academy of Music,* the book by which Mason's teaching assistants were guided, as a "distorted and garbled translation of a little work by Keibler [*sic*] with some additions by Mr. Porter who prepared it for the press."[19]

Day's public opposition may have led the Boston School Committee to reexamine the entire music program. At the time of Mason's dismissal, they were doing exactly that. One of their reorganization plans called for the nomination of a music master by the Committee on Music, but for his actual hiring by the School Committee at large. It is conceivable that some members believed reorganization would be easier if personnel were changed.

When he was appointed to take over Mason's school position, Baker had just published a textbook entitled *American School Music Book: Containing a Thorough Elementary System, with Songs, Chants, and Hymns; Adapted to the Use of Common Schools.* The fact that its publication date (1845) coincided exactly with the "political revolution" in the school system might be entirely coincidental. So might be the advertisement on the back of the book, praising *The Vocal School or Pestalozzian Method of Instruction* by H. W. Day.

James C. Johnson, who should have known the facts, gave an intriguing account of Mason's dismissal. In describing the incident years later, Johnson charged that "two young teachers, outsiders, [felt] it was a great outrage that the important 'offices' should be filled by others and not by themselves; and ... by shrewd political management," they ousted Mason and his associates and introduced themselves in those places.[20] Vague as this interpretation is, it is a model of clarity compared to explanations of others. The common ground in all interpretations is the pettiness and jealousy of Mason's rivals, the weak-kneed response of his superiors, and "political manipulation" behind the scenes.

The "suspicion" that Mason favored his friends by appointing them his assistants was well founded. At the same time, it was natural, arguably even desirable, that his assistants should carry out his principles. A coherent philosophy applied to the entire public school music program benefited the system, the students, and music education generally. The fact that Mason's concepts have survived would seem a final vindication of his work with the Boston public schools.

Mason resigned after correspondence with the music subcommittee failed to reverse their decision. On October 8 the full Boston School Committee held a special meeting at which "a communication from Mr. Lowell Mason was read, complaining of his 'unexpected and unjust dismissal from the office of Master of Music of the Grammar Schools'... and asking... an investigation of the circumstances."[21] The proposal was discussed, but no action was taken. The School Committee did issue a letter stating, in essence, that Mason had served well, thus absolving him of any suspicion of misconduct in office.[22]

The upheaval in the music program was short-lived. In the records of the Boston School Committee of February 12, 1846, this passage appears:

> Ordered: That the Committee on Music be authorized to effect an arrangement by which one half of the schools are taught by Mr. Mason, and one half by Mr. Baker, and that these gentlemen be allowed to make use of their own books in the schools taught by them.

This arrangement took effect in March 1846, but by February 1848, it was impossible for the two superintendents to teach in all twenty schools included in the music program. Baker resolved the problem by teaching in seven of his allotted ten while Mason taught in only two of his ten. Both men hired assistants to teach in the remaining schools.

Mason finally found it necessary to reduce his teaching load to only one school, the Winthrop School, in which 420 girls were enrolled.[23] He remained there until late 1851 when, after long consideration, he resigned from active public school teaching. This concluded his active public school teaching career altogether, though his interest continued, and he occasionally visited classes in public schools in his retirement years.

Publication of Music for Children

Mason's promoting of music education led directly to the issue of such children's books as *The Juvenile Psalmist,* 1829; *The Juvenile Lyre,* 1831; *The Sabbath School Harp,* 1836; and *The Juvenile Singing School,* 1837. For music education to succeed, music teachers had to have appropriate materials. Mason and his associates worked to supply the teachers' needs. Two of the books mentioned above have special distinctions: *The Juvenile Psalmist* was evidently the first music book for Sunday schools published in the United States, and *The Juvenile Lyre* was apparently the first book of secular songs for American schoolchildren.[24]

The Juvenile Lyre presents ideas of Mason and his coeditor, Elam Ives, Jr. According to the preface, music no longer needs to be restricted to an elite few; mounting evidence proves the near universality of abilities to read music and sing. Music training is not only feasible for everyone, but also desirable because it would lead to improved church music. Cultivation of music, the editors add, provides "a source of the purest enjoyment in leisure hours"; it promotes health, for by calming the mind, it invigorates the body; it encourages "habits of order and union" that carry over into other aspects of life; it softens and elevates feelings; it makes pupils kinder to one another and more obedient to their teachers. Finally, echoing theorists from Plato's time to the present, the editors conclude that music "diverts the young from amusements of a questionable character."

These arguments were important in overcoming resistance to public school music training. Over and over Mason argued these points in speeches and writings. And, in common with other pioneer educators, Mason used prefaces to extol music's practical, social, moral, and spiritual effects.

William C. Woodbridge, who probably brought Mason and Ives together, making possible their coediting of *The Juvenile Lyre*, provided Mason with texts collected in Europe and then translated. Because the "full influence of music is only felt where it is combined with appropriate words" (preface to *The Juvenile Lyre*), the texts were carefully chosen. Some of the songs were to be "mere expressions of childish pleasure, descriptions of the warmest and best feelings of the heart; others associate moral and religious instruction with the objects we see . . . [so as to] lead the child 'through nature up to nature's God.'"

In this book, as in others Mason coedited, it is not clear which editor contributed which portions of the book. Some characteristics of the music suggest that Ives may have prepared the manuscript (perhaps even before meeting Mason) as a continuation of his textbook *The American Elementary Singing Book* (completed in 1830, published in 1832). Ives may have joined with Mason in publishing *The Juvenile Lyre* simply because Mason's name was better known.[25]

In addition to these children's song books, Mason promoted music education through supervising others' music textbooks, such as Charles Simon Catel's *A Treatise on Harmony, written and composed for the use of the pupils at the Royal Conservatoire of Music, in Paris by Catel, Professor of Harmony in that Establishment; from the English copy, with additional notes and explanations by Lowell Mason* (Boston: James Loring, 1832) and William Smith Porter's *The Musical Cyclopedia: or the Principles of Music Considered as a Science and an Art*[26] (Boston: Loring, 1834). In neither of these instances can Mason's exact contributions be determined.

During the 1830s Mason experienced the first of many difficulties with people who infringed upon the rights to his printed music. Whether they acted through ignorance or disregard of the law, he was businesslike in calling the matter to their attention, as in this case:

April 28, 1835

Mr. Fleming, Carlisle, Pa.:
I observe you have included . . . music which is copyright and which belongs to me or to my publishers.

I write more at their request and for the purpose of saying to you that we expect that all such tunes and pieces as belong to the *Handel and Haydn Coll., The Choir* or *Lyra Sacra* be immediately left out of your book & that you will stop the sale until this is done.[27]

No further clue to the identification of Mr. Fleming is offered in the letter, nor is it known what his response was. The statute of 1831 provided that musical compositions were protected for twenty-eight years with renewal for fourteen years to the author, his widow, or his children.

Mason was agreeable when compilers treated his music with respect. This is illustrated by a pleasant exchange between Mason and the Reverend Thomas Whittemore (1800-1861), compiler of *Songs of Zion* (1836):

Boston, Oct. 27, 1836

Lowell Mason, Esq.

Sir, I take the liberty to send you a copy of a work I have just published. I would not have troubled you with it; but it occurred to me, since it was printed, that I may in one case have infringed upon a copyright in which I believe you are interested. If I have done so, it was certainly unintentional; and on being apprised of the fact, will make immediate reparation, by removing the pages. It was my intention to avoid any offence in this particular. I remain, Dear Sir, with very high respect,

Yours &c,
Thos. Whittemore[28]

Mason reassured him:

Boston, Nov. 25, 1836

Rev. Th. Whittemore,

Dear Sir,
I rec'd the note & book you were so kind as to send me. The "infringement" if indeed there is any is very small—but had it been much greater I am sure it would have been more than atoned for by the very kind & friendly manner in which you yourself have made it known—& offered "reparation," thus affording abundant evidence that there was no intentional trespass. Who could complain under such circumstances?

Very Respec'ly yrs.,
L. Mason

Ironically, Mason himself often borrowed, arranged, and published music with little or no credit given to sources. Many of his prefaces make proud claims to the effect that he offers the best new music from the best sources (meaning European and British composers with Swiss, Austrian, and German composers apparent favorites). But Mason did not necessarily credit individual sources for pieces he adapted, and for this, he has been justly criticized, even given the relative laxity of copyright regulations in his day.

After music became part of the school curriculum in Boston, the demand for Mason's music books grew dramatically. At about the same time, book publishing was becoming a big business in America. This was virtually an overnight development. During the decade of the 1840s the total books published more than doubled: from $2,850,000 in 1840 to $5,900,000 worth in 1850.[29] Because of the advances in public education, the number of literate people nearly doubled during that same decade.

Music publishing paralleled book publishing generally, but the growth occurred for different reasons. Though music literacy was developing because of public school music, it was not yet a large factor in the music marketplace. Rather, other factors were at work. The continuing interest in sacred music, stimulated by ongoing controversies over the proper style, kept music presses busily turning out books ranging from revival and shape-note books to adaptations of European oratorios. Impetus for publishing also came from the rise of professional music entertainment and the appearance of star performers who attracted public attention. Popular song writing became a big business, in part because of the growing popularity of minstrel shows.

The first large music publishing house in New England was the Oliver Ditson Company, founded in 1835. Before that time most music publishing was done by individual printers who occasionally handled music. Some of those entrepreneurs were also composers and arrangers; others were chiefly proprietors of book and music stores—as, for example, James Hewitt (1770–1827) and Benjamin Carr (1768–1831). According to one count, forty-four different music publishers of this description worked in Boston between 1800 and 1850, most of them running small, short-lived operations.[30] Oliver Ditson himself was affiliated with several individuals and small firms before settling into the company that took his name.

Though Mason produced children's books steadily during the decade, few of them are remarkable for innovations. Throughout his lifetime he kept his "juvenile" books fairly short, usually about one hundred pages long. Most of the selections are simple songs for one, two, or three parts with a few rounds, psalm and hymn tunes, and vocal exercises interspersed. The musical compositions are nearly always short, strophic songs, usually one to two pages long. The prefaces, usually kept brief, stress the editor's judicious choice of pure, wholesome texts. Usually these texts deal with the natural world, the child's everyday life, national holidays, and other topics in which children normally take an interest.[31] The music is usually presented without interpretive directions, without credits to authors or composers, and without accompaniment.

Though its material fits this general description, *The Song-Garden* (1864-66) was innovative in that it was a graded series of textbooks, apparently the first such series of song books for American schoolchildren. The first and second books appeared in 1864, the third and last volume in 1866. The first book was very brief and simple; as would be expected, the second and third books grew progressively more difficult.

Mason's books enjoyed relatively good marketing, considering advertising's limited capabilities at the time. In fact, it was rather unusual that the book *Little Songs for Little Singers* (1840) received little publicity. In an 1855 edition, Mason states flatly that the book was "little advertised and little known and finally went out of print," but that he decided to reissue it after many requests that he do so. No further explanation is given.

Mason's editorial commentary in *The Boston School Song Book* (1841) is more typical. Most of the songs here are entirely new, he says, referring to both tunes and texts. These songs are intended to relieve children from the "severer study of the [music] elements" and to give their voices exercise. Not surprisingly, it is recommended for use with his other classroom materials, such as *The Musical Exercises* (1838). In *The Primary School Song Book,* published in 1846 with Webb, the editors express concern that children learn to sing expressively. Then they propose a more progressive idea: children should begin learning to sing during the preschool years. To this end, the editors address both teachers and mothers, urging the latter to teach rote songs with care to instill correct habits, being as careful as in teaching correct speech. In *The Song-Book of the School-Room* (1847, coedited with Webb) Mason's two main concerns are summarized: children must have a variety of music to keep their musical interests alive, and the music must "exalt, ennoble, purify thoughts, feelings and associations."

Mason's editorial choices reflected the educational standards and objectives of his day. Conversely, through his editing, he shaped musical standards of his day and of subsequent years as well. Although the music he selected for other types of books also influenced many people, the school music books had a particularly powerful, far-reaching impact on public tastes because they reached thousands of impressionable youngsters. These "juvenile" publications impressed Mason's musical tastes upon the American public, just as his writings, personal example, and teacher training programs impressed his methods upon thousands of teachers.

8

The Final Years in Boston

Community Leadership in Music

During his last decade in Boston (1841–1851), Lowell Mason was at the peak of his career, having established himself as *the* leading musician of his region, if not of the entire nation. His teaching in the Boston public schools brought him before the public often, because his classes gave public concerts and appeared at community events. For instance, his students participated in the July Fourth celebration of 1848. As described years later by one of those student-singers,

> Six of the first class girls [from the Bowdoin School]... with a similar number of girls and boys from each of the other grammar schools and the Latin and High schools... assembled at the "Cradle of Liberty." Their part was to... hear patriotic speeches... and under the leadership of Lowell Mason to respond to each speech with a song. These were taken from Mason's "School Song Books:" (1) Oh land of good that gave me birth! My lovely, native land; (2) Friends, we bid you welcome here; (3) Before all lands East or West. That [occasion]... was a red letter day in our school life.[1]

Mason sometimes composed music for special community events. In 1845, for instance, he prepared three short, strophic works for mixed chorus (works that would be categorized as hymns and odes) published that year by A. B. Kidder under the title "Songs Prepared for the City Celebration of 4th July, 1845."[2]

Mason conducted a number of Boston choral groups besides his church choirs. In 1841, he directed the two to three hundred singers who joined the Association of City Choirs. In addition, he was called upon to conduct at special occasions such as the celebration on October 25, 1848 for the installation of Boston's large-scale water supply, a supply drawn from Lake Cochituate twenty miles away. On that program, he conducted three thousand schoolchildren in a song entitled "My Name is Water," with a text by contemporary poet James Russell Lowell (1819–1891). "Thanks be to God" from Mendelssohn's *Elijah* was sung at the very moment an eighty-foot fountain rose. The audience was spellbound.[3]

During his last years in Boston, besides public school teaching, church work, and choral conducting, Mason continued working in higher education, specifically in the training of clergy. It appears that he taught without salary or other remuneration during his eight years at Andover Theological Seminary, 1836 to 1844. Giving up his association at Andover must have been difficult for Mason because he knew his efforts there had been appreciated. For instance, a year before his resignation, he had received this letter with a gift:

Andover, July 17, 1843

Mr. Lowell Mason, Esq.,

Dear Sir:
The vases, which we herewith present you, are offered in token of our warm personal regard for yourself, and of our continual gratitude to you for your invaluable professional labors with us during the past season. When we first expressed to you our hope, that we should feel the inspiration which your name and occasional presence among us might well give to our zeal in the cause of Sacred Music, we did not dare to expect that we should ever have the privilege of coming under your instruction for so long a period—much less, that such a favor would be enjoyed by us without money and without price. But we rejoice, Sir, that you could find it consistent with your many duties thus to favor us; and we desire again and again to assure you that your labors with us have afforded the highest gratification.

We ask you to accept this little token from us...as a memento of our thankfulness. We present it, with our congratulations to you for all the signal good which you have hither done in the Church by your untiring efforts to perfect her holy melodies, and with our prayer that you may long be spared to fill that place in devotional hearts which you now so deservedly occupy.
With the highest respect,
    Yr. ob't Serv't
        J. L. Taylor

Mason's resignation the following year (1844) did not signify that he was cutting himself off from higher education, only that he felt his goals at Andover had been fairly well met. In 1847 he joined the staff of lecturers at the State Normal School in West Newton, Massachusetts. This institution, the first American normal school, began at Lexington, moved to West Newton, and finally to Framingham. Mason remained on the staff there until 1851.

Because he was so well known, Mason had many contacts with aspiring musicians who sought his help. In early 1840 members of the singing Hutchinson family called on him, hoping for ideas to further their concert careers. Mason's advice was short and simple: he told them to buy his latest (song) book. With that, he resumed his work.[4] During the same visit to Boston, the Hutchinsons called on George Webb, who encouraged them to join the Boston Handel and Haydn Society. In short, the Hutchinsons got little help from these prominent Boston musicians.

A little-known incident concerns Mason's contact with the black instrumentalist-composer Henry F. Williams (1813-1903). Early in his career Williams had composed an anthem that was praised by many reputable musicians. Unfortunately many people, Lowell Mason included, expressed doubt that anyone of his race could create so fine a work as that composition. Finally Mason (and others who judged the matter objectively) yielded to the facts and acknowledged Williams' achievement. As he became better acquainted with Williams' abilities, Mason came to admire and respect him. Eventually he voiced his regret that anyone so talented should "be kept down merely on account of the color of his face."[5]

Mason could have used his prestige to break down prejudice in music circles, but he was not a reformer in this regard. In his defense, it can be said that he was very much a man of his times. His religiosity and his rather condescending attitudes toward women are further evidence of this side of his character. (Regarding his attitudes toward women, see, for instance, letter XXIX in *Musical Letters from Abroad,* his discussion of Madam Sontag.)

The Horace Mann Institutes for Teachers

In the 1840s, as before, circumstances of the times favored Lowell Mason's projects. This is particularly true with respect to the development of teachers' institutes under Horace Mann (1796–1859), the first secretary of the Massachusetts State Board of Education. These teachers' institutes are not to be confused with Mason's conventions or the normal music institutes he held with George Root, William B. Bradbury, W. W. Killip, and others. The meetings organized by Mann trained public school teachers, especially those who worked in the lower grades where they handled all subjects themselves. These teachers (unlike those who attended Mason's teachers' meetings) were not specifically music teachers. For speakers, Mann invited leading educators who discussed pedagogy in general and specialists who discussed individual disciplines, as, for example, Lowell Mason representing music teaching.

The idea of teachers' institutes apparently originated in the state of New York in 1843. Horace Mann seized upon the idea, realizing that there were about six thousand aspiring teachers in Massachusetts but only about three hundred places each year in the existing teacher-training programs. He proposed teachers' institutes to the 1844 Massachusetts legislature, but no money was appropriated. Then a private sponsor, Edmund Dwight, offered Mann a thousand dollars for an experimental institute under Mann's direction. That experiment was so successful that the legislature appropriated $2,500 per year for institutes, beginning the following year.[6]

When planning for the fall institutes in 1845, Mann included vocal music among the disciplines to be covered. He wanted Lowell Mason to represent music because he had heard some of Mason's earlier lectures (at least the 1832 and 1834 lectures at the American Institute of Instruction) and had come to admire Mason's teaching philosophy. Inasmuch as Mann contacted him at about the time of the "political revolution" in the Boston Public Schools, Mason must have been particularly gratified with Mann's invitation.

During the following years, Mason and Mann became well acquainted through their work together at institutes. That first fall (1845), Mason was able to attend about half of the scheduled institutes; he definitely was present at Fitchburg and Bridgewater. Of the many letters that Mann wrote to Mason during the course of their association, at least sixteen survive. Of that number, there is one that Abby Mason particularly treasured. Written about three days after her husband had returned from the institutes that fall, it read as follows:

Monday, Nov. 24, 1845, Boston

Lowell Mason, Esq.

My dear Sir,
I cannot refrain from expressing my thanks for your kindness in attending our "teachers' institute," at Bridgewater and giving lessons, in music, to its members. I now see more clearly than I ever did before that a way may be opened, *thro'* Teachers' Institutes, to introduce music into [all] our common schools,—a "consummation most devoutly to be wished."

While witnessing your exercises, as I did during the past week, I resolved to avail myself of an early opportunity to express to you the great gratification I experienced from witnessing your mode of teaching. In your adaptation of the thing to be taught to the capacity of the learner; in your easy gradation from the known to the unknown,—the latter always seeming to spring naturally from, and to be intrinsically connected with, the former, and in your reviews,—more or less extensive,—which seemed to link together the part which had been separately given before;—in all these points, your lessons appeared to me to be models, worthy of the imitation of teachers in all other branches. I have never before seen anything that came nearer to my *beau ideal* of teaching.

With sincere thanks for the valuable services you have rendered, I am, dear sir, very truly and sincerely, Yrs., &c. &c.

Horace Mann[7]

Mason was a staff member of the teachers' institutes and state normal schools for the following seventeen years, long after Mann withdrew from his post in 1848. Mann's successors, Barnas Sears and George S. Boutwell (who served from 1855 to 1861), seem to have appreciated Mason's contributions. Boutwell spoke highly of Mason's work in his autobiography.[8] During the course of his work in those years, Mason worked with many outstanding leaders in education and other fields, such as Calvin Cutter, William Russell (his friend in Savannah), John Pierpont, Charles Brooks, George B. Emerson, Samuel S. Greene, Sanborn Tenney, William H. Wells, D. P. Colburn, Josiah

Holbrook, Asa Gray, James Russell Lowell, Louis Agassiz, Arnal Guyot, and Hermann Krüsi, Jr. (a son of Pestalozzi's associate at Yverdon).[9]

In addition to working in Massachussetts' institutes, Mason lectured on occasion at other states' institutes. In 1847 Henry Barnard, commissioner of the Rhode Island public schools, invited Mason to address the teachers' institute at Pawtucket November 29-December 4. According to the *Boston Musical Gazette* of January 17, 1848, Mason delivered "four lectures in which he exemplified a scientific method of teaching." In 1848 he appeared at an institute in East Greenwich, Connecticut, where he met George B. Emerson, a first cousin of Ralph Waldo Emerson and a distinguished educator.

It is impossible to determine how much Mason was paid for his appearances at these meetings. Some of the surviving letters from Mann mention a sum of money enclosed as payment or partial payment for Mason's work at an institute. The letter dated December 11, 1848, for instance, included $35 as part of his pay for the Springfield, Massachusetts institute just completed. The amounts included ranged from $25 to $35, but some of these sums may have been reimbursements for travel expenses.

Lowell Mason probably made very little money through teaching at the institutes if salary alone is considered. It is equally probable that this additional public exposure led to more sales of his music books. Through the extraordinary success of those books, he made more than enough money to underwrite his other, less remunerative endeavors. Certainly his appearances before the teachers' institutes brought Mason's name, ideas, and materials sharply to the attention of people who selected music textbooks for their schools.

Family Matters

Concurrent with these many endeavors in Boston, Lowell and Abby Mason saw their four sons grow into manhood. Dates and names pertaining to their lives are summarized here:

Daniel Gregory (1820–1869)
    married Susan Belcher Headden (dates unknown)
        Children: Lowell III (1848–1918)
                        Abigail (1852–?)
                        Walter (1856–1858)
                        John Belcher (1858–1919)

Lowell, Jr. (1823–1885)
    married Marie Whitney (1824–1881)
    No children

William (1829–1908)
married Mary Isabelle Webb (1833–1880)
Children: George Webb (1858–1881)
                   Marion Otis (1861–1890)
                   Mary Wilhelmina (1863–?)

Henry (1831–1890)
married Helen Augusta Palmer (1836–1905)
Children: Edward Palmer (1859–1940)
                   Alan Gregory (1861–1934)
                   Henry Lowell (1864–1957)
                   Daniel Gregory (1873–1953)

During the 1840s the older Mason sons were beginning their careers. In 1840 Lowell, Jr. moved to Cincinnati, Ohio to join the book publishing firm of Winthrop B. Smith & Co. His uncle, Timothy B. Mason, who was well established in Cincinnati, may have encouraged the young man to make this move. In any event, Lowell, Jr. soon proved to be a sound businessman and was quickly made a partner. The rise of the book publishing industry at that time coincided with the career of Lowell Mason, Jr., favoring his work, just as the rise of public education had coincided with his father's efforts in music education.

Lowell Mason, Jr. married Marie Whitney during the middle 1840s; conflicting accounts place the event between 1844 and 1847.[10] They lived in Cincinnati until about 1851 when they moved to New York City. In 1854 they moved to Orange, New Jersey, where they resided thereafter. Marie was the daughter of Paul Whitney, a prominent Boston merchant. Though born in Boston, she grew up in Shrewsbury, Massachusetts. It is not known how or where she met her future husband. In later years, though afflicted with deafness, Marie became known as a writer. Many of her short poems were published in magazines of the day, and her father-in-law set some of them to music. At least one, "Mary's Easter," was anthologized as recently as 1942 in Doubleday's *Days and Deeds*.

On January 13, 1851, Daniel Gregory Mason and Lowell Mason, Jr. joined Henry W. Law of Brooklyn, New York as "general partners" in the new publishing firm Mason and Law. "Special partners" were Francis J. Huntington of Hartford, Connecticut and George Savage of Brooklyn, New York. As might be expected, this company published many of Lowell Mason's works, as well as the scores and books of other composers, compilers, and authors. Advertising in the music periodicals of the day reflects extensive publishing by Mason and Law.

Daniel Gregory Mason and Susan Belcher Headden were married on January 20, 1848. Their first child (Lowell and Abby's first grandchild) was a son born November 11, 1848. Named Lowell, III, in honor of his grandfather and uncle, the boy held a special place in his grandfather's affections. He was soon nicknamed "Lolo," and when he learning to talk, he called his grandfather Mason "Dapotee." Many of their letters used these family names.

William and Henry, the younger sons, both studied in Europe in the early 1850s before launching their adult careers and marrying. In the 1840s they were still at home, growing through the teen years. William was already an unusually capable pianist with much performing experience. Among his accomplishments were performances before teachers' conventions he visited with his father.

During this decade William also met his future wife. He described their meeting years later in his autobiography, *Memories of a Musical Life:*

> In 1846 my father was preparing to hold a convention in Augusta, Maine. Mr. Webb was to go with him, and I was sent to his house the evening before they were to start to let him know about the arrangements. Though I knew Mr. Webb very well, I had never had occasion to go to his house. At this time I was seventeen years old. When I was shown into the drawing-room, I saw Mr. and Mrs. Webb and their daughter, a girl then not fourteen. I had not been in the house half an hour before I was deeply in love with her. I found that she was going to Augusta, and I decided at once that I would go, too. So the next day we all started together. She and I grew to be good friends, but the idea of an engagement . . . was not thought of at that time, and while I lived in Germany we were not permitted to correspond. For five years I did not see her; but when I came back I hastened to her father's house. . . .[11]

It is virtually certain that the youngest Mason son, Henry, also knew his future wife from those early years in Boston: Helen Augusta Palmer, daughter of Asher C. and Anne Folsom Palmer, long-time friends and associates of the Masons in Boston.

Departure from Boston

In 1851 Lowell and Abby Mason decided to leave Boston permanently. Their work in that city during the previous twenty-four years had been rewarding, and their sons had enjoyed the advantages of growing up in a culturally and educationally stimulating city. Through the years Mason had made not only an excellent professional reputation, but also a considerable fortune. *The Rich Men of Massachusetts; A Statement of the Reputed Wealth of About Two Thousand Persons with Brief Sketches of Nearly 1500 Characters*, published in 1852 by Redding & Co., Boston, included this entry:

County of Suffolk
Mason, Lowell. $100,000
[roughly equivalent in purchasing power to $1,348,000 in 1983][12]
Commenced a poor man. His professional life is fully sketched in his musical productions which are in every household, and this also accounts for his wealth, which would have been far greater, were his benevolence less. As a teacher he has no superior.

Mason believed that his work in Boston was pretty well completed. The fact that the Masons' older two sons were established in New York City may have attracted Lowell and Abby to that locality; their next residence was in that city. By June 1851, when their intentions became known in Boston, members of Mason's past and present choirs met to arrange a tribute to his work. They decided on a farewell party to which all members of his various church choirs would be invited. A committee was appointed to make arrangements, to purchase a gift, and to request of Mason a farewell address on church music.

The party was held on July 8, 1851 at the Winter Street Church with three of Mason's long-time associates in charge: clergymen Lyman Beecher, Hubbard Winslow, and William M. Rogers. Dr. Beecher complimented Mason's efforts to improve church music. Beecher's remarks, prayer, Scripture reading, and singing formed part of the program, but its central feature was Mason's address on church music.

Mason began by discussing the history of church music in Boston, particularly during the nearly twenty-five years of his experience. He recalled his involvement with church and school music over a forty-year period and his present decision to withdraw from the labors because of ill health. (There are, however, no records of any health problems, and judging from the strenuous trip he and Abby were about to undertake, his health seems to have allowed him to do pretty much as he wished.)

His address went on to cite pioneer "reformers" such as the Reverend Dr. Dana of Newburyport who had led the fight to rid churches of the "miserable musical trash which [then] almost universally prevailed." Boston leaders were also mentioned and their contributions cited. Mason revealed a few personal details as well. He stated that he enjoyed singing the children's songs he had used over the years. In connection with his choir work and the inevitable problems that arise, he observed, "I have always found it possible to calm the agitated waters; and whenever I have failed to control the choir, it has been because I have failed to control myself."[13]

As a climax to the evening, Mr. Rogers, pastor of the Winter Street Church, presented Mason with a large silver vase as a token of the group's feelings for him. According to one of the choir members present at the time, the vase was worth about two hundred dollars.[14] Designed by Charles E. Parker, architect, and executed by Henry Haddock, silversmith, the vase was inscribed on one side with these words: "Presented to Lowell Mason by past and present members of his Choirs, July, 1851." Elsewhere appeared the inscriptions

"Handel & Haydn Soc. Collection 1822" and "Cantica Laudis 1850" (at the time, his last church music collection).[15]

During his last few months in Boston, Mason prepared for his second European trip. Meanwhile, he and Abby were packing their household possessions for moving and storage in anticipation of living in New York City upon their return. Mason continued to teach in one of the Boston schools, Winthrop School, until his departure time.

During these months, quite unexpectedly, a new opportunity developed. Shortly before he left for Europe, Mason was visited by George F. Root, who was then teaching in New York. Root proposed initiating a three-month training session for music teachers. Mason was skeptical at first. "Well," said Root, "I am going to have such a class. You are the proper person to appear at the head of it when it comes to the teaching, but I do not expect you to do any of the work of getting it up; I'll see to that." To clinch his argument he added, "It will be a better opportunity than you ever had to make your ideas of notation, teaching, and church music really known, for you will have time enough thoroughly to indoctrinate people with them." Root commented, as an aside, that if anything would persuade Mason, that would.[16]

No discussion of salary or financial arrangements of any kind took place just then. Root, who knew Mason well from years of association, reflected about the man's view of money gained from his work:

Lowell Mason was the most misjudged man in this respect that I ever knew. He had plenty of money. It came in large sums from his works, but I do not believe he ever made a plan to make money unless when investing his surplus funds. In his musical work it was always "Is this the best thing—Will it be received—Will it do the most good?" . . . He was like a child if any error could be pointed out in his works or defect in his teaching. It was not often that either thing happened, but when it did, it was "Is that so? Let us see," and prompt correction took place whenever he saw he was wrong. . . .[17]

After thinking over Root's plans, Mason agreed to take part in the new teacher training program, soon named the Normal Musical Institute. Root wanted to begin in 1852, with a session running from June through August, but this was impossible because of Mason's trip to Europe, a trip that extended beyond his original travel plans. The Normal Musical Institutes began instead in 1853.

The European Trip of 1852–53

Lowell and Abigail Mason sailed for Europe on December 21, 1851, and arrived in Liverpool on January 1, 1852. According to a letter Mason sent to George Webb, they originally intended to travel only nine or ten months. As it turned out, their trip extended over about sixteen months. Beginning in England, the Masons went to major German cities, plus Zürich, Switzerland, then back to England via Paris. The six-month addition to their trip was a prolonged stay in the British Isles, for when they reached London on their way home, Mason was persuaded to lecture on church music and music teaching. Because these appearances were so well received, he remained an extra six months, lecturing in London and Manchester and Edinburgh, Scotland. On April 2, 1853, Lowell and Abigail sailed for home, arriving April 15 at the East Boston wharf on the steamer *America*.

Mason sent fifty-four informal essays back to the United States as he traveled. These were published at once in various journals, then collected upon his return and published under the title *Musical Letters from Abroad* (Oliver Ditson, 1853; Mason Brothers, 1854). The essays were meant to "serve as a token of remembrance from the writer" to his "numerous pupils and friends" and perhaps to "influence... those who were exerting themselves for [musical] improvement" (preface, iv). Mason concentrated particularly on church music, but also offered some accounts of concerts, festivals, and private meetings with individual musicians, interjecting his ideas on many topics. Individual "musical letters" generally stand alone and can be read individually or in any combination.

Though some of the material in this chapter comes from *Musical Letters from Abroad,* much of it comes from travel diaries which (like those kept during the 1837 trip) remain unedited and unpublished. The diaries show that Mason again visited schools extensively and shopped widely for music to take or send home. The diaries include some personal matters, sometimes providing details otherwise not known about his health, his family, and his impressions. Abby Mason also kept a diary, and from its 126 closely written pages a few remarks are quoted below.

When the Masons began their trip, they were surprised to find that they had a traveling companion to England, long-time friend William B. Dinsmore. During their months abroad they enjoyed his company whenever their paths crossed. Dinsmore, a Boston native, had moved to New York City about 1840 to become a partner in the Adams Express Company. Abby recorded in her diary the circumstances of their departure:

> One pleasing incident I must not omit. Mr. & Mrs. Dinsmore were on board the steamer, I supposed . . . to see us off. After all who were not sailing had gone to shore . . . Mr. D. came up to us. Father [Lowell] said, "The bell has rung!" "Yes," he replied, "we can get back with the pilot if we are left, but I believe I will go & take care of you!" We were indeed surprised & delighted that at least *one* whom we had before known was with us. . . . His daily visit [during the ocean voyage] . . . was quite cheering.

The Masons' first days after arrival in England were busy. Symbolic of Lowell's concerns in 1852 was their visit with William H. Havergal (1793-1870) two days after their arrival. According to Mason's diary, he was "rec'd cordially and talked about church music" with this noted clergyman-musician whose compositions he had often included in his books.

Pleasant though their stay in England was, the Masons were eager to get to Germany where their two younger sons were studying. On January 17 they reached Leipzig, their temporary home for about two-and-a-half months. From there, they made several brief side trips, such as early-April trips to Berlin and Dresden. Most of the time they remained in Leipzig, living at No. 10 Ross Platz where they had a four-room suite for themselves and a second suite nearby for William and his grand piano. These diary entries reveal Mason's delight at seeing William again:

> Leipzig, Jan. 17. Went to Hotel de Barviére [*sic*]. To this Hotel Wm. had directed us. He, not expecting us, had gone over to Mr. Parker's room [James C. D. Parker, a New England musician, graduate of Leipzig Conservatory] & we had to wait until nearly 7 o'clock before we saw him—at that time he came in, & we had a most happy meeting with a dear son whom we had not seen for nearly three years. He is considerably altered—more fleshy—face & limbs fuller—looks quite healthy & more manly than when he left—

> Monday, 19th. Spent the day mostly in walking about with William & Mr. D. [Dinsmore]. After dinner went to Mr. Parker's rooms, with Mother, Mr. D., & Mr. Parker, & William played to us an hour or so. He seems to have improved much, as much as I could have expected. I have certainly never heard anyone play that afforded me so much pleasure as he does.

The Mason's youngest son, Henry, joined them occasionally during their trip. Lowell's entry for January 28 mentions that "Henry left us for Göttingen. Had been with us since last Sat. [24th]. . . . We feel sad at parting with dear Henry today, but it seemed best for him to get back to Göttingen, from where in about a month we expect him to go to Paris." References to Henry indicate that he was with his parents in Paris and London. On July 20, 1852, Lowell remarks, "at 1 called on *Spohr*—and had a pleasant interview of 1/2 an hour. His wife was present, & she speaks English. Henry went with me." On May 7 he records that he had written his older sons at Mason & Law, "asking them to honor Henry's drafts for $100 per mo. beginning June 1 plus an extra $100 for this month."

This is one of Mason's infrequent references to money. He had almost as little to say about money as about his health. Apparently he felt an illness was important enough to record, but not important enough to describe in any telling detail. For instance, in his entry for April 3, in Berlin, he states that "in aft. I was quite unwell & did not go out." A more intriguing entry appears in the June 21 statement, "had my feet operated on." No indication of foot problems had appeared in previous entries, adding to the mystery of the ailment and the operation.

Mason was conscious of his approaching old age and death. On January 8, 1852, he wrote, "This day I am sixty years old.... *Three score* years are gone; Oh, may I feel that my days draw nigh to a close, & that in a little time the places that now know me will know [me] no more forever." He was reminded of death by the news that his Boston friend Daniel Noyes had died in April 1852; soon after that came news of his own mother's death:

Monday, June 21, 1852 [in Frankfurt]

This morning we have received letters from N.Y. via Paris, informing of my mother's death. She was 84 years of age & had lived almost 64 years with my father. She died on the morning of Wednesday 26th May at about 1 o'clock.... She was buried on the Saturday following, at 2 o'clock...[while] we were in Stuttgart.

The sorrow of that occasion was offset somewhat by an entry a few months later, announcing the birth of a second grandchild, a daughter born to Daniel Gregory and Susie Mason on November 8 (1852). This child, named Abigail, was soon called "Abby" like her grandmother.

Of the many musicians the Masons met during their tour, one of the most famous was Ludwig Spohr (1784–1859), composer, conductor, and violinist. Mason renewed his friendship with many musicians he had visited in 1837, including Moscheles, Schneider, Neukomm, and Wilhelm Bach. On April 6, 1852, he called on Bach who "rec'd me very cordially.... I had a most interesting and undoubtedly a last visit of 1/2 an hour." Schneider played five J. S. Bach organ fugues for the Masons. In *Musical Letters from Abroad* Mason wrote admiringly of the rendition:

Schneider... used no fancy stops, made no see-sawing with the swell, no contrasts of reeds and dulcianas, no high-diddle-diddles in his playing. His appeal is always to the intellectual musician. His great point of excellence... is his legato touch. . . .(Letter 23)

On several occasions the Masons met American musicians studying abroad. Perhaps the most prominent of them was Samuel Parker Tuckerman (1819–1890), an accomplished organist from Boston. Tuckerman received the doctor of music degree in 1853 at Lambeth, England. During his career, he edited a number of church music collections, some of which Mason cites as references in his own books.

The Masons met other important music figures of the time, including music theorists Moritz Hauptmann (1792–1868), a professor at Leipzig Conservatory, and Siegfried Wilhelm Dehn (1799–1858), then in Berlin. William Mason had studied with Hauptmann, himself a pupil of Spohr and one-time cantor of the Thomasschule in Leipzig. By the time Lowell Mason met Hauptmann, the latter had heard of him and his work through William who mentions the following episode in his autobiography:

About 1850 Lowell Mason had sent William a copy of one of his recent tunebooks for choir and congregational use (the exact one was unspecified, and it could have been any one of several books). Lowell asked his son to show the volume to Hauptmann and, if possible, to get his evaluation of it. William was shy about doing so and procrastinated until he had received several letters from his father concerning the matter. Finally at the end of a lesson period, William slipped the book onto Hauptmann's desk, mumbling an apology for his father's request and adding that he was afraid his teacher would find nothing of interest in the book. William dreaded his next meeting with Hauptmann, but was surprised and relieved when his teacher greeted him saying, "Mr. Mason, I have examined your father's book with much interest and pleasure, and his admirable treatment of voices is most musicianly and satisfactory. Please give him my sincere regards, and thank him for his attention in sending me the book."[1]

When he himself met Hauptmann, Lowell was impressed with the man's "kindness, gentleness, and courtesy," but even more with his modesty: "Although standing at the very head of musical science, he has, as yet, published no work of importance on harmony; he says that he waits for more experience, so that when he publishes a book, *it may be of some value.*"[2] Mason adds that certain Americans who presume to write music theory books ought to exercise similar restraint.

Mason's meeting with Professor Siegfried Dehn, director of the music library at the Royal Library in Berlin, was particularly memorable. Mason describes Dehn as a "very learned musician," and that he was. Dehn, both a theorist and a pioneer musicologist, published works of the sixteenth-century master Roland de Lassus, analyses of J. S. Bach's fugues in the *Well-Tempered Clavier,* a twelve-volume set of vocal compositions from the sixteenth and seventeenth centuries, as well as his *Theoretisch-praktische Harmonie-lehre* (1840), his most important publication. Mason reports in *Musical Letters from Abroad* that he and Dehn looked over the Royal Library holdings together even though they could not communicate well because of the language barrier. Dehn proudly showed his guest the rare, early volumes of Lassus' *Psalms.* Wishing to make his feelings clear despite the language problem, Dehn "took the volumes into his hand, and touching me, to call my attention, gave them a very intelligible and affectionate kiss!" (Letter 31)

Mason's reports of the trip reflect his special fondness for the music of Handel and Mendelssohn. He repeatedly refers to their works, their excellent text settings, and (most of all) their effective oratorio writing.

> Handel's music meets the wants of all classes; the learned and unlearned are alike gratified in its performance; those who have made the greatest progress in art and science find enough in Handel to fill their minds and to draw out their feelings; and like the poetry of Shakespeare, it so delineates human nature, or is so conformed to it, and is so common-senselike in its character, that it can hardly fail to be appreciated even by a child.[3]

Though he writes at one point that *Israel in Egypt* is Handel's greatest work (an opinion not shared by most critics), Mason refers to *Messiah* far more often. That work prompts one of the most emotional passages in all of Mason's writing:

> Great is Handel's oratorio of the *Messiah!* Great are its wonderful and soul-stirring themes! Great in musical inspiration! Great in its moral power! Ye choirs who seek for music of a high order in the oratorio form, purchase Handel's *Messiah!* There is nothing on earth like it! Be not satisfied with anything short of this.... The music is indeed difficult; it cannot be performed without labor, but the labor bestowed will be productive of rich reward.[4]

Mason was especially impressed with the *Messiah* overture as performed by the Birmingham Festival orchestra: "We have (we are ashamed to confess it) sometimes thought the overture unworthy of the oratorio, but it was because we knew it not."[5] Part of his enthusiasm for Handel's *Messiah* was admittedly due to its text, but considered overall, comparable works fell short in his sight. When speaking of an American music society that chose Haydn's *Seasons* over *Messiah,* contrary to Mason's specific advice, Mason says that they "chose a shilling piece when they might have had a gold sovereign."[6]

Seeing Mendelssohn conduct in 1837 added to Mason's admiration for the man and his music. His references to Mendelssohn are numerous and complimentary. Not infrequently he mentions that a Mendelsohn work was the main attraction of a concert.[7] Inasmuch as the concerts the Masons attended were often three to four hours long and offered a broad range of musical styles, the fact that Mendelssohn's music is singled out as the most appealing is significant. Of course, Mason might also have been influenced by the British enthusiasm for Mendelssohn.

Mason's reverence for Beethoven is apparent whenever the composer's name is mentioned.[8] His diary entry for June 22, 1852 indicates that he, Abby, and William

> had left Frankfurt... going to Paris via Bonn, Cologne, and Brussels. At Bonn [they] stopped to see Beethoven's birthplace... one of the greatest artists. [They] stood and gazed upon the monument in perfect silence and with intense interest. No musician... can look upon this statue without a deep feeling of reverence and admiration, amounting as nearly to worship and adoration as may be rendered to the highest manifestations of human genius.

Mason adds that they left Cologne on the following day, having been accompanied to the railroad station by William, who waited with them for the departure of their train. "It was hard to part with William. We met him in Leipzig... and have been with him daily... five months and six days—and now we part with him to return... home and he to remain a year or two longer." Abby noted in her diary that they had ridden their last few miles with William mostly in silence, "our hearts too full to speak."

Two dominant impressions emerge concerning Mason as a music critic. First, he was detailed and precise in writing about musical styles and practices with which he was familiar (for instance, church music), but vague in dealing with music that was new and unfamiliar to him (for example, Beethoven's Ninth Symphony, which he heard for the first time at the Birmingham Festival in September 1852). Second, he was seldom negative in his statements (though he was highly opinionated), and when he was negative, he usually explained his reasons.

A sampling of his writing is sufficient to illustrate these conclusions. The following passages from his diary entry of January 9, 1852 show the precision of his observations:

> This morning... went to the Foundling Hospital where we attended Public Worship. We got there at 20 m. before 11, & found the children all in their places—about 370 in all. 200 Girls on one side of the organ & 170 Boys on the other. The Service commenced at 11 with an organ voluntary; and a lighter more frivolous piece of organ playing I never heard. It was an attempt at a kind of Overture, entirely secular & destitute of every thing from beginning to end like organ style, or like sacred music. Now the flute, now the reeds, with staccato, or sudden Pianos & Fortes, without dignity, without character, without the slightest particle of reverence, and even without sense. I have heard the organ abused & degraded many times, but never did I hear such a complete burlesque as this—the climax of all that is ridiculous & absurd in the use of the noble instrument in public worship.

In the chanting there was the *merit* of *keeping together,* & also of the absence of drawling in the cadences. The cadences were very quick, even quicker than I have heard before, but the effect was good. But little attention was given to words—on the chanting note they were not decently spoken—they were clipped, with wrong vowel sounds, & careless pronunciation.

It is interesting to compare this passage with his published version (*Musical Letters from Abroad,* Letter 2). The published version follows the diary passage closely.

Another example of Mason's careful observation comes from the diary entry of April 7, 1852, in which he records his visit in a school:

Berlin. Visited one of the public schools. About 300 girls 6-14 yrs. old. 6 classes. Each has own room and teachers. All under 1 man's supervision. Male and female teachers. Heard 3 groups sing. Smaller kids taught by rote. All singing began with chorales. Some sing in unison, but by 3 and 4th classes, in 2 parts, higher classes in 3 parts. I did not see a single pupil who was not engaged in singing. Their voices were brought out fully—they are taught to use them with firmness, decision and certainty. The songs that they sang (not chorales) were sung in considerably slower time than I had been accustomed to. . . . They all seemed delighted with the exercise....The teacher had a violin...but used it only to give out the pitch....Children did not sound the pitch before beginning.

By contrast, when confronted with the daring concepts of Robert Schumann's Symphony #3, Mason wrote only as follows:

March 18, 1852. Thursday. Have just returned from the 19th Gewandhaus Concert. Robert Schumann's new Symphonie was played conducted by himself. I have no words to describe the grandeur of this music. There are five movements—the 4th—a short slow movement appeared to me wonderfully grand. The 2nd movement is perhaps most pleasing. But throughout it is most wonderful.

Mason sought to be fair and accurate, often admitting that he could not evaluate a composition adequately after only one hearing, a perfectly reasonable view. Yet, the impression remains that Mason simply did not understand the European musical climate of the 1850s and did not grasp the importance of Schumann's latest work, nor the works of Schumann's contemporaries with the exception of some works by Mendelssohn.[9]

When Mason felt that negative comments were in order, he was generally cautious. His disapproval often concerned some particular details that did not fit into context, for the total effect of a musical work was consistently one of his major concerns. Other criteria included the appropriate matching of texts to music and the proper decorum of the performers. On certain occasions he objected to specific aspects of a musical arrangement, though again, the objections were based on the violation of the mood of the whole work.[10]

According to his own statements, Mason greatly enjoyed most of the performances he heard during the trip. Though he was especially interested in sacred music, he was enthusiastic about other types of music as well. He favored the Leipzig Gewandhaus Orchestra and the Royal Opera Orchestra in Berlin among performing groups. The Berlin Singakademie's renditions of *Der Tod Jesu* composed in 1755 by Graun and Passion music by J. S. Bach (not further identified) impressed Mason deeply. He also praised the choir music at the DomKirche or Cathedral in Berlin and the military bands in Munich.

Mason could be outspoken regarding music which he disliked, as evident in the January 9, 1852 diary passage quoted above and in this passage in *Musical Letters from Abroad* (Letter 4):

> A flute concerto is a flute concerto whether in the Gewandhaus, Hanover Square rooms, Tripler Hall or the [Boston] Melodeon; and although it may not always be played by Herrn *W. Haake* (who certainly did his duty well), it is always the most dry and uninteresting of musical performances.

Mason had distinct standards for choir performances. He strongly disapproved of nasal singing, straining of children's voices, faulty enunciation, and inappropriate conduct during public performances. He says that too often children are made to "exert their tender vocal organs to the utmost, strive for a loud noise, and perhaps the execution of something that seems very difficult," causing them to suffer severely at the time and to form bad habits that may last a lifetime, adding that he objects to "the kind of nasal, or feline quality of tone... [that is] anything but pleasant" in any group's singing.[11] Despite its importance, he maintains that "good utterance of words . . . in singing... is much neglected."[12] He calls attention to the danger of exaggerated emphasis on certain sounds; for example, distortion of the letter "s" can cause a hissing sound.[13]

Mason wrote often about the conduct of choirs during a performance. Proper conduct, as exemplified by the St. Thomas School Choir in Leipzig, is contrasted with the undesirable conduct that he had seen all too often:

> There is an entire absence of that sleepiness, drowsiness, inattention, and foolish levity too often witnessed in our choirs. No looking about, or whispering, or laughing, or silliness; but close attention is ever manifested. I wish I had words to point out that consecration to the work, that deep, heartfelt interest which these choir members seem to possess; so that it might be sought for by our American singers.[14]

He also urged soloists to conduct themselves in accord with the mood of the texts they sing and to take their positions as leaders seriously: "Solo singers... should, in every look and action, do honor to their office... [which, in church] should be regarded as sacred as is that of him who ministers at the altar of religion."[15]

One of the major events of the trip was Mason's purchase of the library of the organist-composer, Johann Christian Heinrich Rinck (1770–1846). The first mention of this matter appears in Mason's diary entry for April 29, 1852: "Rec'd today a Catalogue of Rink's [*sic*] Musical library, together with a letter from A. G. Schenck Rinck... offering it for sale to me." Rinck's collection included 830 manuscripts and 700 volumes on hymnology. Among its holdings were several rare items, such as a volume printed in Venice in 1589, another from Heidelberg in 1596, and a book of songs printed in Paris in 1755. Because Rinck had been a pupil of Johann Christian Kittel, who was a pupil of J. S. Bach, Rinck had had close connections with Bach's sons and successors and their materials. Through these connections he had acquired "manuscripts from sources close to Bach himself. Included in Rinck's library were the engraved *Partita I* of 1726, with one exception Bach's first printed work,"[16] and thirty-three J. S. Bach chorale preludes for organ, unknown to modern scholars until discovered in the Rinck materials by musicologist Christoph Wolff in 1984.

The Masons visited Darmstadt especially to see the library, and Mason purchased the entire library, apparently with little or no hesitation. In reporting this purchase he was extremely modest, though surely he realized that he had captured a wealth of material at a tremendous bargain:

> June 18. Paid 500 florins for Rinck Libr. to George Rinck, son of Ch. H. Rinck. Procured a man... to assist in packing.... We packed five large sized boxes of books.... Got a bill of sale with a duplicate. Paid with one Frankfurt Bank note for the entire amount.

This amount was the equivalent of about $275, a tiny sum compared to the value of the research material Mason procured for American scholars.[17] He himself had little use for the materials in Rinck's library. In his *Musical Letters from Abroad* report of the purchase, Mason alluded to the use of the material by others:

> The lover of music and of its progress amongst us will be glad to know that it is already packed, and will be on its way to America in a few days.... There are now many young men who are beginning to feel the necessity of a more liberal education for the profession of music than has hitherto been supposed important.[18]

The Masons acquired another rare and valuable addition to their library during their final days in Paris. On July 5 the Reverend and Mrs. Pilatte (whom the Masons had known in Boston) gave a farewell party for them. As a part of the evening, Mr. Pilatte gave Lowell a Bible published in 1567, containing the original Psalms of Marot and Beza with the tunes.

On July 12 Lowell, Abby, and Henry Mason left for London. They arrived late that night at the Queen's Hotel in that city. The following day Lowell and Henry went out early to find lodging. They called first on Nathan Richardson, another Bostonian studying abroad. Pianist-composer Richardson had studied in Leipzig with Moscheles and Dreyschock, but turned his attention to teaching and later to piano pedagogy. He had preceded the Masons from Paris by a few days and had found himself suitable quarters. Lowell and Henry were pleased to find out that the same building had a vacancy which suited them well, so they returned to Abby Mason at once and began to move into their temporary home at No. 1, Tavistock Street. Here they were to remain for almost nine months, a longer stay than was at first anticipated. Later the same day, Lowell visited Vincent Novello, his son Joseph Novello, Charles Purday, and others whom he had met during his 1837 trip. These men were still active publishers and musicians except for Vincent Novello, who had retired in 1849.

Mason became engrossed in the fall with teaching and lecturing, chiefly on "congregational singing, although he gave some lessons in his incomparable way in the elementary principles of music."[19] Among many instances recorded in his diary are these two samples:

> Dec. 3, 1852. 22nd lesson at Home & Colonial [School], 14th with a P.F. [pianoforte, presumably]. Gave a lesson to a class of little ones about 7 years of age in the presence of the teachers, they being assembled . . . to witness it. Began with melodies and only went on as far as one and two. Evening—gave a practical lesson on psalmody in the Chapel of Hon. & Rev. Baptist W. Noel. Lecture was 1 hr. long, introduced 3 tunes—St. Anns, Denfield, and Boylston. We used "Mason's Handbook of Psalmody," i.e., a specimen sheet of it. All seemed to be much pleased with the tunes and the manner of conducting them. Another meeting is to be held on Fri. next. I stood in the . . . pew and was surrounded by the Deacons, the leader of the Sng., and a few others who occasionally asked questions. I never spent a more agreeable hr. in a professional way; it seemed to me, that I was doing the very thing for which I am best qualified; and it is certainly the work which I most delight to do.

> Dec. 7. Went by invitation to Mr. Mayo's residence about 3 or 4 mi. away where at his invitation a company of 25 or 30 men and women had assembled to hear me explain the inductive teaching. I spoke to them 1 and 1/2 hrs. nearly. Mr. Mayo had obtained a blackboard. The company consisted of well educated and apparently wealthy people. Home by 11 o'clock.

Mason's diary indicates that he presented evening "lessons on psalmody" at the following places on a regular basis: at Mr. Noel's Chapel, fourteen lessons from Friday, December 3 through March 4; at the Portland Chapel, St. John Wood (to a class of about 200, he adds), thirteen lessons from Wednesday evening December 8 through March 2; at the Gresham Street YMCA, Monday evenings (sometimes alternately on Saturday evenings), twelve lessons ending February 28, 1853; and at Mr. Binney's Weigh-House Chapel, eight lessons from Tuesday, January 11 through March 1.

Mason attained such a large following partly through advertising, a sample of which described him as one who

> had attained a very high position, not only as a Professor and teacher of Music, but as a Composer, Harmonist, and Editor . . . extensively known in his own country as an advocate of a CONGREGATIONAL form of Psalmody. It is rare to find this large experience

of... Psalmody and intimate and practical knowledge of our own forms,—and this feeling of its *religious* importance, combined in one individual with acknowledged musical eminence. ... We have, therefore, been very desirous of having the benefit of Mr. Mason's experience and instruction, during his sojourn in England.... [20]

In short, as he told his friend George Webb in a letter dated January 28, 1853, Mason found himself unexpectedly engaged in teaching and soon had Monday, Tuesday, Wednesday, and Friday evenings tied up with teaching or lecturing on church music. He was also teaching at the Home and Colonial School where "I always give two and sometimes three and four lessons a week." At the same time he was evidently collaborating with others on a music book to be published in London about 1853. It is therefore not surprising that he had little time to see "musical men or attend concerts."

One incident in January 1853 took Lowell and Abby out to see a special concert. Miss Arabella Goddard, a pianist who was scheduled to perform, was unable to appear, so William Mason was invited to London on short notice as a substitute. This opportunity came about because the concert manager, a Mr. Benedict, had heard from Lowell Mason about his talented pianist son.

Lowell states in his letter to Webb that the critics were favorable to William's performance for the most part, and that those who were not should be disregarded because William had had little preparation time and no choice in the selection of the repertoire. Lowell adds that he did nothing to make friends with the music editors in advance, although he had been advised that William would be handled roughly if there were no sovereigns thrown in the critics' way beforehand. Perhaps most revealing of all is Lowell's statement that he wanted this explanation of the event passed on to John Sullivan Dwight. Then, if Dwight should see any unfavorable reviews, he would understand the circumstances. The explanation was not, however, meant for publication in *Dwight's Journal of Music.*

Many tributes were offered to Lowell Mason during his second European trip. One which meant a great deal to him was described in his diary as follows:

March 5, 1853. Went by special invitation to a meeting of the YMCA. Meeting designed as an expression of their gratitude to me. Rev. Mr. Parker presided. Tea was provided. Grace sung before and aft. partaking. 35-40 young men present. Their secretary spoke for 10 min. referring to my labors and closing by presenting an expression of their feelings, signed by all of them. Also presented a Bible. Spoke in answer for 10 min.

Mason had little to say about his journey home, though his few diary entries indicate that he was uncomfortable at least part of the time: "April 9, 1853. Had severe Rheumatism—Want of air in State Room—exposed to drafts. At night suffered much." It is evident from his reactions upon arrival that he was delighted to get home and see those closest to him: "Friday, April

15. Arrived in E. Boston wharf . . . met by Mr. Reed, Julia [Reed] and Lowell [Jr.] waiting on the wharf." That afternoon he called on Webb, Chickering, Melvin Lord, and Mr. Dana. Monday the 18th he went to Medfield and visited his father and Abby's mother, spending three days there. On April 23 he went to New York; he mentions specifically seeing Daniel Gregory, Lowell, Jr., and Lolo. The following day he was "unwell," but George and Towner Root called in the evening with Mr. Cady, who later became a partner in the Root & Cady music store in Chicago.

The final statement in Lowell's travel diaries—quite characteristically—points succinctly to the future: "Mon. April 25. Normal Musical Institute opened at 10 A.M. I gave an introductory address."

George F. Root, Lowell Mason, and William B. Bradbury
(Reproduced from the copy in the Music Library at Yale University)

The Widening Circle of Mason Influence

The Normal Musical Institutes

The idea George F. Root had presented to Mason in the fall of 1851 was finally implemented in the spring of 1853. Having persuaded Mason that his idea was valid, Root had gone to the firm of Mason and Law, where he persuaded Daniel Gregory and Lowell, Jr. that the institutes would provide a more thorough understanding of their father's ideas and, consequently, would stimulate book sales. The publishers grasped this argument immediately. Their endorsement took the form of nationwide advertising of a three-month training session to be held during the summer of 1852.

When Lowell Mason wrote from abroad, saying he had so much work to do in England that he couldn't return until later in the year, he advised Root to go ahead without him or to wait until the summer of 1853. His sons quickly assured Root that if he would put off opening the institute for a year, they would take care of all expenses incurred by the delay, plus the costs of advertising it again the next year. Root agreed, saying that he did not want to begin "without the master"; the abilities of "the master" notwithstanding, Root was the guiding force in planning and administering the institutes. Announcements of the delayed opening were sent out to the points where an 1852 institute had been advertised.

Unlike the musical conventions that preceded them, the institutes involved a three-months' enrollment to provide the most thorough teacher-training curriculum available for music teachers at the time. The opening of the first institute, named the New York Normal Musical Institute, was widely covered in contemporary music periodicals. *The Musical World and New York Musical Times,* a weekly journal edited by Oliver Dyer and Richard Storrs Willis, gave this report in its April 30, 1853 issue:

> The most original musical institution of the day has...quietly sprung into existence...the first musical establishment in the world having for its specific object the education of teachers. All foreign conservatories are designed mainly...for artists and composers. They

do not *teach the Art of Teaching* and prepare persons...for this occupation. About fifty intelligent and somewhat experienced pupils...have already presented themselves. The locality is the large and beautiful Hall...next [to] Grace Church. The sessions commenced last Monday, and are to continue for three months, from 9 until 1. Mr. Lowell Mason ...lectures from 9 until 10 on the art of teaching—R. Storrs Willis (Tuesdays and Thursdays) from 10 until 11, on Harmony and Composition—Mr. Geo. F. Root from 11 until 12 on the culture of the voice, and Mr. W. B. Bradbury from 12 until 1 on Part-Singing....Other teachers are engaged for...private pupils: Mr. Zundel for organ; Mr. Dodworth for Band Instruments and Mr. Howe for the melodeon and piano.

Willis (1819–1900), who had been a pupil of Mason's, was himself a compiler and editor of music collections, but he attained distinction as a music journalist during the 1850s with this journal. The passage quoted above went on to editorialize that the success of the institutes was beyond question, considering the large advance enrollment and the interest many others had expressed in future sessions.

Though not mentioned in this particular article, Thomas Hastings was a major figure in the New York Institute. Other issues of this journal and other contemporary sources described his involvement. For example, one front-page account of the institute acknowledged that "Mr. Hastings has communicated sound and experienced views as to the *side-culture*—mental and physical—of the musician."[1]

One key figure mentioned in the article above was William Batchelder Bradbury (1816–1868), a former member of Mason's singing classes and Bowdoin Street Church choir and a frequent associate in Mason's later activities. Mason had procured Bradbury's first job. "At the age of twenty he was still singing in Mason's choir when one evening at recess the latter laid his hand on Bradbury's shoulder and said, 'William, I have had an application for a teacher at Machias, Maine, to teach three large singing schools, besides private pupils, and I believe you are just the man for the place.' "[2] This episode launched a career that in many ways paralleled Mason's.

Bradbury helped instigate public school music programs in New York State, starting with free singing classes for children. He composed popular hymn tunes, some of them still widely used: for instance, tunes set to the texts beginning "Just as I am, Without one plea"; "He leadeth me"; "Sweet hour of prayer"; "Saviour, like a shepherd lead us"; "Tis midnight, and on Olive's Brow"; and others. Bradbury produced about sixty books containing vocal music, ranging from glees to hymns to children's sacred and secular songs. Like Mason's books, some of these were commercial successes; *The Golden Chain* (1861), for example, sold over two million copies. Bradbury worked with Hastings, Root, and others in the "Mason circle" in teaching and editing. His work with the conventions began in 1851 in Somerville, New York; his more extensive work with Mason began in 1853 at the New York Normal Musical Institute.

Bradbury was a charismatic and capable teacher. "Tall, gaunt, with red hair and immense glasses,"[3] he was a striking man, but also a man with a volatile personality. References to his career indicate clashes with his associates. All things considered, Bradbury was apparently one of Mason's most versatile and colorful associates.

After a successful first session of the New York Normal Musical Institute, the founders established four successive terms to cover the academic year, beginning that September (1853). This front-page announcement in *The Musical World and New York Musical Times* of December 10, 1853 gave details on the program:

NEW YORK NORMAL MUSICAL INSTITUTE

The academic year commences on the 15th of September, and closes on the 15th of July.... The ten months of the academic year are divided into four terms, of about eleven weeks each, commencing ... September 15th, December 1st, February 15th, and May 1st.

THE FIRST, SECOND, AND THIRD TERMS

are devoted especially to vocal and instrumental training, in small classes and private lessons, and are under the direction of

Mr. George F. Root.

The fourth term, which may more especially be called

THE TEACHERS' TERM

and which commences May first, is under the

DIRECTION OF

MESSRS. LOWELL MASON, GEORGE F. ROOT, AND WILLIAM B. BRADBURY,

and is devoted particularly to Lectures on Teaching, Harmony, Church and Secular Music, Vocal Cultivation, Musical Taste, Musical History, Elocution, &c., in connection with thorough class and chorus practice....

TERMS:

Private lessons, Vocal or Instrumental, per Course $25.00
Class-Exercises of First, Second, and Third Terms, per term 12.50
Lectures and Class Exercises of the Teacher's Term 25.00

Payable in advance.

A course in private lessons consists of two lessons per week for the entire term. The class lessons and exercises are every day. . . .

Thus, in the twenty years between 1834 and 1854, Lowell Mason progressed from the brief teachers' classes at the Boston Academy of Music to three-month institutes designed for teachers and performers. In his later years he stressed the need for longer, more intensive music training, up to several years' study:

> It is strongly recommended to those who wish to become accomplished performers and especially those who intend making music their profession, to commence the musical year and go through the entire course....As a general thing even with some previous knowledge...two or three years will be required to fit one to take a good stand as a teacher and performer.[4]

Without detracting from the earlier teachers' conventions, Mason, in his mature judgment, advocated more thorough training, such as that offered at the New York Normal Musical Institute. In evaluating the New York program, John Sullivan Dwight observed that "among psalm-book makers and mass teachers there is no one like him [Mason]. . . . The Normal Institute is probably...his crowning effort, to concentrate and build up into some distinct form of permanency the results and methods of his extensive and in many respects original experience."[5]

Like the conventions before them, the institutes quickly spread across the country. By the middle 1850s the focus of Mason's attention (insofar as institutes were concerned) came to be the North Reading, Massachusetts, Institute that Root organized in 1856. The reasons for this shift of location are not altogether clear, though the high cost of living in New York City and its inhospitable summers have been suggested.[6] Root had returned to his hometown, North Reading (about twenty miles north of Boston), and found it convenient to have the institute in that friendly, hospitable community. Reports indicate that residents thronged to the choral programs, often bringing along their music-loving neighbors from nearby communities. For example, the Henry Ward Beechers, the Lyman Beechers, and Harriet Beecher Stowe and her husband Calvin Stowe, then living seven miles away in Andover, came to performances upon occasion. Reflecting on these choral programs years later in *Dwight's Journal of Music,* A. W. Thayer observed that "Thousands carried away with them their first and never-fading impression of the glorious power and beauty of a chorus of Handel, sung by a thousand voices with orchestral and organ accompaniment."[7]

Whether Root's relocation was a cause or an effect of the growing importance of the North Reading Institute cannot be determined. Nonetheless, at North Reading, Root, Mason, Bradbury, and their associates continued the work begun in New York. They were soon joined by George J. Webb, who still resided in Boston.

At North Reading additional teachers came into the Mason group. Chief among them was William W. Killip (b. 1832), an organist-choir director who became a confidant of Mason's during the latter's declining years. Killip lived in Geneseo, New York and ran a clothing store until 1857 when he gave that up to become a full-time musician. Killip had first seen Mason at a musical convention in Rochester, New York. Mason was there with Artemis N. Johnson, Root, Webb, and his son William Mason (the latter only three years older than Killip himself). Killip's attendance at that convention was a turning point in his life, for he came under the spell of the Masons at once. Years later he recalled that William Mason "played the organ *surprisingly* to us hayseeds. He played the piano to the delight of everyone, setting the girls crazy. He played the 100th Ps. tune and Yankee Doodle and a few other things all together."[8]

Killip wrote in considerable detail about the North Reading Institutes in letters to Lowell Mason and later to Lowell's grandson, Henry Lowell Mason. Killip admitted that Lowell's "open preference for me" made him very proud, "more proud than anything else in my long life." Each day they walked together from the school to Root's house; every Saturday afternoon they went to Boston together. Each Tuesday and Thursday of Killip's last year at North Reading (1858), he drove the horse and carriage to Andover for Mason, enabling Mason to work with Andover Professors Edwards A. Park and Austin Phelps on *The Sabbath Hymn and Tune Book* (1859).

Apparently the Roots entertained institute leaders in their home. Killip described an incident in which Mason was at the head of Root's "long dining table, and there were some ministers, as well as scientists and statesmen there." Killip was near the foot of the table, but he could hear from the head of the table much "earnest talk about sin against the holy ghost." He continued the story:

> Mason, I think, took little or no part, but it got warm. Presently he called out, "Killip, what is the sin against the Holy Ghost?" I said, "I am an Episcopalian, and everybody knows that we have nothing to do with religion." Then the man... tried again, "Well, what is the *very worst thing* that is done in all the world, in your opinion?" Whereupon I replied, "Oh that is easy. Singing below the pitch is the *very worst thing* I know." All laughed, and the discussion dropped. He [Mason] was much pleased and told me afterward that the discussion was disagreeable to him.[9]

Killip wrote of Mason as a "strictly honest and fearless man" who was not disposed to religious controversy. He was also a punctual man, "on the job to a second every time." This characteristic Killip mentioned in contrast with Webb, who, he said,

> was *not energetic,* in fact, was a little lazy. He must have his cigar and paper and a little leisure. [At the North Reading Institutes] Mr. Webb gave private lessons, and we were

always late. He was fully engaged every hour, and beginning 15-20 minutes late, made every lesson late. Apologies, explanations, etc. taking time, we were paying $2 for about 45 minutes and four of us engaged him for one hour three times a week and arranged among ourselves who should get the lessons.[10]

Webb must have been an easy-going man, for despite talent and hard work, he was constantly overshadowed by Mason. His disposition (and that of his wife) is suggested by this biographical footnote: In 1852 Webb's brother Arthur, his wife, and their nine children emigrated from England. In Philadelphia, on their way to a new home in Illinois, the parents and youngest child died of typhoid fever. The George Webbs immediately opened their home to the eight orphaned children, the eldest of whom was eighteen. They reared this large second family as well as their own two daughters. A descendant of the Arthur Webb branch of the family, Mary Sturgis Gray, recounted these and other details in an unpublished biography (1937).

According to all reports, the curriculum of the North Reading Institutes was comparable to that of other institutes. Elias Vosseller, a student in 1858, wrote to Henry Lowell Mason on April 19, 1913, describing the institute he had attended. He recalled that Lowell Mason not only taught church music, but also led the opening devotional period, often including an anthem he had composed. Mason played the piano during those periods. Later in the day, he led the study of oratorios with Webb accompanying at the piano. Mason showed that he "had no patience with anything frivolous in the church service, but taught that all must be dignified, orderly and devotional"; further, he had only scorn for "comic songs" in any form.

A writer in the *Boston Musical Times* (1860), in an article signed "An Old Normal," gave a similar, but more detailed outline of the daily agenda. According to that source, the program ran like this: At 8:30 Lowell Mason conducted devotions; at 8:45 he answered questions that had been handed in previously; from 9:00 to 10:00 he gave a lecture on the principles of teaching, showing how to draw information out of the pupils. At 11:00 Root had a class in vocal training; at noon Bradbury had a class in harmony. After a dinner recess from 1:00 to 2:15, George B. Loomis gave instruction in sight-singing. Practice teaching by members of the student body was conducted from 3:00 to 4:00, after which an hour of singing "the works of the masters" concluded the day.[11] Private lessons were undoubtedly included, though the correspondent did not mention them.

George B. Loomis became a leading pioneer music educator in the Midwest. In 1866 he began teaching music in the Indianapolis, Indiana public schools, having been recommended for the job by Lowell Mason. In 1877 Loomis helped form the Indiana Music Teachers Association, one of the first such organizations. He also published a widely used series of textbooks, *Loomis' Progressive Music Lessons.*

By 1860 the relationship between Root and Bradbury had disintegrated. Although a full explanation may never come to light, rivalry sprang up from time to time in the Mason circle, prompted (more often than not) by professional jealousy and those sure-fire motivators, money and power.

Killip alludes to one episode that contributed to the Root-Bradbury split. North Reading, Killip admitted, was a poor place for the institutes because of a lack of facilities. Capitalizing on this fact, Bradbury hired a man unknown in the area to visit surrounding communities and obtain subscribers to a petition asking that Bradbury come and establish an institute in another town. The signers were also pledging themselves as students in that (tuition) school. Many of the signers were Root's admirers who did not realize that in this instance Bradbury was competing with Root. Killip himself was no longer a part of the North Reading Institute, having organized his own institute at Geneseo, New York, starting in 1859, so his understanding of this rift (which developed, it seems, in 1859) was less than complete.

Lowell Mason, by his own admission, detested controversy and squabbling among his associates. When it occurred, he tried to remain aloof. His feelings, with the Root-Bradbury feud as a case in point, came through clearly in a letter he wrote to Killip on February 26, 1860:

Grieved was I to read, for the paper told me of deceptions, falsifications, perversions, double-dealings, misrepresentations.... So I was in a strait betwixt [the] two, and there I am still. You know I have feelings of friendship for Mr. Root and also for Mr. B.—the friendship continues notwithstanding all the drawbacks. They never either of them see me, but they get a severe lecture of reprimand for the cause they pursue in their profession. Oh, that I could reach them and my own heart too with those great words, "Thou shalt have no other gods before me."

And, dear Sir, I am not excluding the friend of Mr. R. and/or Mr. B. I am . . . truly your friend. I formed an affection for you at N. R. [North Reading] which is still unbroken.... As for Mr. Webb, God forbid that any root of bitterness or of indifference should ever spring up between us. . . .

I cannot ... go into the awfully dark controversy. I cannot say even, who appears to me to be right and who wrong. Do you see those *hungry dogs*—One of them has got a bone—how they snarl and growl and bite and fight for it? Trickery, guile, shakiness, fraud, etc. are bad for men, very infinitely worse than those dogs' habits are for dogs. So I cannot go into detail of Yr. letter, yet there are many points on which I would not be unwilling to converse were I to see you. I thank you for the story you have told me; it differs not much from what with my knowledge of parties my imagination could, in the general, have bro't up to mind. . . .

I will tell you something of the state of things. . . . Mr. R. very soon after our last normal (1858) turned *round* so far as Mr. B. is concerned—it was a . . . right about face. I was not in the secret at all, but I could not help knowing the fact. I do not blame him for this, only I cannot see his consistency. I had been pleading for B. with him a year or two, but he was bitter against him. But now, all at once, without any apparent reason, he changes; I say without reason but there is a reason not difficult to imagine by those who are near the Book-Sellers. I soon heard there was a co-partnership in the Book business between them—a counter agreement by which they were to publ. together. My Sons being deeply interested...consulted with me...and (I must not dwell upon details) after some time of travail, I authorized Mason Bro. to make any arrangement they saw fit by which I should also be brought into the co-partnership. The result is now, that we are all three of us in anothers publications—i.e., I am as much pecuniarally interested in Mr. R.'s and Mr. B's Books as my own—I mean of those which are to come. The first by Mr. R. will come as we suppose this coming summer. This arrangement has, of course, influenced us as to *schools*. We have agreed to hold two or three Normal Schools together. First at N.R. we all expect to go there. Two other places have been talked of—vis. Geneseo and Chicago. . . . I leave it principally to Mr. B. and R. to decide. It is my . . . belief. . . *we shall not come to G.,* but that we shall go to Chicago. I have said to them that I cannot go to G. to interfere with you and . . . be in opposition to you. I think . . . you shall have that field to yourself so far as B., R. and I are concerned.

I hate . . . politics and chicanery . . . and I give thanks that I have been preserved from them in a great degree.

On August 2, 1861, Mason wrote Killip from North Reading that Root "has improved much in deportment." He added that Root "is the best class teacher of vocal training that I know of. . . . I believe one would learn ten times as much of class teaching (vocal training) from Root as from B. [Bradbury]." Root's teaching ability was praised by other contemporaries as well.[12] During that year, Mason specified that he, Root, and Loomis "constitute the whole board of instruction thus far [at North Reading], though Mr. Webb is as he was—always most civil and kind to those around," suggesting that Webb was present as well. Addressing Killip in that letter of August 2, 1861, Mason added, "Your beloved friend Mr. Bradbury is not with us this season. The prospect of making something was not a sufficient inducement. He has some good points that you do not see—yet as a teacher he is certainly inferior to Mr. R. [Root]."

Mason's letters to his grandson Lolo indicate that he had been in Chicago the previous fall (1860) with Bradbury, but among the many activities he recounted, there is no mention of any institutes. In writing to Killip in 1861 he admitted that "quite a number of our pupils have left us to go into other schools." Indeed, many of the pupils were forming their own institutes, compiling their own tunebooks, and becoming leaders in other areas of music as well. Among those who deserve mention in this regard are Luther O. Emerson, Theodore F. Seward, and Charles Callahan Perkins.

Perkins (1833-1886) was an artist and an art historian as well as a musician. The first American to be elected to membership in the French

Academy, he wrote, among other things, *Tuscan Sculptors, Italian Sculptors, Raphael and Michaelangelo: A Critical Essay* (1864, 1877, and 1878, respectively). He collaborated with J. S. Dwight on *A History of the Handel and Haydn Society,* writing the first three chapters while Dwight handled the rest. Perkins also won respect as a music teacher. As Mason remarked to Killip in the letter of August 2, 1861, "Mr. Perkins, I doubt not, is very good for he caught his manner of vocal training from Root himself."

Leaders of the institutes were often inconvenienced and uncomfortable while *en route* to the institutes. In personal letters to Lolo, Mason described some of his travel experiences in detail. For example, from Provincetown, Cape Cod, April 21, 1857, he wrote as follows:

Dear Lolo,
    My beloved Grandson,

Last Friday I left Boston...and arrived at evening at Yarmouth. Here I stopped at the Tavern all night—had supper, talked a while with the people & went to bed.

Saturday morning, Mr. [William?] Russell & myself got a man to bring us down the Cape; so we rode along and when we got to Orleans we stopped & got some dinner,—Baked Beans & pudding.

Then another man took us to the Town of Wellfleet; then a boy took us as far as Truro. Here we stayed all night. I had a room assigned to me, a very small room; it is so low that I can almost touch the top with my head when my hat is on; and it is so small that I can only just turn round to wash myself. On Sunday, the wind blew hard, but I went to church in the morning, climbing over the high sand hills to get there. . . .

I slept in my little room again on Sunday night. On Monday morning I went to the Teachers' Institute, & taught an hour & a half—then went back to the Tavern. At 2 o'clock I started in a wagon with an old white horse who could not go much faster than a walk with a boy to drive, for this place.

I never before rode over so strange a way. For a good part of the way there is no road, except what is made by the sea side, on the beach. The wind blew, the rain poured, & the poor old horse could only take a few steps at a time and then rest....[We] got to this strange place, where I now am, stopping at the Pilgrim House.

Before we got here it rained fast, and we have had a real easterly storm ever since. The wind blows in from the sea furiously, and... it is snowing fast. . . .

I expected to go back to Truro this morning, but no one can perform the journey [in] such weather with safety. . . .

I was to have lectured last night but who would go out in such a terrible storm? So it was put off. It has been appointed again for tonight, & altho' it snows & blows, yet I think some people may come out to the lecture.

This morning I tried to kindle a fire in my room; the wood was all prepared with kindling &c., but the terrible N.E. wind blew so much that all the smoke came out in the room, and I was obliged to jump up and run out before I could dress & call in the chambermaid. She opened the window & put out the fire, and after a while I went in & dressed myself. . . .

. . . notwithstanding the weather, I have kept very well thus far; I have felt rheumatism *a little* but nothing to speak of, & have kept quite free from cold.

Your most affectionate Dapotee
Lowell Mason[13]

Despite the difficulties of travel and the frustration of quarreling associates, Mason actively participated in institutes until at least 1862, the year he reached age seventy. In that year, according to Root's account, Mason taught at his last "normal," a six-week session in Wooster, Ohio. Though Root was present, the account is disappointingly sketchy. Root mentions "good attendance" although there were "always officers around," referring to officers of the Union Army. "The war meetings detracted from the attention of the group," Root reports, though he provides little information about these "war meetings." He then shifts to a topic dear to him, saying that his new war songs helped to recruit and "rouse the enthusiasm of the people especially as sung by our choir."[14] Root became famous (and prosperous) composing popular Civil War songs.

Thus, Mason continued actively training teachers into 1862. All the while, however, he kept in mind his goal of reforming church music. Through his publications, speeches, comments during discussion at the institutes, and comments in personal conversations, he tirelessly advanced that ideal along with others in which he believed.

Promotion of Congregational Singing

I heard the congregation singing hymns . . . so that the voices were as the voice of one man; the grand chorus filled the house of the Lord. . . . I came away wishing that the people of America could . . . know what we mean when we speak of congregational singing . . . and hasten to take the appropriate . . . measures for its introduction.

Lowell Mason, *Musical Letters from Abroad,*
from Leipzig, May 1852

As he grew older, Lowell Mason worked ever harder to improve church music, especially congregational singing. As early as the 1840s his publications increasingly emphasized sacred music and particularly tunes for congregational singing.

Mason's most successful and popular books of that decade were *Carmina Sacra* (1841), *Songs of Asaph* (1843), *The Psaltery* (1845), and *The National*

Psalmist (1848)—the latter two coedited with Webb. Mason also published several series of pamphlets, such as *The Choralist* (1847) and *The Hymnist* (1849), which—like such earlier works as *The Seraph* (1838–40)—contained music for use in the churches. In 1850 Mason issued three collections which are among the most important of his entire career: *Cantica Laudis* with George J. Webb; *The Hymnist* (entirely distinct from the 1849 pamphlet); and *The New Carmina Sacra*. *The Hallelujah* issued in 1854 was another major work.

The number of books issued, their widespread acceptance, and the resulting prestige that accrued to Mason are important, but so is the insight these volumes provide into his thinking about church music. Furthermore, at every opportunity, he educates his readers about practical means of improving music in their own churches. He argues that correct editing is essential but goes on to other basic considerations, such as the use of a moderate vocal range. In the preface to *The Modern Psalmist* (1839), for example, he says, "Psalmody has often been written too high—favorable, indeed, for screaming, but unfavorable for singing." In *The National Psalmist* (1848), he addresses specific problems in a question-and-answer format: How shall a new tune be introduced to the congregation? What number of voices is required to constitute a choir? How should the singing in a Sunday school be conducted?

Though many of Mason's writings reveal his concern for congregational singing, he is especially articulate in the prefaces to his tunebooks. As defined in *The National Psalmist*, good congregational participation means "the united voices of the whole people in a well known and appropriate tune, and this mostly in unison, each one singing the melody." A weak voice singing the melody, he continues, can too easily be overwhelmed by a nearby strong voice handling a harmony part. The person with the weak voice may become so discouraged that he drops out. In congregational singing everyone should sing the melody, and the melodies should be easy. In *Cantica Laudis* the editors go so far as to mark tunes according to their level of difficulty. In all cases, the organ's role is supportive, sustaining the voices.

By 1848, the issue date of *The National Psalmist*, Mason had concluded that congregational singing is not just desirable, but essential in church music. Choir development is directly related in that good congregational participation requires the leadership of a strong choir; moreover, the choir must make enhancing the worship experience its chief objective lest choir performance sink into mere exhibitionism.

That exhibitionism in church music was anathema to Lowell Mason is clear from his earliest to his latest writings. The foundation of his thinking is simply that music must be subordinate to worship. Music must fit the texts; indeed, it should enhance the texts. Performances must always be expressive of the texts. Church music must seek to heighten worship, not to display artistry; it must call attention to the Object of worship, not to itself.

These ideas were far from original with Mason; on the contrary, they can be traced through centuries of thought by Christians whose views are otherwise divergent. Mason's thinking was directly influenced by Thomas Hastings whose *Dissertation on Musical Taste* (1822) Mason had absorbed in his youth. In addition, Mason's experiences shaped his views so that by the 1840s, his conclusions rested on his life's work.

In the 1840s Mason urged the revival of Anglican chanting. Widespread in colonial America, chanting was a casualty of the diminished influence of the Church of England during and after the Revolutionary War. At its peak of popularity, Americans' use of chant extended beyond the Anglican (Episcopal) church to other denominations.

A few of Mason's predecessors had tried to reinstate chanting to its former prominence. Andrew Law (1749–1821) produced the first American tunebook to include chant, namely, *Rudiments of Music* (Philadelphia, 1783). One of the first American books to consist almost entirely of chants was published anonymously in Salem, Massachusetts by Joshua Cushing in 1814 with the title *Chants, Occasional Pieces and Psalm Tunes, for the Use of the Protestant Episcopal Churches in the United States.* Jonathan M. Wainwright (1792-1854) and Dr. George K. Jackson, among others, urged the use of chant in the early nineteenth century as well, but with only limited success.[15]

These various, isolated efforts to encourage chanting made some inroads, as did Mason's earlier books in which chants were included. In 1842 Mason took another step toward promoting chant by publishing his *Book of Chants,* all of them Anglican style but meant to be used by any Protestant congregation.

This book includes instructions on chanting, plus remarks extolling its advantages. Mason openly admires both Gregorian plainsong and Anglican chant, stating his belief that chanting would enrich the worship experience in American Protestant churches. The texts in his *Book of Chants* (1842) include hymns as well as psalms, for he argues (here and elsewhere) that chanting can be the most effective means of handling certain excellent texts. In *The Choral Advocate and Singing-Class Journal* of June 1851, he presents views about the appropriate uses of texts:

> It is true, indeed, that some metrical pieces may be better *chanted* than *tuned;* but then it will almost always be equally true that the same piece will be better *read* than *chanted.*

> A bad hymn is better *chanted* than *sung to a tune,* and better *read* than *chanted,* and better *read in silence* than *read aloud.*

> It may be also proper to remark here that a *bad hymn* may be a *good religious poem;* and also that *a religious poem* containing very little *thought,* and being quite destitute of *technical theology, argumentation,* or *logic,* may be a *good hymn.* We advise those who have a desire to cultivate chanting, to do so mostly in connection with the Psalms.

Mason's enthusiasm for chanting far surpassed that of most Americans then or later. Even Lowell Mason could not convince most American churchgoers of the desirability of chant. Nevertheless, he continued to advocate chanting and to provide chants in his tunebooks throughout his career.

Judging from his voluminous writings from the 1840s and later, Mason's ideas on church music remained constant. This is evident in his reports from abroad, collected and published as *Musical Letters from Abroad* and in a twenty-six article series called "Choirs."[16] Most of these articles appeared in *The New York Musical Review and Gazette* from February 1858 to February 1859; three additional items intended for this series remain in manuscript form in the Lowell Mason Papers. In this set of essays, Mason elaborated upon the ideas expressed in his 1826 address and in the prefaces to his anthologies.

A concise, but comprehensive statement of Mason's final ideas appears in a twenty-three page essay entitled *Song in Worship*. This work, published posthumously in Boston in 1878, covers both basic principles and practical situations. These are the main points:

1. *"There is no good reason why the choir should not be willing to act as the servants or helpers of the people."* This emphasizes the congregation's importance by subordinating the choir's role. After all, Mason argues, the first example of Christian song occurred just after the institution of the Last Supper. "And when they had sung a hymn, they went out into the Mt. of Olives." Mason asks whether this singing was for music's sake, then answers his rhetorical question:

   > The thought is blasphemous. Oh, no! It was a religious song...bringing into a lively exercise the confidence . . . needed in that mysterious and trying hour.... But we learn from this first...song, not only what should be the true character of church song, but also what should be the...manner of the song-service.... Was it by a select choir?...No—But *congregational singing.*

2. *The Christian church has historically vacillated between congregational and choir leadership.* Mason traces this path briefly, including the rise in America of "unsingable music" (presumably fuguing tunes) and contrasts that with continued congregational singing in Europe. Citing Luther for authority, Mason argues that "the people were supposed to have something to do in public worship as well as the minister, and a principal part of that which was assigned to them was the singing of psalms and hymns."

3. *"The pastor's influence is most important"* in promoting congregational singing. During the singing he must set the example.

He is not to be leafing through his sermon, making pencilled changes, or ignoring the singing. Nor should others be preoccupied.

4. *"Every one should consider it his duty to unite vocally in the song....* The songs and the prayers should not be regarded as mere appendages, incidentals, or as condiments to the sermon; they are forms of worship, and should be made acts of real worship."

Mason's ideas on church music met more opposition than would be supposed in light of the sales of his books and the popularity of his compositions, hymn tunes in particular. With the inception of choirs in the late 1700s, American congregational singing had all but disappeared. Mason himself said that he had not heard congregational singing during his first twenty years (around 1800). By the middle 1800s the situation had improved little despite efforts in that direction. By that time, paid singers led choirs in the more affluent, fashionable churches. These singers, often drawn from outside the church membership, frequently had little concern for the churches they served or for the edification of the worshippers. The paid quartet of solo singers also enjoyed a certain vogue.[17]

Obviously, the practice of paying outside talent to lead singing contradicted Mason's concept of church music, as did the use of a quartet rather than a larger group. Remembering American practices, he reflected in an essay published in *Musical Letters from Abroad:*

A quartet is beautiful in its place, and in connection and in contrast with a choir, may be truly effective in church music, but save us from that form of song in the house of God, which consists in the monotony of a four-voiced performance, without the light and shade afforded by a chorus.[18]

Mason had a chance to put his ideas into practice upon his return from Europe. On May 15, 1853 he became music director at the Fifth Avenue Presbyterian Church in New York City, a large, new building at Nineteenth Street. As had often been the case, Mason worked with an outstanding clergyman, this time James Waddel Alexander (1804-1859), still represented in hymnals by his translation of "O Sacred Head Now Wounded."

Mason persuaded the church to get rid of its choir and orchestra (the latter known to chat and tune instruments during the sermon) and to use precentors and an organ instead. By October 1855 the congregation had a new organ built by George Jardine & Son. In a letter to the organ builder, Mason described the instrument as "the best... of its size and contents which I have ever known."[19] Instead of a traditional choir, Mason had a number of precentors (six, according to one report) spread out in the sanctuary to encourage congregational singing. This strategy evidently worked: "The whole people join in, supported by the stronger voices which are placed in the front side seats."[20]

This experiment was short-lived. Mason soon moved to his new home in Orange, New Jersey, and New York City churches continued as before with little congregational singing. A report published in 1861

listed musical forces in New York's major churches. Of 86 non-Episcopal, Roman Catholic, or Lutheran congregations, only five—four of them Presbyterian—had adopted organ-supported congregational singing. By contrast, thirty-one, including the parish for which William Mason was organist, had quartets; six of the latter . . . were Presbyterian, and two of that six . . . still refused to permit the use of an organ in their worship, even while employing the professional quartet. . . . Even the Fifth Avenue Church could not resist the tide much longer. . . . In the early 1880s the parish engaged a quartet for the first time. It had no other choir until 1926.[21]

Lowell Mason must have been discouraged by the relatively slow progress made toward congregational singing. In addition, on several occasions he felt that his emphasis on congregational singing and his attitudes about choirs were being misunderstood. He defended his stand in a series of articles appearing in *The Choral Advocate and Singing Class Journal* from 1850 to 1853. Later he expressed these ideas verbally and in musical practice at his church in Orange, New Jersey. The minister there at the time, George Blagden Bacon, summarized Mason's ideas:

Pre-eminently, Dr. Mason's work was, in the best sense of the word, a popular work. More and more . . . he aimed to do for the people, not what they most desired, always, but what, according to his judgment, they most needed; less eager to gratify their present taste than to improve and elevate it . . . he maintained these two positions: *1st, That the tunes used in the churches should be such that all could sing them—and 2nd, that they should be subordinate to the words used, should be the fit and natural expression of the words.* I think that in insisting on these two principles, he sometimes went to an extreme of plainness and severity . . . and that the tunes which he prepared with too exclusive reference to them, were sometimes, for that reason, unsuccessful. I believe he thought so, too; but I am sure, that these two principles are sound and true. By them at any rate, he wished to stand, and did stand, to his death.[22]

Soon after returning from Europe in 1853, Mason began work on another sacred music collection. Completed in August 1854, *The Hallelujah* is musically somewhat more sophisticated than his previous books. As noted in the preface, the music includes a greater variety of metric patterns and more venturesome harmony, particularly in the more frequent use of the supertonic and mediant chords. A greater variety of cadences appears, resulting in less reliance on the standard $^6_4$ chord in cadences. Progressions so "characteristic of the genuine school of church music" are used because they are "much more soft and euphonious," but the "genuine school of church music" is unidentified. Possibly the reference is to Palestrina, Purcell, and Tallis, composers "unrivalled for the simplicity and sublimity of their church harmonies," according to Mason in *The Psaltery* (1845). In *The Hallelujah,* he simply argues for a "much more soft and euphonious" sound. Intervals of fourths and ninths (carefully prepared) are more often used, as are minor keys.

The Hallelujah also features instrumental interludes for use between stanzas of hymns. According to the editor, these passages are provided for performance and for examples to show organists that interludes need not be mere repetition of the final musical phrases. Mason's interludes generally consist of elaborated cadences closing on the tonic or dominant to lead smoothly into the stanza portion. Not infrequently these passages begin on the closing chord of the hymn and end on its opening chord. Mason adds these interludes occasionally, not consistently.

After a five-year lapse of relatively little publication, Mason produced an altogether different type of congregational music book in 1859 with *The Sabbath Hymn and Tune Book for the Service of Song in the House of the Lord.* His coeditors were Austin Phelps and Edwards A. Park, noted professors at Andover Theological Seminary.[23]

The Sabbath Hymn and Tune Book has the vertical format of the modern church hymnal, i.e., pages are longer than they are wide. In this book the texts and tunes are printed together. Though Mason had not followed this custom, many American editors had issued choir books with tunes (with or without texts) and congregational books with texts only. Though the tunebook vogue was dying out in 1859 and the use of separate books for tunes and texts was less common, tunebooks continued to appear in which only the first stanza of each hymn was printed, thus requiring singers to hold a tunebook in one hand and a text collection in the other unless they could place the two books on racks in front of them (an accommodation often built into choir stalls at the time).[24]

About 1860 American publishers also experimented with placing the tunes on the top half of a page, texts on the bottom half, then cutting the pages horizontally so that the half pages could be turned separately. In this way a given text could be matched easily to any tune anywhere in the book, assuming, of course, that the poetic and musical meters coincided. Mason did not indulge in this practice because it contradicted his belief that texts and tunes should be carefully matched for overall effect.

The Sabbath Hymn and Tune Book departs from custom in several ways besides format. The book has a more detailed preface than any previous work by Mason, though again, the preface is a platform for the editors' views of church music. The book also contains more thorough indexing than Mason's previous works. These indices list tunes alphabetically and metrically, texts according to first lines, and compositions according to types (chants, anthems, doxologies, and other categories). The book offers three or four texts for each tune with alternate texts usually on the bottom half of the page and the tunes on the top. Moreover, Mason uses keyboard scoring with the melody in the soprano line as in modern practice, but alto and tenor parts are printed in smaller notes than the outer voices. The four parts are complete and free of the antiquated figured bass found in earlier books, yet singers are visually encouraged to follow the melody line (soprano) or the bass line.

Publication of *The Sabbath Hymn and Tune Book* was prompted by a volume of 1,300 texts and tunes entitled *The Sabbath Hymn Book,* compiled by Henry Ward Beecher. Upon arriving at his new charge at Plymouth Church, Brooklyn, New York, Beecher found that the choir had completely usurped the music program. Furthermore, their renditions, all unaccompanied, were poor no matter what music they attempted. In hopes of reviving congregational singing and of providing more suitable choir tunes, Beecher began to edit tunes and texts he felt were both appropriate and singable.

Despite local success, the book had its detractors, including Professors Park and Phelps who questioned Beecher's heavy reliance on Watts and Wesley texts. Believing that much of Watts' theology was outdated, they turned to works of the American congregationalist Ray Palmer and the Scotch poet Horatius Bonar. Mason had known Palmer from at least 1830 when Mason set Palmer's best known text, beginning "My faith looks up to Thee," to his tune Olivet. Bonar (1808-1889), a Presbyterian minister, issued a series of three books titled *Hymns of Faith and Hope* from 1857 to 1866. Both Palmer and Bonar are mentioned repeatedly in Mason's correspondence during the preparation of *The Sabbath Hymn and Tune Book.*

Park and Phelps' work on texts is scholarly as compared to work in other contemporary hymnals, Beecher's included. The Andover professors explored the sources of the texts and "did not hesitate to apply literary criteria and treated their materials with scholarly precision." Their belief that "hymnologic taste" had been elevated by the Romantic Movement and that Christians should welcome new songs of a lyric quality was quickly embraced by many of their contemporaries. The book itself received "almost unqualified praise from many eminent clergymen and . . . it was adopted and used in many congregations."[25]

Mason actively courted critics and others by sending out complimentary copies. This factor and the reaction of some of the reviewers abroad are evident in the following letter:

South Orange
15th Aug. 1859

Rev. Dr. Park,
We are at length getting something from England. You will be gratified with the notices in Evangelical & Brit. Quarterly. Also with the one from Dr. Warwick, Dublin, & especially with that from Mr. Jno. Angell James which, I believe, exceeds, in laud, anything which we have had before.

I have this day finished letters to Dr. Warwick & to Mr. James, thanking them in the name of the Editors, & sending copies of the "Hy & Tune Book."

I have also sent a copy of Hy Book to Rev. Jno Caird of Marlow [?], who preached before the Queen, & who lately pub. a book of Sermons.

Would it [not] be a good thing to get Her Majesty to speak favorably?

I have also written to D. [John Sullivan Dwight?] rather gently hinting at a notice from him, & sending him a Hy & Tune Book.

I hope all these things will meet yr. approbation. Was the return of sales equal to yr. expectation? It has well nigh got us out of debt, which is more than I expected so soon. [This "debt" is unexplained.]

Very truly yrs.
Lowell Mason

The contents of *The Sabbath Hymn and Tune Book* appeared in several forms besides the original described above. The texts were published alone under the title *The Sabbath Hymn Book,* the tunes alone in *The Sabbath Tune Book.* In addition, *The Sabbath Hymn and Tune Book* was issued in a Baptist version identical to the original edition except for the addition of thirty-one Baptist texts set to eleven hymn tunes. These tunes were also used in other parts of the book, set to various other texts. The extra Baptist texts necessitated nine extra pages, extending the book to 519 pages as opposed to the 510 of the original edition.

Publishing a Baptist version was apparently Mason's idea. In a statement printed at the front of that edition, Francis Wayland states that Mason approached him with the request that he prepare a version suitable for Baptist use. Wayland, a friend of long standing, had been the first president of the American Institute of Instruction. He later became the president of Brown University, Providence, Rhode Island. In accord with Mason's request, Wayland examined the book prior to its publication and prepared the Baptist version for release concurrent with the regular edition. Noting the changes, all suited to his church's doctrine on baptism, Wayland endorses the book for use by Baptists in church or family worship or in their private devotions. His statement, opposite the first page of the preface, is dated September 1858.

The Sabbath Hymn and Tune Book, though successful in all forms, was particularly successful in the standard version with texts and tunes printed together. As early as May 1, 1860 Mason wrote to Park, expressing his delight with the book's popularity:

More than 40,000 copies sold in a year! . . . I doubt very much whether there was *ever* a hymn book before, of which so many sold the first year. . . . [The book] is making its way. Where it is *understood* it is liked. I know full well there are many who understand not, & that the people are "perishing for lack of knowledge." Opposition comes occasionally; but my faith rests on what... must be, & *that* it must be. Thus far it has prospered.

So successful was this book that in 1866 Mason and his associates issued a new edition, essentially the same in format and contents but somewhat smaller in size. Mason did alter a few of the tunes and substituted some new selections for a few of the less-well-received tunes. The new edition's close relationship to the original is apparent even in its name, *The New Sabbath Hymn and Tune Book for the Service of Song in the House of the Lord.*

Lowell Mason as an Editor

Three qualities characterize Lowell Mason as an editor:

1. He was closely in tune with the book market, its fluctuations and its opportunities, and he made a fortune.
2. He was a perfectionist who insisted upon having his materials published exactly as he wanted them to be. He constantly corrected "final proofs."
3. He guarded his copyrighted materials carefully.

Each of these points is clear from surviving correspondence.

In a lengthy letter to George J. Webb, sent from London on January 28, 1853, Mason discussed opportunities for book publication. The letter was recorded in its entirety in Mason's diary, indicating that he wanted it preserved for his own records. As quoted from his diary entry of that date, the letter reads as follows:

Dear Sir,
I find that owing to the great changes in relation to musical publications the Cantica Laudis [1850] is not likely to do much more. I expect very little from it hereafter. I doubt whether it will pay in all $1,000 next season.

I find that I cannot bring out a new book at present, certainly not by next autumn, so that this work will probably quite run out before I can do anything more. I have thought that perhaps you might like to bring out a book next autumn, either by yourself or in connection with someone who can aid you, and that it would be best therefore for our connection to be dissolved, i.e. so far as it relates to the pub. of books together.

In addition to the above I may remark that my sons have desired me to make for them... perhaps in two years or more, a book by myself—They desire that I would leave them a book of my own exclusive editing, not knowing when or how they shall publish. This I have of course an inclination to do for them. [It is impossible to determine which book developed in response to this request because many were produced after 1853.] Taking these things into view, I thought I ought to write you a note to the above effect, that you need not feel yourself confined by our agreement.

There are many books which ought to be pub. in Boston. It is hardly probable I shall ever do more in this way there, but if anywhere in N. York.

I look back upon our intercourse (professional and personal) with great pleasure & shall always cherish for you a deep feeling of respect and affection and so also for all the dear members of your family, all of whom I truly love. When we meet we will converse freely on these & other things.

Yours as ever
    Lowell Mason

Just how successful was Lowell Mason in the sale of his books? Figures vary, but here is a reasonable estimate:

Carmina Sacra and its revision, *The New Carmina Sacra,* sold at least 500,000 copies from 1841 through 1858.
The Hallelujah sold 150,000 copies from 1854 through 1858.
Seven other books sold over 50,000 copies from their publication dates through 1858:
    The Boston Handel and Haydn Society Collection of Church Music
    The Choir
    The Boston Academy Collection
    The Modern Psalmist
    The Psaltery
    The National Psalmist
    Cantica Laudis
Many other books sold over 10,000 copies.[26]

Mason's determination that his materials be published exactly as he wanted them is shown by the correspondence between Mason Brothers and Melvin Lord of Boston in 1855. The following letters concerning Lord's printing of the latest edition of *The New Carmina Sacra* illustrate that point:

September 1, 1855

Dear Sir,
We hope you are not introducing any new tunes into New Carmina.... Father objects decidedly to any others being admitted except after his examination. He also notices... you have changed some of the names of the tunes.... Please have these altered as we wish to use the same names as in the Hallelujah. We are suffering for want of books.

Truly yours,
    Mason Bro.

* * * * * * * * * * * * * *

September 3, 1855

Dear Sir,
We enclose a note from father and the proofs with his corrections. He is very strenuous about the matter and speaks much more strongly even than he has written. *All these changes must be made before publication at whatever cost of delay*...which of course must fall to your percentage.

We are daily hearing complaints of the admission of many tunes into New Carmina....We never intended...any alteration other than the insertions of a few tunes from Hallelujah.

Yours truly,
   Mason Bro.

* * * * * * * * * * * * * *

September 5, 1855

Dear Sir,
Father is positive in the matter. Britain, Irvine, and _____ [illegible] must not appear in the new edition of Carmina—also the names altered from Hallelujah must be restored. . . . The new tunes put in from the Hallelujah should not have been on two staves but it is too late probably to remedy this. . . .

We propose to advertise New Carmina very extensively in the South and West—if you will allow us to charge [you]...one-half the expense.

Will you please let us hear from you on this subject as soon as may be as advertisements should be put out at once.

Yours truly,
   Mason Bro.

According to the unpublished memoirs of Edward Palmer Mason (Henry Mason's eldest son) who worked with Lowell Mason, Jr., the latter was a pioneer in the use of modern advertising techniques. He was, at the very least, a skillful businessman. This letter and others indicate that Mason Brothers recognized and cultivated the "Bible Belt" decades before the region was so named by H. L. Mencken.

Lowell Mason's careful attention to his copyright privileges occasioned a number of letters, including this one sent to Bradbury with an identical copy to George F. Root:

Library Room,
South Orange, N. J.
October 10th, 1861

Mr. Bradbury, Dear Sir,
It gives me much pleasure to be able to send you a copy of Asaph [just published]; with it,

accept my thanks for your kind contribution and be assured that I shall be ready to reciprocate the favor when there is an opportunity.

Will you allow me now to call your attention to a subject no less important to you than to myself, but one that has not been *practically understood* or properly acted upon by many editors of music books before. I refer to property in books, or as we commonly say, *copyright,* or *copyright property,* by which I understand the "rights" (both legal and moral) which one has in that which he originates in his own mind, or which he lawfully and properly procures from others. This property extends both to music and to words or poetry. It is with regard to the latter, (words) that there has been, if I mistake not, a want of attention, and in which I think the rights of editors have been not infrequently infringed. In my present book, Asaph, there is much that I claim as original, both in music and in words. Almost all in the secular department, and much in the Psalms and Hymn Tune, and also in the Anthem and Motet departments.

Now, My Dear Sir, I do not believe you will find it in your heart to find fault with me, when I say that I cannot consent to any one's taking or republishing either words or music without the consent of editors or publishers; and I am especially unwilling to allow a separation between words and music—i.e. for any one to take words which are . . . originally adapted to music, and set the same to other or new music. This is a point on which I feel decided, and I cannot consent that *my words* shall be divorced from that music to which I have united them, *or in any way taken and republished without special permission.*

Now, dear Sir, I have tried to write plainly, but I also write with most friendly feelings, and I believe in accordance with the great principle of doing as I would be done by. I address this letter *verbatim et literatim* both to you and to our mutual friend, Mr. Geo. F. Root, for *we three* are especially interested in these things.

I have written in my own name but with the full consent and approbation of my _____ [illegible].

Yours very truly as ever,
    Lowell Mason

P.S. This letter I have shown to the Publishers of our books.

The Mason Sons

In his publications after 1850, Lowell Mason was assisted by his two eldest sons in the publishing business. The New York City firm of Mason and Law (discussed in chapter 8) operated from 1851 to 1853. On February 14, 1953 a new company was set up under the name "Mason Brothers." An announcement in *The Musical World and New York Musical Times* read simply:

The subscribers will continue the Publishing and Bookselling Business at the old stand (23 Park Row, opposite the Astor House) under the firm of MASON BROTHERS.

Signed, Lowell Mason, Jr.
Daniel G. Mason

The new organization continued publication of Lowell Mason's works as well as other publications ranging from English and French dictionaries to histories, school and college texts, and a journal called *The New York Musical Gazette*. Like Mason and Law, Mason Brothers advertised widely and prospered.

On January 29, 1868, Mason Brothers reorganized to include Henry Mason, Lowell and Abigail's youngest son. The articles of partnership indicate the following provisions: the firm is to continue under the same name and in the publication and sale of books; the capital stocks shall be $75,000, a third of which was put up by each of the three partners; profits and losses are to be shared equally by the partners; none of the parties can become bound in any way as security for the good of any other person without written consent of the other parties; the partnership can be terminated at any time, provided three months notice in writing be presented by the person wishing to terminate his association; in the event of the death of any of the partners, the surviving partners shall have the right, if they so elect within sixty days of the decease, to purchase the interest of the deceased partner according to the value to be ascertained in accord with procedures laid down in this document and taking into account all the liabilities outstanding.

This last clause turned out to be extremely important, for in less than eighteen months one of the partners, Daniel Gregory Mason, died suddenly. Thus, on June 24, 1869, the partnership was dissolved, but the surviving partners agreed to continue the business under the same company name. This arrangement did not last long because later that year Lowell, Jr. and Henry were both deeply involved in the work of Mason & Hamlin, an instrument manufacturing company. The holdings of the publishing house were sold at a good profit to the Oliver Ditson Company with the plates of Lowell Mason's work alone valued at over $100,000 (roughly equivalent in purchasing power to $887,000 in 1983).[27]

As has been indicated, Mason Brothers advertising promoted Lowell Mason's work in institutes and in book publication. Special efforts were made to promote his publications in the South and West, though the advertising was nationwide. Letters by Mason and his sons reveal a sensitivity to advertising others seemingly lacked. To cite but one example, in a letter dated May 1, 1860, Mason suggests that Dr. Phelps should send out his "charming little book" (not further identified) "with more power [in the] South and West."

Immediately after his graduation from Harvard University in 1881, Edward Palmer Mason went to work at Mason & Hamlin with his uncle, Lowell, Jr. There he remained in various positions until 1890, observing Lowell, Jr. closely from 1881 to 1885, when the latter died. According to Edward's memoirs, Lowell, Jr. was one of the first businessmen to calculate the expense of reaching given groups with specific types of advertising.

Of Lowell and Abigail's four sons, William attained the most prominence, for he became one of the most celebrated concert pianists in American music history. After five years study in Europe with Liszt, Dreyschock, and Hauptmann, he returned to the United States in 1854 and became a concert artist. Described in *Dwight's Journal of Music* "not merely [as] a brilliant virtuoso but [as] a fine musician,"[28] he toured widely as a pianist through 1855, then settled near New York City where he joined Theodore Thomas, Carl Bergmann, Joseph Mosenthal, and George Matzka in the Mason-Thomas Soirees of Chamber Music, a series of concerts that continued until 1868. Subsequently he also developed a wide following as a teacher and composer.

William established his family in the 1850s. In his *Memories of a Musical Life,* he relates that upon his return from Europe he "hurried to Boston, and went... to the house of Mr. Webb. This had been my constant purpose ever since... I left America in 1849. In due course Miss [Mary] Webb and I became engaged, and were married on March 12, 1857."[29] William and Mary had three children.

The year 1857 brought a second wedding to the family, for in December, Henry married Helen Augusta Palmer. In June, Lowell had traveled from his home in New Jersey to Cambridge, Massachusetts to lecture on congregational singing. Henry, who was then twenty-five, was with him part of the time, at least during a visit at the Asher Palmer home. The Palmers and Masons had been close friends ever since Anne Folsom Palmer and Asher Palmer had sung in Mason's Bowdoin Street Church choir in the early 1830s. This visit sparked Henry's interest in the Palmer's daughter Helen, and after a six-month courtship, the two were married December 24, 1857. They had four sons.

The youngest of the Henry Masons' sons, Daniel Gregory, wrote about his parents' courtship, marriage, and family life in *Music in My Time and Other Reminiscences.* Noting that music was a part of their daily life, he added that his father was a fine pianist: "In his touch was something of that clinging, singing, caressing quality that make my Uncle William's... the most beautiful touch I have ever heard; and their father, Lowell Mason, used to say that his talent [Henry's] was almost as marked as William's had it only been developed."[30]

The marriages of their sons evidently pleased Lowell and Abigail greatly, as did the cordiality that existed between members of their family. Lowell's letter to Daniel's wife just after Henry and Helen's wedding reflects this feeling:

January 5, 1858

Dear Susie,
I catch a moment just to thank you for your very kind note giving an account of the reception of our new daughter and sister, already beloved, as Christians say. Mrs. M. had written to me that you were the presiding genius on the occasion and this way things were in fine order—for all this too, I thank you, for I desire most sincerely that Helen might receive a hearty welcome.

It is a circumstance of my life that gives me *very great pleasure indeed* that my sons and families are so harmonious and that they live together so pleasantly and socially—and that if there are often things that happen that are to be regretted, yet on the whole there is a great degree of peace and union amongst the whole. This, I repeat it, gives me great satisfaction. I often think of it with gratitude to God. . . .

Father L.M.

Henry Mason built his career in instrument manufacturing with the firm Mason & Hamlin. As noted above, Lowell, Jr. became involved in this company too, as did several of Henry's sons in later years. Lowell Mason had a major role in establishing Mason & Hamlin. The firm came into existence in this way:

In 1854 Lowell Mason met Emmons Hamlin at the Oliver Ditson Music Store in Boston, apparently by chance. Hamlin (1821-1885), a native of New York, had moved to Boston in 1852. Previously he had built melodeons with George A. Prince & Co. in Buffalo, New York. Exercising his mechanical ingenuity, Hamlin perfected the voicing of reeds and increased the potential array of reed organ stops. Henry Mason, who had just returned from studying in Europe, had no definite plans for the future. His father suggested to Henry that he and Emmons Hamlin set up an organ manufacturing firm, specializing in reed organs.[31] To help them get started, Lowell Mason and Oliver Ditson each loaned the young men five thousand dollars.

By 1861 Mason and Hamlin had developed the cabinet organ (or reed organ) in its generally accepted form. This instrument became enormously popular in America and, in fact, became the most widely used of large musical instruments. By 1900 Mason & Hamlin produced about 80,000 organs per year. The instruments were of such fine quality that they won the highest medals and premiums at world's fairs. In 1882 the company expanded to piano manufacturing and excelled in that area as well. Through an improved method of stringing, these pianos had an unusually pure and refined tone, along with greater durability and decreased liability to getting out of tune.

In 1862 Mason Brothers secured an interest in and the New York agency for Mason & Hamlin. In 1868 the company was incorporated under the name "Mason & Hamlin Organ & Piano Company" with Daniel Gregory Mason, Lowell Mason, Jr., Henry Mason, and Emmons Hamlin as stockholders and directors. When Daniel Gregory died the next year and publishing activities ceased, the surviving partners gave undivided attention to instrument manufacturing. Lowell, Jr. became the president of Mason & Hamlin at the time of its incorporation in 1868, a post he held until his death in 1885. He was succeeded by Henry Mason, who retained the position until his death in 1890.

At that time, Henry's eldest son, Edward Palmer Mason, succeeded to the office. This talented member of the family was largely responsible for the improved method of stringing applied to the Mason & Hamlin piano. He later established his own independent piano manufacturing firm in the Bronx, New York. He wanted to make an apartment-sized grand piano with a fine tone and succeeded in a model he called the Edward P. Mason Recitalgrand.[32]

Edward's successor at Mason & Hamlin was his younger brother, Henry Lowell Mason, who led the long-established firm until 1929. By 1900 Mason & Hamlin had a paid-up capital of a half million dollars and factories in Cambridge, Massachusetts with about five hundred employees. In 1929 Mason & Hamlin merged with the Aeolian American Corporation with factories in East Rochester, New York. Still later this firm became a part of the American Piano Company.

The Mason Library

Lowell Mason collected books and music assiduously throughout his adult life. Many of these materials were essential in his editing and teaching; some added to his professional growth indirectly, while for others he had little use. Yet he respected learning, treasured the materials he gathered, and absorbed all he could.

Though his formal education had been limited, Mason attained a broad, thorough education on his own so that by 1858, he was described in *Dwight's Journal of Music* as standing "before the public—from the world-renowned professors at Andover to the dwellers in the squatters' cabins in the West—in a position held by no other musical man in the country." And how did Mason attain that stature, given his background? The writer ("diarist" A. W. Thayer) went on to answer that question:

> If you should ever go into his library, you will see there at a glance to what his success has been due. You will find that whatever came from the press bearing upon sacred music and the science of teaching it, found its way at once to his study; and the notes and marks in books

and periodicals prove how carefully all were perused.... The consequence was, that as time passed, his mind became so stored with information on all these points, that he is a welcome companion to men of the highest culture in other departments of knowledge.... You may not like his music.... That is a matter of taste—the public does, and purchases it. But that is not to the point.... [Mason's preeminence comes from] nothing but his devotion to his profession, and his determination to avail himself of every means of extending his knowledge of it.[33]

Mason's knowledge was recognized by Union Theological Seminary, New York City, where he was an instructor in sacred music during the year 1854-55. Further recognition of his learning came in the form of an honorary doctorate in music presented *honoris causa* by New York University in 1855. This was the second time that this particular degree was granted by an American institution, but it was the first such degree to be granted with distinction.[34]

In 1855 Mason participated in community actions which, it was hoped, would bring a New Jersey State Normal School into Orange, his newly adopted city of residence. Citizens offered land, money, and equipment to the prospective school. Mason offered the use of his private library, then valued at about $35,000, plus free music lectures to the students.[35] Ultimately the school was built at Trenton, to the disappointment of Mason and other Orange residents.

Mason's library would have been a splendid addition to any normal school's facilities, for it was one of a very few significant music libraries in the country at the time. According to a report published in September 1854, this was the situation:

In the public libraries of this country, among from 80,000 to 100,000 volumes, scarcely fifty books can be found which range under the head of musical literature. Besides the [sizable music] collection of Mr. Albrecht [of the Germania Musical Society] which is considered the most complete in America, we only know of but three more in this country; the first is owned by Dr. LaRoche, of Philadelphia... the second belonging to Mr. Lowell Mason... the third is the musical library of the Harvard Musical Association of Cambridge....[36]

Mason's private library was "by no means confined to such works as he could read or use," according to Alexander Wheelock Thayer, the eminent Beethoven biographer who worked in the library for a time. Rather, Mason accumulated "for the use of others ... with the intention of making a collection which after his death should be deposited in some institution of learning for the public benefit."[37] According to his wishes, Mason's survivors contributed his entire library to Yale University, New Haven, Connecticut.

Some of the works in the Mason Library are music books by his contemporaries, books similar to his own works. Many of these books were gifts to Mason. Admirers and associates gave him other valuable books from time to time, knowing that he appreciated such gifts. In this way he acquired many collector's items. For instance, the famous work by Thomas Walter (1696-1725) entitled *The Grounds and Rules of Musick explained, or An Introduction to the Art of Singing by Note* (1737, Third Edition) was sent by a donor from Stockbridge, Massachusetts with this letter:

April 11, 1858

Lowell Mason, Sir:
This had a title page which bore the date of 1737. If it is so old as to be new to you, it may amuse you; if not, it may at least serve to mark the improvements of a century of Music—to which you have contributed a full share. Accept it with sincere regards of

S. Rockwell

Of course, all of Mason's publications are included in his library. Overall, the collection contains a heavy preponderance of vocal music. The instrumental music included is principally for organ and piano, and most of the European works for organ come from the Rinck collection.

Mason searched for music materials all his life, especially in England and Europe when traveling, but his interest did not stop there. In 1855 he heard that Professor S. W. Dehn of Berlin wanted to sell his personal music library. It is probable that Thayer's letter to *Dwight's Journal of Music* alerted Mason to the possibility of making this purchase, for Thayer had written Dwight, pleading that somehow the Dehn collection be purchased and brought to America.

The Dehn library was rich in works by the German Baroque theorists Johann Mattheson (1681-1764) and Friedrich Wilhelm Marpurg (1718-1795). Dehn, the distinguished music scholar whom Mason had met at the Royal Library in Berlin, had collected materials for many years, developing one of the finest private libraries in Europe at the time. Mason immediately decided to make the purchase, and for the entire collection he paid the remarkably low price of $97.[38] As was the case with the Rinck library, Mason had no personal use for most of the material, but considering its value to American scholars, the purchase was a tremendous bargain and a rich investment for future generations.

The relationship between Thayer and Mason offers insight into Mason's personality. Thayer had begun to gather materials for his definitive study of Beethoven during a two-year trip to Europe in 1849 to 1851. Lack of money brought him back to America where he took odd jobs to earn money for further research abroad. In 1852 Thayer was in New York City working on the staff of the *New York Tribune*. At some point between 1852 and 1854 he was also employed to work in Mason's library where, according to his own account, he was cataloging.[39] This employment must have occurred in 1853 or early 1854 while the Masons lived in New York City.

Thayer and others were allowed to use Mason's library quite freely, provided they made proper arrangements. Thayer, who had written critically of Mason before meeting him, later admitted that his tastes differed from Mason's and that he had run into differences of opinion with Mason. Nonetheless, they shared a love of learning and respect for music scholarship. Mason believed in Thayer's Beethoven project and helped underwrite Thayer's research in Europe. Though Thayer acknowledged Mason's "essential aid" in the dedication of the first volume of his Beethoven biography (1866), Mason's patronage received general public recognition only after Mason's death. Thayer then acknowledged openly that Mason had loaned him "a handsome sum . . . to be repaid at convenience, without interest, to enable the writer [Thayer himself] to pursue his studies in Europe."[40]

Within a year after Mason's death, his entire library was presented to the Yale University Divinity School. The exact reasons for selecting Yale cannot be determined. George Blagden Bacon, son of Leonard Bacon of the Yale Divinity School and the Masons' beloved clergyman during their years in Orange, may have influenced the choice. The fact that William Mason was awarded an honorary doctorate from Yale in 1872 may also have played a part.[41]

A formal letter dated March 15, 1873 and signed by Lowell Mason, Jr. explains the reasoning behind the gift:

> The family of the late Lowell Mason, *Mus. Doc.*, ask leave to present herewith his library of Music and Music literature to the President and Fellows of Yale College, for the Theological Department.
>
> It is the accumulation of a life-time devoted with rare zeal and industry to labors for the advancement of sacred music, and elementary musical instruction, and will be found especially rich in the former of these departments.
>
> That all the people might enter fully and heartily into the use and enjoyment of music in the praise of God was a paramount object of my father's life, and he believed this could be realized only as the churches should become enlightened as to the best religious use of music; and that such understanding must come largely through the instruction of pastors.
>
> It is hoped that this disposition of Dr. Mason's library may help to furnish a means for the preparation of many for such teaching, and so serve an object which he held to be so important.

The Lowell Mason Library should be distinguished from the Lowell Mason Papers (also at Yale) upon which much of the material in this book is based. The Mason Papers include correspondence, diaries, programs, handbills, manuscript music, clippings, scrapbooks, miscellaneous writings, and memorabilia. These materials were organized, referenced, and listed in a register compiled by Adrienne Nesnow in 1982 under a grant from the Research Resources Program of the National Endowment of the Humanities. Henry Lowell Mason's manuscript biography and documents pertaining to his research are included, as are papers of William Mason.

The Lowell Mason Library (or Collection) includes a shelf count of about 10,300 books and other items. In 1874 Joel Sumner Smith of the Yale Library staff began a catalogue of the Mason Collection. After devoting more than four thousand hours to this complex task, he had a manuscript consisting of 678 pages, "a model of completeness and accuracy."[42] Having been put to little use in the Divinity School, the collection was transferred to the School of Music in 1917 when completion of Sprague Hall made space available. In its new quarters the collection was kept together until 1933. At that time it was determined that portions of the Mason Library should be incorporated into the Yale Music Library, provided that all of Mason's books be distinguished with a special bookplate.

This has been done gradually, as time has permitted. Of the 10,300 items, about 2,000 have been incorporated into the Music Library.[43] Special effort has been made to transfer books with publication dates earlier than 1800 and those having particular value in connection with some aspect of music (e.g., theory, opera, music periodicals, and others). Many scholars have used the materials. "Lowell Mason could only be gratified at the extent to which his library is being put to use. . . . What was to him a working library has become, through the passage of time, a library for reference and research."[44]

11

Lowell Mason as a Composer-Arranger

An Approach to Evaluation

In 1853 John Sullivan Dwight bemoaned that "our Masons and our Bradburys are esteemed the greatest composers in the world by thousands and thousands of our inland population."[1] Now, over one hundred years later, the music of these men is engrained in the lives of "thousands and thousands of our population"; indeed, Mason's tunes and those written by his contemporaries form a core repertoire for American Protestant congregations.

Mason's best known hymn tunes (composed or arranged) and the texts to which they are usually set include the following:

Tune	Text
Antioch	Joy to the World, the Lord Is Come
Bethany	Nearer My God to Thee
Boylston	A Charge to Keep I Have
Cowper	There is a Fountain Filled with Blood
Dennis	Blest Be the Tie That Binds
Hamburg	When I Survey the Wondrous Cross
Laban	My Soul, Be on Thy Guard
Malvern	Jesus, Where'er Thy People Meet
Mendebras	O Day of Rest and Gladness
Missionary Hymn	From Greenland's Icy Mountains
Olivet	My Faith Looks Up to Thee
Sabbath	Safely Through Another Week
Watchman	Watchman, Tell Us of the Night
Wesley	Hail to the Brightness
Work Song	Work for the Night is Coming

Many of Mason's tunes have been quoted in musical works, including compositions by Charles Ives (1874-1954). They have also formed the basis for many arrangements, such as Seth Bingham's organ settings, "Seven Preludes or Postludes on Lowell Mason Hymns."[2]

Mason's musical style became the norm for American Protestant hymnody from his time on. He established a "moderate" hymnody between other styles prevalent in the 1800s: on the one side stood revival music, shape-note music in the South and Midwest, and (after about 1860) gospel music; on the other side was the operatic style of vocal music by soloists or small groups in the wealthier churches of eastern cities. Mason objected to certain aspects of both these styles, and the success of his tunes and books rivaled and, to a considerable extent, supplanted these styles and practices.

Mason's compositions put into practice his ideas about music's role in worship. Fundamental to understanding his music is the distinction he made between *church music* and *music in church,* between spiritual potential and artistic quality. In his practice as a church musician, in his speeches and writings, and in his editorial choices as a tunebook compiler, Mason was consistent and insistent about these distinctions.

Mason's musicianship has not always been interpreted in light of his objectives. For example, Frédéric Louis Ritter (1834–1891), whose view was that of an oratorio society conductor, assessed Mason's musicianship accurately from the technical standpoint, but missed the point of Mason's work:

> As a composer... he strove towards simplicity in melodic and harmonic treatment.... His tunes are smooth, of simple rhythmical construction, of rather prosaic expression, which alternates with commonplace sentimentality. There is not much originality about these tunes. The harmonic treatment is confined to the closest related chords and is, in general, correct. There is not much individual life in his four-part arrangements. Alto and tenor have a predilection for stationary existence. Here and there a modulation into dominant or subdominant, and occasionally into some parallel minor key, is indulged in. He was not much of a contrapuntist; this was, perhaps to his advantage.... Mason observed in his church music "simplicity and chastity" to a distressing degree.[3]

Ritter overlooked the difficulties Mason and others faced in reviving congregational singing and in providing music for that purpose. Ritter did admit grudgingly that many of Mason's tunes "are popular with congregations, whose capacity, as congregational singers, they do not exceed. And this is in some ways a merit."[4]

Even those who understand Mason's objectives have found thorough, objective evaluations of his music difficult, mainly for these three reasons:

1. No one knows the precise extent of his composing, but it was prolific. Henry Lowell Mason tabulated his grandfather's hymn tunes, analyzing them as to their origin, date of composition, and publication. He concluded that there were 1,697 hymn tunes, 1,210 of

them original, and 487 arrangements, totals which are in some dispute in light of recent research.[5] Children's songs, anthems, glees, choruses, chants, madrigals, rounds, and other pieces sacred and secular—all these stand apart from the tabulation.

Besides the sheer volume of the known material, there is the more perplexing problem of determining what else Mason actually composed. Many of his compositions are permanently unidentifiable. He often published his tunes anonymously for a time so that they could "run on their own merits." Eventually he claimed some of them, but often he did not. Thus, many of his works do not carry his name to this day.[6]

2. Mason's music is stylistically indistinguishable from the music of many of his contemporaries. This generalization applies equally to all the types of music he composed and arranged. One contributing factor was his willingness to adopt whatever rhythm, melodic patterns, harmonies, or forms suited his purposes. Practicality was endemic to American musicians during Mason's era (particularly in his own circle). Mason himself was both a champion and a victim of this approach to music.

Contributing to stylistic uniformity was the consensus among Mason and his associates as to the kind of music desirable for specific purposes. Though they had their differences, these writers (Hastings, Bradbury, Root, Webb, Woodbury, and others) all endorsed simplicity, clear text projection, and ease of performance. As a consequence, they imposed a blandness of style and a narrowness of dimension upon a mountain of music. Of course, their music was calculated to appeal to the public and to fill utilitarian needs. It was cogently argued that a book "too good" in terms of its music would suffer from fewer sales.[7]

3. Critical examination of Mason's musicianship has often been unreliable because of the prejudices of his contemporaries and the incomplete data available to later researchers. Mason's contemporaries might be excused because they were too close and too involved in the issues of their day. In addition, a sense of inferiority (expressed as indifference, if not disdain) with respect to American music pervaded thinking at the time. These factors have all contributed to the superficiality of attention to Mason's music.

Mason's own attitudes contributed to the lack of critical attention given his compositions during his lifetime. He did not believe his music deserved critical attention for its own sake. He thought of himself not as a composer, but as an educator who composed and arranged music as needed to educate children, churchgoers, and members of choral groups.

Considering these three factors, how should Mason's work as a composer and arranger be evaluated? First, one should keep his total career in perspective. Because he promoted participation in music and appreciation of "better" music, he worked with concepts larger than the musical style of any one individual, including himself. Richard Storrs Willis summed up this view of Mason by saying that "we do not . . . regard him as a great musician, a great composer, a great artist; he does not . . . regard himself as such. The great object of his life has been a far different one . . . *the musical education and instruction of the masses.*"[8] Keeping Mason's total career in perspective averts exaggerating his compositional skills in misguided attempts to elevate American music of the 1800s. It also averts equating the popularity of Mason's hymn tunes with aesthetic values they do not possess.

A second step to evaluation is cautious interpretation of remarks by Mason's more knowledgeable contemporaries and successors. Some of this commentary was based on music which has since fallen into disuse. Critics of the 1800s had the advantage of placing Mason's music in the context of the times, offsetting the disadvantage of being too caught up in the temper of the times for full objectivity.

The third and most objective step toward evaluation involves precise musical analysis of selected works. Modern researchers have undertaken chordal, rhythmic, and melodic analyses in efforts to define the "Lowell Mason style." Two of the more comprehensive studies of this type support these generalizations:[9]

Mason's hymn tunes—the most accessible, durable, and relevant of his works—illustrate his compositional practices: syllabic settings most of the time; chordal style; diatonic melodies in the middle of the vocal range; diatonic harmony, usually in a major key with few sharps or flats; harmonic progressions with little chromaticism or modulation; simple, basic rhythm patterns; and much repetition of phrases.

Mason's choral music is somewhat more elaborate, having a number of varied sections. He sometimes set popular hymn texts to new music for each stanza. Such "through-composed" settings, meant for choirs, were called "set pieces."[10] Imitative writing is used infrequently, and when used, departs from the usual syllabic settings. Mason's choice and handling of motifs is often reminiscent of the European composers he admired. For example, the anthem "O Look to Golgatha" relies on an arpeggiated figure ("Mannheim rocket") for its dramatic opening and for unity throughout.[11]

Mason defended simplicity for church music in both his published and personal writings. In a letter to the Reverend Edward N. Kirk on January 27, 1859, he explained his ideas in this way:

Some have complained of the Simplicity of Hymns, and of the familiarity of expression, etc. You do not thus complain, for you like to be familiar with Him whom we address.... Here [in America] we worship a god afar off too much. Some say we have too many Hymns. There can hardly be too many, provided they all express the true spirit of worship. It is a great mistake for a minister to confine himself or his people to a few *very select, extraordinarily beautiful* hymns.... The whole range of Hymnody is not too much if we would train Christians to a large, liberal, truthful, high and holy standard of piety.

Mason's Style in Hymn Tune Composition

Rhythm

According to Lowell Mason, the most nearly ideal rhythm for congregational music consists "mostly in tones of equal length" with "longer initials and terminals [to] enable people to begin and close the line together."[12] Yet his rhythmic patterns are seldom that simple. He uses the quarter note as the basic beat about three-fourths of the time with the half note as his second choice. Tunes almost invariably end on a strong beat.[13] Syncopation is rare, and when it does occur, it is mild; for examples, see the tunes Antioch, Ariel, and Ward.[14] Mason favors triple meter which he describes in the preface to *The Choir* (1832) as "easy of execution, effective and universally popular." One critic regards triple meter as "almost an obsession" with Lowell Mason.[15] An upbeat appears in about four-fifths of the most frequently used hymn tunes.[16]

Melody

Analysis substantiates a conclusion obvious to those who look at Mason's tunes in any hymnal: diatonic melodies are used almost exclusively. Ascending and descending intervals appear with nearly equal frequency. The major second is by far the most frequently chosen interval, followed by the perfect fourth and the minor third. Thereafter the frequency falls off sharply to major and minor sevenths, which are rare. Diminished and augmented intervals are simply not found.[17]

Mason's sparing use of dissonance underscores the diatonic melodies. Frequently no dissonance appears at all or, if it does, only as a passing tone or (less frequently) a double passing tone. The form of dissonance most acceptable to Mason seems to be the unaccented passing tone. Suspensions appear in some instances with the 4-3 suspension favored; according to one analysis, it is used seven times as frequently as the 9-8 suspension.[18]

The melodies almost always end on the first, third, fifth, or octave, emphasizing the tonic chord. Keeping the vocal limits of the average churchgoer in mind, Mason usually restricts the melodic lines to the span of an octave or a ninth. The highest note in the soprano line is d^2 preferably, with e^2 as an absolute limit.[19]

Harmony

Mason's harmonic concepts are reflected first (and most superficially) in his marked preference for major keys. No particular ones are preferred, but those with four or more sharps or flats are avoided, perhaps as a concession to the amateur organists of his time. More importantly, he uses primary chords thirteen times more often than secondary ones.[20]

Mason begins nearly every composition with the tonic chord, usually in root position. Thereafter he leans heavily on inversions of primary chords. The tonic chord appears in the first inversion as often as do all other chords combined. The first inversion of the dominant and supertonic are used about a third as often as the tonic, with the mediant chord being least frequently found in its first inversion.

As would be expected, the second inversion commonly appears in cadences, specifically in $I-IV_4^6-I$ and $V-I_4^6-V$ patterns. Less frequently he includes a II chord in a cadence pattern. Pedal and cadential $_4^6$ chords are used eighty-three times in sixty hymns examined in one study.[21]

Reliance on second inversion chords is one way to keep the bass line smooth. In the bass lines of Mason's hymns, by far the most common interval is the unison, accounting for more than a third of the intervals as compared with the fourth and fifth, each of which is used about a quarter of the time. It must be noted, however, that Mason makes only limited use of second inversion secondary chords. Though his use of seventh chords is generous, it is not excessive when compared with practices of his predecessors and contemporaries.[22]

Mason's limited use of secondary and seventh chords further applies his doctrine of simplicity. Basing his harmony on European standards of the Haydn-Mozart era (or earlier, as his remarks in the preface of *The Psaltery*, 1845, suggest) he keeps chromaticism limited principally to modulation and seldom modulates except for brief moves to the dominant. One study shows that in twenty percent of his cadences Mason uses a secondary dominant. The authentic cadence is used as the final cadence in fifty-eight of sixty hymns examined.[23]

A few conclusions can be drawn regarding Mason's harmonic practices: First, he knew the prevailing rules of harmony. This cannot be said of some of his predecessors and contemporaries. He showed an "intelligent understanding of harmonic usages...and though he did not consider himself a theorist, applied conscientiously what he did know,"[24] always in ways faithful to his purposes.

Second, he worked hard at being correct. When a reviewer of *The New Carmina Sacra* (1850) criticized him for allowing hidden parallel fifths and octaves and for neglecting to fill in all tones of certain chords, Mason responded at once, assuring the reviewer and his readers that the defects would be corrected in subsequent editions since they were simply oversights. But he added,

> I remember that when I was younger and knew less than now, I have *corrected,* as I thought, some of Handel's work, by filling up the chords according to the school rules; but after I had made the additions . . . I have found that the passage was really more effective as Handel left it . . . and I concluded *that Handel knew very well what he was about!*[25]

Mason went on to argue that being "correct" was secondary to being effective.

Third, Mason's harmonic practices deviated little from his first to his last works. No evidence of a trend can be found in his harmony or in any other aspect of his composition. Mason was conservative by comparison with his contemporaries during the 1840s and later. Despite his contacts with European musical practices through his sons' study, his own travel abroad, and his tireless study of the music he collected, Mason continued to use a harmonic vocabulary corresponding more nearly to the Haydn-Mozart era than to the Schumann-Chopin-Berlioz period in which he lived.

Form

Mason's hymn tunes usually adhere to a simple, conventional form consisting of sixteen measures broken into four phrases of four measures each, usually in AABA or ABAB pattern. The regular, almost rigid use of this simple form results at times in an imperfect union of poetic and musical phrases. Occasionally Mason deviates from this pattern and from his usual rhythmic patterns to use modified fuguing tune techniques, as, for example, in Antioch and Harwell. In general, however, he adheres to the regular (simple) form, fitting the concept expressed in *The National Psalmist* (1848) where he advocates "the plainest and easiest tunes" for congregational use.

Text Setting

For texts Mason drew on sources ranging from famous poets, such as Isaac Watts, to little known contemporaries, such as Ray Palmer. Mason was consistently concerned that the texts be edifying. In nearly every case he used syllabic settings. Short melismas grace the "Hallelujah" refrains added to some of his hymn tunes. Other deviations from syllabic writing are rare.

Mason's Style in Children's Songs

Mason's hymn tunes and his music for children are stylistically similar. Furthermore, his music for children is generally indistinguishable from that produced by his contemporaries.[26]

The primary aim of the children's books was to teach the pupils to read music. To this end, the books generally included charts, diagrams, and teachers' aids ranging from question-and-answer review sections to pedagogical tips. Pictures and drawings appeared occasionally. The music provided both practice and performance material. Over the years, the children's collections used less one-, two-, and three-part writing and more four-part writing.[27] When three-part writing was used, the music was written for two treble voices plus baritone.

Rhythm, melody, and harmony are simple in the children's songs. Mason relies on the tonic and dominant (including the dominant seventh) for about eighty-seven percent of the chords used. The supertonic and subdominant chords account for another nine percent, leaving other chords scarcely represented.[28]

Mason exercised special care in selecting texts for children's songs. American textbook compilers of his era favored certain topics for the texts of children's songs: nature, religious, seasonal, moral, and patriotic subjects (in decreasing order of frequency). These five categories account for ninety-five percent of the song topics in public school music texts of the 1800s. Interest in religious songs persisted until the 1880s but dropped off sharply thereafter. In some instances, special sections of the books were reserved for religious songs (for instance, in *Mason's Normal Singer,* 1856). In all these respects, Mason adhered to the prevailing practices and public expectations.

Usually Mason's songs for children were as simple in form as his hymn tunes. Most were short, strophic songs, sometimes with a refrain. The most common form was AABA or AA^{1}BA^1 with four measures of music in each of the four sections.

Mason's Arrangements

Lowell Mason was an arranger during his entire career, beginning in Savannah when he compiled *The Boston Handel and Haydn Society Collection of Church Music.* In that work he adapted approximately thirty tunes from Gardiner's *Sacred Music* for use with new texts. Believing that he "drew from the best sources," he took thirty additional tunes from Haydn, Mozart, Beethoven, Pleyel, Tallis, Viotti, Ravenscroft, Pergolesi, and Paisiello.[29]

Mason admitted that he altered materials for his books whenever he felt alterations were desirable. This happened constantly because he wanted his books to suit his purposes. Certainly Mason's sources and intentions could be no secret when preface after preface announced both to his readers. The scope of his arranging, his defense of arranging (as opposed to composing), and his concern for students' full development are evident in this portion of a letter to W. W. Killip dated February 26, 1860:

> I am not idle. I have been engaged for three or four months past, in *getting out secular music.* I am much dependent upon the good German writers—among whose works I find an exhaustless store of beautiful pieces—which are already—or may be by a little arrangement adapted to the wants of our people. I have been fortunate in procuring the aid of several persons who can furnish words—by translating, or by imitating, or by originals—and I have now written out ready for [the] printer over *100* beautiful part songs and glees—*all new— words and music*—of various grades of difficulty.... Yet *difficult* pieces I care not for, since there are enough already. I have many more in pt. done; so that I have not less than *250* pieces—which may be soon finished and I am still gathering in at the rate of from *two* to *four* a day. Now in doing this work, I fully believe that I am doing good, vastly more so, than as if I was composing myself. There are some people, who seem not to care what others have done—they ignore all that has gone before, and depend upon what they can do. I would not be so—I would rather go out of myself.
>
> I have no particular plan in relation to publication; I feel quite satisfied when I get a good piece fairly copied out music and words . . . whether I live to pub. it or leave it to others is a matter of little consequence. I do not work for mere money—I do really desire to do that which shall improve my fellowmen. Do you not sympathize with me somewhat in this? Arise, then, my dear young Friend, and . . . engage in this . . . work heart and hand. Introduce the best music you can; make your teaching thorough as you can, *educational,* reaching the *moral* as well as the *intellectual* and *physical.* Do not stop as many, very many teachers do with the *sensuous* and the *physical* (almost all vocal teachers, trainers of voice, etc. stop here)—but look to something higher—even to the highest development of the human. . . .

Mason's arrangements, like his compositions, were meant to facilitate participation and to satisfy his concepts of tasteful, appropriate music. In church music this meant ease of performance so that everyone could participate and a lack of ostentation so that the music would add to worship, not detract from it. Mason knew that Americans were still musical amateurs, despite advances being made in public school music (at least in major cities). Arrangements of works by "distinguished European composers" were not just tolerated but welcomed by the public, a striking example of American practicality and dilettantism.

Mason's arrangements range from slight modification of the original to such an overhaul of the original that it is unrecognizable. He defended his arranging practices many times, including in *Cantica Laudis* (1850), coedited with George J. Webb. In the preface to that work, Mason and Webb contend that many lovely themes are useful, though their original forms might be impractical and unsuitable for church use. They note that the words "arranged from" can mean little or much arranging. "The greater part of the tunes without any name affixed are taken from classic writers, or have been suggested by passages from them, and have only been composed by the editors." Then, in italics for emphasis, this note is added: "*Therefore, they are found nowhere else and hereby are claimed as property.*" Whether Mason wrote these statements himself or simply approved what Webb had written is unimportant (as well as impossible to determine), but Mason thought along exactly these lines and had he not agreed with the statements, they would not have been published.

Starting with themes he considered workable, Mason tailored rhythm and harmony, almost surely simplifying one or (more likely) both, then adding or deleting measures to maintain regular phrase patterns.[30] He kept accompaniments restrained, making only modest demands on performers. Choral parts were generally kept within normal SATB boundaries. Mason sought to preserve the mood of the original insofar as possible, or in the case of hymn tunes or children's songs, to mold the text and the music into a unified whole.

One final point illustrates Mason's methods as a composer-arranger and the difficulties of analyzing his musical output. Many compositions cannot be definitely categorized as "originals" or "arrangements" because the line between the two is so thin with respect to Lowell Mason's music.

In the third edition of *The Boston Handel and Haydn Society Collection of Church Music* (1825), Mason attributes the hymn tune Hamburg to the Benedictus from Novello's Evening Service. Because Mason used Gregorian and other chants for his arrangements fairly often, it was not unusual that he would draw on this source.[31] But one can argue in this instance that Mason wrote in the spirit of the chant rather than arranging it.[32] The first and fourth phrases of the hymn tune follow chant lines fairly closely, but the second phrase is entirely different from the corresponding portion of the chant. The third phrase duplicates the first phrase. Thus, the entire composition is, at most, only partially derived from its model. Actually Mason recast a part of a chant in the mold of hymn tunes of his day, using a pattern of repetition not found in the original and interspersing newly composed material. He ended up with an impressive, durable piece of music—and with an illustration of the interrelationship of his composing and arranging.

Such composing-arranging was apparently acceptable to thousands of Mason's contemporaries, judging by the sales of his books over many decades. An anonymous writer expressed this view in *The New York Evening Post,* shortly after Mason's death in August 1872:

> He has been termed a compiler, rather than a composer; and a compiler he certainly was. But he drew his ideas from the best sources. He took fragments from Handel, Haydn, Beethoven and other German composers, and from these extracts he devised the melodies which for the last half-century have been sung in every church in America. Nor did he wholly neglect original composition.... To produce the melodies which have been for fifty years the medium of Christian praise ... is no ordinary honor.[33]

Lowell Mason in His Last Years, c. 1870
Engraving by G.E. Perine, New York
(Used by courtesy of the Trustees of the Boston Public Library)

12

The Retirement Years

Life at Silver Spring Estate

Lowell and Abigail Mason moved to a seventy-acre estate just outside South Orange, New Jersey in late 1854 or early 1855. By April 1855, they were settled in that park-like setting named for an ever-flowing spring and brook that trickled through the grounds. Their house, a large, three-story Victorian structure, was inviting with a spacious porch spread across the entire front and centrally located steps leading to the front door. Ornate wood carving graced the trim; a bay window on the side of the house and vines growing on the porch columns added to its appeal. This comfortable home was conveniently located about fifteen miles from New York City, roughly an hour's travel time.

The estate included a stable in which Mason kept his dogs, horses, and carriages. In a letter to his grandson Lolo on September 3, 1855, Mason told of his four horses and four carriages: "First a great carry-all that holds six persons—then a Rock-away—then a covered Buggy—then a new Buggy without a top." Hired helpers, some of whom became family friends, maintained the stable, the house, and the grounds.

Mason arranged working space in the house; he described to Lolo a "nice large room ... where I make my psalms." A visitor later noted the "rows and rows of books [and] the large table in the center piled high with manuscripts, its undershelf loaded also." Treats were kept there for children who visited him. On a day when Marion Davis Collamore (the daughter of his neighbor, Davis Collamore) visited, Mason looked up from his work and "with severe expression pointed to ... a mysterious box kept amidst his books and said just two emphatic words, 'Eat that.' Then he resumed his writing. . . . Inside the box for that day the visitors found prunes."[1]

Soon after settling into their home, the Masons began to improve the property and to build a second house (later known as Cosy or Cosey Cottage) for the Daniel Gregory Mason family. In writing to Lolo on August 31, 1855, Mason described the work being done:

The men yesterday cut down and dug up by the roots four or five apple trees, because they were right in the way of where your new house is going to be; they are digging the cellar and will soon have it done. We have got a new wall almost done on the road, in front of the house, and the men are now building new gate posts, with a red kind of stone—the other day it rained so much that our pond became very dirty, and we have been cleaning it out; now we have nice clean water in the pond and two nice rustic seats where we can sit down and look at it. We have got a rustic bridge into the garden and another new bridge made of stone since you were here.

Daniel Gregory, Susie, and their family moved into Cosy Cottage as soon as it was completed (around January 1, 1856) and remained there for seven years. Then they traveled in Europe and, upon their return, settled in New York City. Lowell, Jr. and his wife Marie seem to have lived with Lowell and Abigail in the big house at Silver Spring for at least part of these years. The William Masons resided elsewhere in Orange during the 1860s and 1870s, and in 1870 the George Webbs moved there to be near their daughter, Mary Webb Mason. Thus, Lowell and Abigail had family and friends nearby. Of the immediate family, only Henry, Helen, and their sons remained in the Boston area.

During these years in Orange, the Masons were active in the Orange Valley Congregational Church. Both Lowell and Lowell, Jr. were charter members; both served as deacon, as members of the standing committee, as Sunday school superintendent, and as precentor (the latter office being held by one of them until 1876).[2] The church grew out of a Sunday school established in 1854, with official organization of the congregation in April 1860.

Writing to his friend Ray Palmer on May 31, 1860, Lowell indicated that by a vote of 37-26 the group had elected to become Congregational, though "we have Presbyterians all around us." Mason, who was selected to help prepare the rules of government and the articles of faith, sought Palmer's advice on these matters. After expressing confidence in Palmer's "fair, deliberate judgment," he added, "I am a . . . very great friend to Bible and Bible expressions. Brevity seems also to be an important thing too much overlooked."

This latter remark coincides with ideas expressed a month later in a letter to Dr. Leonard Bacon (1802-1881), professor at the Yale Divinity School. Bacon's son, George Blagden Bacon, had preached in the church on a trial basis. Mason admitted that when he went to hear the young man, he expected to have his patience tried. Instead, he was happily surprised to hear clear, forthright sermons. Mason frequently expressed his distaste for "metaphysics and philosophy" in sermons. George Bacon must have agreed because he pleased Mason during the remaining years of the latter's life, and, in fact, became a Mason family confidant.

The Masons led the church music program at the Orange Valley Church. William selected the organ and raised funds for it, partly through a special benefit concert he and Theodore Thomas gave on March 12, 1868, a concert that netted five hundred dollars. A five-thousand dollar organ was installed later that year. William played that organ without accepting salary until "his failing health made it necessary for him to go abroad"; meanwhile his musicianship "made the Orange Valley Church famous far and wide."[3]

A new church edifice, built of blue trap rock from Orange Mountain, was dedicated on June 26, 1868. Two years later the congregation installed a set of ten chimes in the church tower. Private subscription underwrote their cost ($4,200). The largest bell, placed at the top and weighing 2,432 pounds, was presented in the name of Dr. Lowell Mason.[4] These chimes were first rung at a meeting of the Conference of Congregational Churches on June 18, 1870, a meeting moderated by Henry Ward Beecher, one of the sons of Mason's former associate Lyman Beecher.

During the late 1850s, family matters absorbed much of Lowell's attention and energy. The birth of Daniel Gregory and Susie's second son, Walter, in early November 1856 started a chain of events through which Lowell's devotion and sentimentality became especially apparent. The joy of this birth helped offset the sorrow of Johnson Mason's death on November 12, 1856. Lowell and Abby were in Medfield with Lowell's father at the time of his death and through the day of the funeral.

Though Mason's former acquaintances in Medfield were nearly all gone by 1856, a few close friends remained, including George and Mercy Prentiss Davis. In addition to those ties, Mason had business interests in his hometown. Remaining fragmentary records reveal that he had purchased pieces of real estate in earlier years and that he had put some of the deeds in his mother-in-law's name. In a letter to Hinsdale Fisher on August 21, 1840, he agreed to purchase the Adams house for $850 and asked that the deed be made out to "Hannah Gregory who owns the Davis place." He offered to rent the Adams house to Fisher's "society," suggesting that Mason managed Mrs. Gregory's property but let her live on the income it produced.

Various neighbors had helped Johnson Mason during his last years. These kindnesses were acknowledged in several ways. The Rhodes family, who lived nearby, received a turkey unexpectedly one Thanksgiving from the Lowell Masons.[5] A letter written by Abby on August 2, 1856 thanks George and Mercy Davis for giving "the aged ones" rides to church. The Davises lived adjacent to Johnson Mason or with him at the last. The climax to the Mason-Davis relationship came in a letter Lowell wrote them on November 19, 1856:

> We shall not attempt to express our gratitude...for your long continued kindness.... The debt we owe you we can never expect to pay. Yet as a manifestation of our feelings, in part, we must be allowed to present to your daughter, Mary, the pianoforte now in your house as her own personal property.[6]

He added that the instrument had cost $150 when he purchased it.

On January 30, 1858 Lowell wrote a long letter to his two eldest sons, urging them to be more frugal. The letter shows that while the Masons lived in affluence, other values dominated their thinking. The solid relationships within the family are also evident as the aging father expresses himself openly, knowing his sons will understand:

> My dear sons, Daniel G. and Lowell,
> The great thing, that which is always on my mind, is your spiritual good.... I may safely say with regard to both [of you], as with regard to myself also, that we are far, very far from what we ought to be.... Perhaps I cannot do better at this time than to say a few words on...*self-denial* and yet it is a point upon which I am...most unqualified *practically* to utter a word, for how little do I know it in my experience?... I will press towards this mark...the control of the inner man: especially of the fancy, imagination or undue desires after the good things of the world, although they may be quite lawful. ...
>
> Our living...is most expensive; and here I am not going to advocate a penurious, miserly course; you know me too well to suppose this for a moment, but let our income...be what it may, we are not justified in such extravagant expenditures. I feel sure that any judicious sober-minded man would say that our expenses are far too great; not only too great for the amount of money which we may control...[but] too great for our own best good perhaps.... [Daniel's] children are growing up without knowing what self denial means; they have everything that they merely wish for.... I may be justified therefore in saying that they are too much cradled in the lap of luxury.... I may ask how much money is expended on each one or on the three, annually? How many unnecessary books, toys, etc., are purchased—looked at—thrown to make way for something new. ...
>
> But with respect to ourselves, too, we ought to cut off little indulgences.... The table...is too luxuriously supplied.... Plainer food and less of it would often be better.... [Regarding] apparel. We might be much more economical here. Ladies and gentlemen are extravagant, the *dresses* abound too much—there are too many new ones bought without any regard to price, or to the real pecuniary ability of the purchaser.... Mother never sought gratification in this way. I have sometimes forced upon her comparatively rich things, but she has never sought for them, and has denied herself often. But I do not know that the ladies are much more in fault than the gentlemen—I would recommend that the gentlemen set an example.... How many coats a year? For myself one; but this may not do for you. ...
>
> I have read over this letter; it is very unsatisfactory to me, and yet, I think, imperfect as it is, I will send it; for my sons will not misinterpret it. ...
>
> And now I pray for God's blessing upon you...to write to you is almost the only thing left for me to do.
>
> Affectionate father,
> Lowell Mason

But Lowell was soon distracted from these comparatively minor concerns by the serious worry over his infant grandson Walter who became ill in February 1858 and seemed "to wilt away, drooping along from day to day without improvement."[7] Inasmuch as the fifteen-month-old boy had been a healthy, playful child, it was with surprise and alarm that the family watched his strength wane. On the evening of February 16, Lowell visited Cosy Cottage, and as he later recalled,

> I went into the room where I last saw him alive, then in the last struggles of death, his little frame trembling all over.... I knelt by him—the Doctors Beyham [?] and Richards were standing watching over him. My heart was full... as it never was before, for death had never come so near me until then. I got up and bid him goodbye forever—no... not forever, but for all that which we call time.... I left the house and went to my bed. At about two [A.M.] Dr. Richards came up and told me of the death of the beloved one which had taken place at one.[8]

In his memo book for February 17, Mason wrote simply, "This morning... died my lovely little grandson Walter... aged 15 months and 16 days—a little angel sent by God on a mission of love; he has done his work and has gone to his Father... above."

Expressing his grief over Walter's death, Mason wrote letters brimming with religiosity and sentimentality (qualities characteristic of his era and of his personality). In a letter to Killip on February 22, 1858, he wrote,

> On Friday last we buried my dearly beloved little Grandson.... It has been a sore trial to us all. Death has never come so near to me before. I have been married more than forty years and never lost a Child or Grandchild before. We sang the... hymn at the funeral of the dear little one, "As the sweet flower scents the moon, etc." My son, the father of the departed one, starts today for a Western business tour.

Daniel Gregory Mason traveled for four or more weeks, going at least as far as Chicago. In a letter March 10 his father refers to Daniel's spiritual struggles and reveals an evangelical zeal for Susie's "conversion":

> Dear Son,
> I have felt from the beginning that the death of our beloved one would be the turning point with you and probably with Susie. You know not how thankful I feel that you seem now to be viewing the whole matter rightly—press forward and be watchful—be vigilant for the enemy is constantly on the lookout for our fall. But now it is a great thing to bring in Susie—I cannot be reconciled to anything short of her becoming a Christian indeed. For this you must labor; it is not too much perhaps to say that in all human probability her salvation is placed in your hands. . . .
> Your affectionate father,
> Lowell

On October 28, 1858, Susie gave birth to her fourth and last child, John Belcher Mason. Yet grief hovered over their family. It was becoming increasingly evident that their daughter Abigail (born in 1852) was mentally retarded. Lowell's letter to Daniel Gregory on March 24, 1863 deals with this sorrow as fully as any passage in the extant family letters (the matter seems not to have been mentioned often):

> Elizabeth has just returned from Orange where she saw Susie and she brings the news that Abby is to go to Saxonville. I am glad. She will be in a quiet place, and I doubt not will receive the kindest attention. Poor little Abby, my heart bleeds. She can never *here* be a partaker of those pleasures which come from intellectual and musical culture or certainly only in a very small measure. All that can be done for her is to make her physical condition as happy as may be, and this I believe they will try to do at Mr. Stone's.

Neither Elizabeth nor Mr. Stone is otherwise identified. It is not clear whether Abby was placed in a public or private institution or in a private home. She apparently did not live a normal life span, for in 1889 Abigail Mason referred to the daughter of the William Masons as her "only granddaughter."

Through all these years Lowell maintained a close relationship with his grandson Lolo. Much correspondence passed between them, particularly during the fall of 1860 when Mason traveled to Chicago, St. Louis, and Louisville. Mason focused on things eleven-year-old Lolo could appreciate, such as food he savored and scenes he enjoyed. Mason was lecturing and teaching in churches, normal schools, teachers' institutes, theological seminaries, and public schools. Some of his letters mention these activities, while others give insight into his feelings, habits, and personality. "The Lake Michigan water," he wrote October 9, "is very good but not so good as our Silver Spring water." The previous day he had commented on finding sweet sickle pears and mentioned his breakfast of "a little sausage, fried mush, corn cake, and potato with coffee," eaten heartily, it seems, though "I was not much hungry." On October 11 he reported having eaten oysters and "now suffering for it, for they almost always hurt me."

During his trip Mason visited many friends and acquaintances, such as E. Towner Root in Chicago. Part of the time William B. Bradbury was with him in Chicago. On October 8 Mason reported this amusing incident to Lolo:

> You tell Uncle Lowell that Mr. Bradbury has drawn in a lottery a beautiful silver tea set . . . one coffee pot, two teapots, sugar, cream, and [?] bowl, worth perhaps a hundred dollars. He bought a ticket at a fair and gave one dollar for it, and last Saturday evening the lottery was drawn and Mr. Bradbury drew the prize. I told Mr. B. that he would make money anyhow, that if he should be taken and stuck in the mud in the lake with his head down, he would find out how to make something. He is all the time at some money making business.

Descriptive reporting to Lolo continued during the St. Louis portion of the trip. In that city Mason stayed at Barnum's Hotel at the corner of Second and Walnut Streets. He remained in St. Louis only four or five days before going on to Louisville. At the levee Mason saw "ever so many steamers . . . all large . . . carrying many passengers. I went aboard one and had the idea of riding down the river myself!" But that same evening, October 24, he went to a church and "spoke to the vestry full of people until past nine," having spent the forenoon with "one or two schools...to visit." From St. Louis, Lowell gave one of his rare comments on his well-being; despite the rigors of traveling and teaching and despite approaching age sixty-nine, he said simply, "I go on—getting tired in the day and resting at night."

Sometimes Mason gave his grandson detailed information about his professional engagements:

October 24, 1860, 11:30 A.M.

I have this morning been out to visit the high school. I met about 200 children from 12 to 16 yrs. of age. I talked to them, asking them questions and sang to them for about an hour. The superintendent of schools was with us. After we came out and as I took my leave of him, he told me my visit to the St. Louis Schools will long be remembered, that I had won the hearts of a thousand children and young persons, who would forget me never. These school visits have been very pleasant and successful. I have now done with them, as I suppose forever; I am glad to have met the children of St. Louis and shall never forget them.

I have now only one engagement remaining...to lecture at the Rev. Porter's [?] Church this evening. I am tired and need rest. . . .

Less correspondence is extant from Louisville, though a letter dated October 26, 1860 indicates that Lowell had seen his brother Johnson, Johnson's wife, one of their daughters, and her husband. The disappointing lack of detail in many of his letters is offset by occasional frank revelations. In a letter to Lolo nearly two years later, Mason expressed his feelings about the Civil War:

August 7, 1862, Wooster, Ohio

There is a great deal of war enthusiasm here now—men are enlisting now much faster than before the President's call for drafting. They think they had better enlist and get the various bounties, rather than be drafted and have to go without any bounty. I feel solicitation for your father, and for uncles Lowell and William. I do not feel as if I can give them up to go to the war—nor can they either of them be spared. I hope they will, if drafted, find substitutes. I had rather pay for substitutes than have them go—but dear Lolo, perhaps were you 24 years old and had a suitable education I would not object to you going, for it is surely the duty of all the people to aid in putting down the rebellion and young unmarried men are the ones upon whom we may chiefly depend. . . .

Mason seldom aired his political views, though in a letter to Killip on December 9, 1861 he wrote,

As to your political views I speak nor *for* or *against* them. I do not know—I am incapable of judging what is best. But I have for many years doubted the success of our republican [government]. . . . We are too democratic—more restraint is needful. There is not intelligence enough among the people to sustain universal suffrage, etc. *But again I say I do not know.* What will be the result of the war? I think it will purify to some extent. I do not agree with you that we cannot subdue. I believe we can but it may require a "long pull and a heavy [?] pull and a pull together." It is a terrible state of things. . . .

Mason had assessed the painful realities of the Civil War more accurately than had many of his overly optimistic countrymen in 1861. Perhaps the most characteristic comments he made on the subject were expressed in a letter to Daniel Gregory and Susie on May 10, 1864: "I have felt as you do in relation to this contest in our country. . . . My prayers are continually that there may be the termination of battle, bringing submission on the part of our foes and peace, with righteousness, truth, freedom to the land."

Mason's continued love of children is apparent in letters of his retirement years. He recalls taking Lolo at age five or six downtown on the omnibus, tumbling him headfirst in the snow, and going for walks with him. Ignoring his own alarm at the overindulgence of his grandchildren, Mason often alludes to gifts he has sent them. Perhaps his most unusual episode of indulging them concerned the pony he purchased and kept for Lolo, seemingly in 1859, even though Lolo was away in school in New York City. Playful letters refer to the cost of keeping the animal, alluding to the tab being run up for Lolo, then adding, "to relieve you of all the trouble. . . I have transferred the pony to myself, thereby paying the bill." Mason was proud of all his grandchildren. In 1859, for instance, he wrote (again to Lolo), "Uncle Henry [was] here a few days ago. Eddy, 'a fine looking one,' bids fair to be as fine a little grandson as any of you. I have now four grandsons and one granddaughter."

Mason's interest in children extended to children of friends, such as Frederick Root, son of George F. Root. Frederick recalled years later that when Lowell was a house guest in their home in North Reading, Massachusetts, he often "unbent to be humorous and entertaining to the children." Later he added, "but he was also serious with us. . . . It usually fell to me to drive the conveyance which he took for his frequent calls on Professor Park. . . while they were collaborating on *The Sabbath Hymn and Tune Book*." On one of the trips with Frederick to Andover (about seven miles away) Mason reflected on teachers being promoted downward:

> When you study and work with a subject as long as I have worked with music, Frederick, everything takes on a clearness and a simplicity that isn't apparent to you when you are young. There are undoubtedly other subjects about which this is true, but music is certainly such a one. In place of new, inexperienced teachers teaching the beginners, it is these older and more competent teachers who should be introducing the subject. Therefore, my boy, I would start the new teachers in the upper grades and promote them down, a class or a grade a year, as they ripened in service.[9]

As the decade of the 1860s got underway, Lowell Mason became more and more an old man. Though his retirement removed him somewhat from the professional concerns that had so long absorbed him, he continued to be interested in his profession. A poignant statement of his sense of retirement appears in a letter to an organist who had appealed for help in finding a position. Apparently the two did not know one another. Nonetheless, Mason sent this kind letter:

October 14, 1861

Mr. Thomas Bissell,
Dear Sir,
With all my heart I wish I could help you, but I am now so much out of the way of all musical men and doings that my opportunities are rare and small. I live fifteen miles out of New York and seldom go into town so that I am wholly cut off from musical associations and influences.

I shall re-enclose your letter to my sons, asking them to make inquiry for you, but I must tell you frankly that there are not a few who *profess* to play the organ in N. Y. looking for places. I doubt not that my sons shall do what they can, and I shall request them to throw in an advertisement for you gratis, and I think they will do it. My son, Daniel Gregory Mason, is himself an Episcopalian and may therefore be more likely to hear of a place in an Epis. Ch. . . . .

Lowell Mason

The Final Years

The evening of his life was long and tranquil. . . . The churches and universities had recognized his work with grateful and public appreciation; and privately he had the singular felicity of a home . . . [that] was the continual resort of friends and pupils of his earlier days, who came to testify their obligation to him, and their love and reverence for him.[10]

Lowell Mason's final years were spent in nearly complete retirement, yet he occasionally taught, composed, lectured, or visited public schools. For instance, he was a guest teacher in a Springfield, Massachusetts high school sometime between 1867 and 1869. Frank H. Foster, a member of that class, recalled that Mason began by asking questions about keys and intervals. Foster felt compelled to answer because no one else dared to speak up. After Foster's fifth or sixth answer, Dr. Mason said, "Why, that boy answers like an old musician!" Then he sang a song to illustrate a point, and the class felt more at ease. Foster remembered Mason as "a rather large man with a fresh complexion, white hair and blue eyes, with the most benevolent and winning expression and charming manner."[11]

Visits to schools were emotional experiences for Mason and for those whom he met there. For those who were being visited, the venerable Dr. Mason was an aging celebrity, someone to see (probably) for the last time. For his part, visiting a particular place often brought back pleasant memories of past associations, starkly contrasting with the realization that he would probably never return. A newspaper account dated June 27, 1867 from Oswego, New York related a "very interesting occasion" in which Mason's visit to a school was marked with speeches of tribute and the presentation of a gift to him, an ebony cane with a "beautiful gold head." Much moved, with tears running down his cheeks, Mason accepted, saying, "It is just what I wanted . . . and will sustain me physically. Nothing could have been more appropriate."

Despite old age, Mason maintained his charm and sense of humor. During a visit to one church, he took a little boy, about six years old, on his knee and was about to teach him a hymn. The child's mother apologized, saying that the boy could not sing. Said Mason, jokingly, "Didn't he ever cry when he was a baby?—Then he can sing!"[12]

Mason tried to help those who requested his help. In a letter to Melvin Lord in March 1865, he referred to a Mr. Wilder of Bangor, Maine, editor of a tunebook Mason Brothers was about to publish, adding,

> I have at his request written a number of tunes for it, and I am requested to allow him to pub. 1/2 doz. of Mr. Zeuner's tunes from Mss. [manuscripts Mason Brothers and Lord owned]. I told him that it would not be proper for me to grant that request without consulting you, and at his request, as also that of my Sons, I now write to ask your permission for him.[13]

For the most part, however, Mason removed himself from active involvement in musical affairs; instead, his final years were spent mainly with family and friends. By 1866 Abby wrote that he was "decidedly in his old age and reminds me so much of his parents."[14] His increasing sentimentality is shown by the following excerpt from a letter to Daniel Gregory on January 11, 1866:

> It was a real comfort to me to receive your note congratulating me on my 74th birthday. . . . I look back with wonder and with gratitude . . . to the way in which thus far I have been led. . . .
>
> All the way of my life I have been blessed and protected, and provided for and now in my old age I have children caring for me with tender solicitude.
>
> A wife too, the wife of my youth, the mother of my children still preserved, and still as ever bent on good to all around. Surely I have cause for gratitude.

One of the happiest occasions of Mason's last years was the celebration of his golden wedding anniversary on September 3, 1867. A description of the event appeared in the *Orange Chronicle* of September 14, 1867:

> One of these very infrequent occasions, a golden wedding, took place last week in Orange. . . . A large gathering of friends from Orange and from Mason's life was assembled at

Silver Spring.... The house and grounds were filled with flowers and with music. [Music was provided by Theodore Thomas and his orchestra.] Men eminent in the musical world were present to express their great reverence for Dr. Mason's great services... and men distinguished in the church were present to express their grateful sense of his distinguished services in behalf of the culture and improvement of our public worship. Great as these services have been, it is probable that time will make them still more highly appreciated.

A singular fact connected with this celebration was the presence of the entire bridal party... with only a single exception. There were six in all, the bride and her two bridesmaids, the bridegroom with his two friends. Only one of the groomsmen has passed away.... The others were all present.[15]

Within a month after this celebration, Mason was in Boston briefly, but had returned to Orange by October 8 when he wrote to Melvin Lord, offering the first reference to his failing eyesight: "I owe you an apology for neglecting so long to write, and also for omitting to call on you when in Boston. I write but little now for my eyes only enable me to do so on a bright & clear morning." By the time of his death, Mason was almost blind.

One of the most detailed accounts of his declining years appears in Abigail's letter of March 3, 1868 to Hattie Mason Hillyer, daughter of Johnson Mason, Jr.:

Your uncle was greatly interested in your letter. He thinks more of remaining friends and early associations as business is mostly laid aside. He often speaks of the day your father spent with him at an institute. . . . He gradually loses strength. He rides to Orange occasionally but he has not been to Church for three months. The least draft gives him a cold and that prostrates him at once. He went to Medfield last September [1867] for two days and called to see several friends feeling that it would be his last visit.

Mason continued to travel in spite of the difficulties involved. In June 1869 he was honored by the executive committee of the National Peace Jubilee and Great Musical Festival in Boston under the leadership of Patrick S. Gilmore (1829-1892). In its formal invitation, the executive committee quoted a motion passed unanimously during a planning session:

Voted, that the venerable Dr. Lowell Mason, who has done so much, during a long and useful life, in behalf of the art of music, be invited to unite with us in our... musical celebration... as our *honorary guest.*[16]

Mason's reply, dated May 29, 1869, includes this passage:

I beg leave to present to the Executive Committee my grateful sense of the distinguished honor conferred upon me.... Unless detained by physical inability, I shall certainly do myself the pleasure of attending at least a part of the most interesting exercises proposed ... but ... the infirmities of age are upon me, and indeed I know not what will be on

the morrow. Should anything occur to prevent my attendance, I shall endeavor to give you
early notice....Should I be able to come, my home will be with my son in Brookline.

He did attend the Peace Jubilee, but the happiness of the occasion was
eclipsed within days by the unexpected death of Daniel Gregory Mason on
June 24, 1869. "For a few months his health had been failing, and in April . . . he
left New York for Carlsbad, whither he was directed by his physicians, with the
hopes of a speedy and permanent cure. His malady, however, did not yield to
the medical treatment of this celebrated resort" and he left there for
Schwalbach, Germany, where he died.[17] Daniel Gregory himself seemed to
believe he was stronger; a few days before his death he had written his
associates in New York that he would be back with them in September.

The death of his eldest son must have been a devastating blow to the aging
Mason, but remaining letters offer little comment on the subject. Of course,
cataracts were gradually blinding Mason, so he wrote few letters, and those few
were often written in crayon on wrapping paper so that he could see a little
better. This practice made his correspondence cumbersome and hard to
preserve. Further, some of his close friends had died and others (such as the
Bacons and Webbs) lived nearby. Mason probably wrote to George F. Root,
then in Chicago working at the music firm of Root and Cady, but
unfortunately, their correspondence was lost in the great Chicago fire of 1871.

Mason continued to be interested in his family and friends despite failing
vision and other infirmities. He remained more and more at home; in August
1870 he wrote that he had not been out to communion services at his church for
about a year.[18] His days were brightened by visits from friends such as
Theodore F. Seward, who recalled that Mason liked to reminisce about his
career and to pore over his professional work as his strength allowed. Seward
and Mason issued *The Pestalozzian Music Teacher* in 1871 based on
approximately sixty articles published serially in *The New York Musical
Review and Gazette* between 1855 and 1857. Mason was the author, but he
gave credit to Seward, his friend and former pupil, for help in getting the
material ready. The final form actually required little effort. Seward remarked
that revision took longer than necessary because Mason had such a good time
working on it.[19]

Seward also noted that Mason wore a velvet skullcap (in which he was
sometimes pictured) when there was "the least hint of frostiness in the
atmosphere."[20] Others remarked on the "invariable skull cap, knit scarf and lap
robe"; the knit scarf that "he wore in summer and winter" was at least fourteen
inches wide, had gay colors at the ends and a long fringe.[21]

Mason continued his correspondence as well as he could, adding at times
something like, "I can hardly see to write, & thus must apologize for the
appearance of my letter." [22] In a letter to John W. Dickinson, principal of the

State Normal School in Westfield, Massachusetts about eight months before his death, Mason spoke of his health, activities, and interests:

December 12, 1871

I think that on the whole I am gaining though I have an occasional drawback. My sickness has left my mouth and teeth in a shattered condition, and my sight has been much impaired by it. I ride out every pleasant day, and go up to Mary's and Susie's, post office . . . etc. Martin my servant and waiter [Henry William Martin] is *always on hand;* he is very intelligent and had a much better school education than myself. He has read all Shakespeare's plays, much of Milton, and has quite a considerable knowledge of books. . . . He has been in Europe, Africa, and America and was born and educated in Asia.

A typical letter to a grandchild appeared in those last months as well. Like so many others, this one dwells upon matters a child might enjoy and admonishes the reader to "be good." Addressed to Henry's second son, then about ten years old, the letter was dated December 1, 1871.

My dear grandson, Allan Gregory Mason[23]
A charming letter came to me yesterday from you, thanking me for apples "just what you wanted." Well, I did not know that you wanted them, but seeing some large, red, fair apples, I thought of my dear grandchildren in Boston or Brookline, and I thought that they would be pleased with them. So I had them sent to you. And now I am fully repaid for my trouble by the receipt of three little letters, one from each of my grandchildren in Brookline. Thanks, dear Alan, that you contributed one to the number. Now when you eat one of the large red apples think of your old grandpa and grandma in Orange. They often speak of you, always pray for you, and never cease to love you dearly. *Be good*—good to father and mother and brothers. Never be cross and ill-natured, and speak kind words and do kind deeds, one to another, so will you be happy and blessed.

Your affectionate grandpa,
    Lowell Mason, almost eighty years

And much love to papa and mama, and Eddy and Henry

In the final few months Mason's mind wandered from time to time. These lapses were, however, of short duration, and for the most part he thought clearly. He was able to appreciate the honor bestowed upon him by his hometown, Medfield, in naming a new public school building for him. Upon hearing that a tablet was to be placed over the main entrance, reading "Mason School," he wrote in December 1871,

Such an honor *I* do not certainly deserve, but I need not say I shall feel most grateful for it, and shall try to do a little to express my gratitude for such a distinction. Perhaps the next Summer I may see this building if life and health be spared, though I feel no assurance that I shall see my native state again.[24]

Less than three months before his death, Mason reported at length on a meeting with his former adversary, George W. Lucas. Mason dictated a report of this meeting for his secretary to send to Melvin Lord. It shows Mason's attitudes and his lucid state of mind:

Orange, N.J., May 23, 1872

Melvin Lord, Esq.,

Dear Sir,

About three weeks since just as I had sat down to dinner, at the ringing of the doorbell, I was told that an old man had entered the house and wished to see me. I said to the servant, "Ask the man his name," who replied, "He refuses to give his name, but says you know him very well." At that moment, the inner door opened & without being invited, he entered where we were sitting round the dining table, came right up to me, put his face very near to mine, saying, "Why, don't you know me?" Mrs. Mason, who was sitting at the opposite side of the table, said, "Mr. Lucas" and notwithstanding his shabby...appearance, I then recognized him; he immediately commenced a random harangue, consisting mostly of broken assertions, telling how he had labored with me & for me until as our dinner was all getting cold, I asked him if he would take some dinner, thinking I would fill a plate, & put it at another table. He said he would lay aside his overcoat, sit in the other room, take a cup of tea & get rested. Mrs. Mason immediately ordered a cup of tea; he retired (but not out of sight). We proceeded with our dinner. A bottle of claret stood on the table, which I told the servant to remove. After we were through eating, I said, "Will you come now & take some dinner"; he replied, "Yes" & came & took his seat at the table.

Mrs. Mason filled his plate; when he commenced eating, he resumed his talk, which really was little more than a repetition of the same thing over & over again. He told me that he had not come to beg money from me, but he was determined to see me. He said I need not have had the bottle removed, for he had done drinking. I took occasion to say in reply to his assertions of friendship, "Mr. Lucas, I have heard repeatedly of the abuses you have heaped upon me in your public addresses, etc." "Oh," he replied, "you have been misinformed"; this kind of unmeaning talk continued until I began to think it was time for him to go & I said to him, "Mr. Lucas, where are you going tonight?" When he said, "How much are you going to give me?" I answered, "I have given you as much as I ought to give you already." He then pulled from his pocket a two dollar bank note & a twenty-five cent bill, saying "There is all the money that I have." I then handed him a ten dollar bill & having taken the precaution to have a carriage at the door, I told him, "If you go now, you may perhaps reach Albany before morning." He had before told me that he would like to go to Albany, & then cross over into Massachusetts where he was known & would be taken care of. He got in, & was driven to the station, where he would take the cars for New York; the above is a very brief & imperfect report of the conversation I had with him, but the substance of it is correct.

Yesterday I received a paper published at Pittsfield, Mass. "The Berkshire County Eagle" containing an article about Mr. Lucas, which I have cut out & will send you; the paper is dated May 16; it would seem that Mr. Lucas went directly from here to Pittsfield, & there resumed his old habits. [Here Mason added in his own handwriting] I have tho't that you would be interested in the above narration. What a poor miserable creature has Lucas become? Thanks to Him who has made us to differ.

By Amanuensis,
    Truly yours, Lowell Mason[25]

Of the extant Mason letters, this letter has the latest date. It is reasonable to suppose that following that May 23 Mason declined in strength, though his mind remained clear to the last.

On Sunday evening, August 11, 1872, "just at an hour when... in many homes throughout the land, households were praising God in tunes that he had taught them—just then, peacefully," Lowell Mason died.[26] He had lived eighty years, seven months, and three days. Lowell, Jr., who was traveling in Germany with his wife at the time, commented upon hearing the news that his father's life "had become a weariness to him, and... [now] he is freed from those infirmities of the flesh which tried him much."[27]

The funeral was held the following Thursday afternoon (August 15). A procession consisting of carriages and the hearse moved from Silver Spring estate to the Orange Valley Congregational Church where the service began at 2:30. A prelude of quiet organ music preceded the service. The organist was a Mr. Boyce, "well known organist of Dr. Hall's Church, New York City."[28] The singing was led by C. F. Whiting, precentor of the Orange Valley Church (substituting for Lowell Mason, Jr.), S. E. Perkins of the Madison Avenue Baptist Church, New York City, and J. A. Johnson of Orange. Floral arrangements adorned the pulpit, the chancel, and the rosewood casket. Approximately five hundred persons heard the sermon and eulogy by George B. Bacon, including the observation that "no man is worthier of perpetual and sweet memories in all... Christian churches than he whose life and work were so closely interwoven with their worship."[29]

After the service, "amid the tolling of the church bell the procession moved to Rosedale Cemetery, where on a slight elevation, in a single tomb, now rest the remains."[30] On that peaceful hillside simple stones mark the resting places of others who were close to Lowell Mason during his life: Abigail; Lowell Mason, Jr. and his wife Marie; William Mason and his wife Mary Isabelle Webb Mason; Mr. and Mrs. George J. Webb, and their other daughter, Caroline.[31] The stones marking Lowell and Abby Mason's burial places read simply

LOWELL MASON, MUSICAL DOCTOR

Born January 8, 1792
Died August 11, 1872

ABIGAIL GREGORY
His wife

Born July 21, 1797
Died October 11, 1889

Lowell Mason's devotion to his church was memorialized by the family after his death by a stained-glass window in the sanctuary. This window, depicting David "catching on his harp the inspiration of celestial music from angels hovering over him and surrounded by a throng of musicians," carried the inscription "Let the people praise Thee, O God; Let all the people praise Thee!" Beneath these lines is a simple statement: "In Memoriam, LOWELL MASON, Mus. Doc.," with birth and death dates.[32]

Immediately after his death, words of tribute poured forth in the press. Indeed, within the first month after August 11, "the announcement of Dr. Mason's decease has already been carried to every hamlet in the United States. It is an event in which the whole nation is interested, for his name has become a household word.... Not by musicians alone... is it held in reverence."[33] In the words of one columnist,

the spirit of Lowell Mason still lives.... His religious melodies are among the most admired in America. They are heard alike in many of the elegant metropolitan churches, in the village meeting houses and in the camp-meeting groves.... It is especially to Lowell Mason's credit that he understood the requirements of our religious musical public, and that he ably responded to them; and it is to their credit that literally "his praise is in all the churches."[34]

Epilogue

Lowell Mason was ... at the head of the great *musical movement* in America.... He has done what very few could have done. *No foreigner* could have effected it—a man was necessary who understood the *people:* a man who had practical American common-sense enough, and intellectual force enough, and ... religious principle enough, to command the respect, arouse the attention and enlist the sympathies of the peculiar classes he addressed. No mere composer could have done this—no artist—no performer. A strong-minded man was necessary—a teacher, in the best and most comprehensive sense of the term.[1]

When Lowell Mason began his career, Americans had little opportunity for music instruction. Isolated attempts by well-intentioned but inadequately trained singing-school masters were, for the most part, ineffective; certainly they were hampered by the lack of suitable materials and a workable methodology. This situation changed with systematic music education in the public schools, staffed with teachers trained in an appropriate pedagogical system and equipped with specially designed instruction books. These books, the teacher training, and the educational philosophy were, to a large extent, the result of Mason's work.

When Mason began, congregational singing had virtually died out in American churches, and choirs were undisciplined both in conducting themselves and in performing their musical duties. Mason alerted laymen and clergymen alike to the urgency for reform, and he supplied congregations and choirs with manageable new materials. By precept and by example, he worked toward a revival of singing in American churches.

When Mason began, societies of amateur musicians struggled with the limitations imposed by a scarcity of music appropriate to their abilities and desires. He encouraged an upsurge in their performing by providing suitable music in a variety of publications.

When Mason began, Americans had no music criticism per se, very little music journalism, and almost no music scholarship. Through his writings, through his encouragement and patronage of others, and through the gift of his music library to succeeding generations, he opened doors for those who were to surpass him in these areas.

When Mason began, American musicians had to rely heavily upon imported musical instruments to attain top quality and upon imported music publications to attain a wide variety of materials. During his lifetime, Mason helped secure music resources for Americans, partly by undergirding his sons' work with Mason & Hamlin and Mason Brothers. Also, by promoting increased musical participation in America, Mason stimulated the market for a wide range of music products, thereby opening opportunities that American industries met swiftly and well.

Above all, when Mason began his career, American musicians had neither spokesmen nor examples; they had neither direction nor purposes other than meeting the immediate needs of the choir loft, the school room, the local music society, or the family parlor. Mason, along with his dedicated associates, gave musicians and nonmusicians alike a conception of musical participation for all Americans. This conception rejected the aristocratic view of music as a province for the talented, privileged few; rather, it established the democratic ideal of bringing musical participation within the reach of every American.

The music Mason offered to his countrymen followed established standards of propriety with respect to both texts and musical construction. While insisting upon music that was meaningful and within the potential grasp of performers and listeners, Mason nonetheless avoided pandering to the lowest possible level. While encouraging participation, he refused to do so at the expense of such basic requirements as music reading and expressive performance. The standards that Mason upheld removed him, therefore, from the narrow rigors of conservatory-oriented professional musicians and from the zealous amateurism prevalent in certain segments of American society.

Even a superficial view of America today confirms that music activities are vast, far-reaching, and thriving. Public school music programs alone involve millions of students, teachers, and supervisors. To these numbers must be added the music publishers, instrument manufacturers, retailers, composers, arrangers, and editors who provide necessary materials. Church music affects additional millions, and private music organizations reach untold numbers of others. Finally, a mass market for all types of music through various media touches all Americans one way or another.

These music activities have their roots in the work of pioneers such as Lowell Mason. Mason's goal of music participation for all remains a guiding principle of our musical culture. Many of his pedagogical ideas survive, as do many of his hymn tunes. Americans are increasingly conscious of the foundations laid for American culture and, at last, are acknowledging the founders of that culture. Surely in American music, Lowell Mason stands as a towering figure of his time.

Because of his importance, it is fitting that Lowell Mason's life and work should be further studied and that the findings should be widely circulated. His contributions deserve recognition, not continued near obscurity. Yet, in some ways, tributes to Lowell Mason already surround us.

The finest tribute to his work as a composer-arranger lies in the tunes deeply entrenched in our folk culture; millions who have never stopped to read his name in their hymnals know his tunes by memory through repeated usage. The finest tribute to his educational leadership is the music program of American schools—ranging from the first rote songs of our preschoolers to the most accomplished performances of our university choirs. The finest tribute to Lowell Mason's total career is the enormous public support Americans now extend to music and musicians, support that owes much to his pioneering efforts and timeless ideals.

> He was emphatically, *a man of his times*—a man who was needed, and had to *be*—to awaken the slumbering music among the masses of this country, and commence, on a large scale, that general, elementary culture, which was indispensable before greater musical results could be hoped for. We therefore pay this sincere tribute to Mr. Mason, who has labored hardest and best at the first oar of musical progress.[2]

Appendix A

Chronological Listing of Major Events in Lowell Mason's Life

This listing covers major events in Mason's life and career, excluding publications covered in Appendix B. Activities that extended over several years are mentioned under the initial year. For details on these and other events in Mason's life and work, consult the Index below.

1792

Birth, January 8, Medfield, Massachusetts

1805-06

Attends local singing schools

1807

Teaches his first singing school in Athol, Massachusetts

1808-10

Directs the choir in his church; leads the town band

1812

Composes his first musical work, the anthem "Ordination"

1813

Settles in Savannah, Georgia; begins work in a dry goods store; gives first musical performance in Savannah; opens his first singing school there

1815

Becomes choir director and organist at the Independent Presbyterian Church, Savannah

1817

Begins music study with Frederick Abel; begins presenting concerts with his church choir

Marries Abigail Gregory September 3 in Massachusetts

1819

Has first newspaper item on music published; becomes a bank clerk (1819 or 1820) at the Planters Bank

Leads the musical portion of dedication services at the church with President James Monroe in attendance

1820

Birth of son, Daniel Gregory Mason, May 8

1821

Travels to Boston, meets G. K. Jackson; signs contract with the Handel and Haydn Society for issue of his tunebook

1823

Birth of son, Lowell Mason, Jr., June 17

1824

Composes first major hymn tune, "Missionary Hymn"

1826

Delivers a major address on church music in Boston, October

1827

Moves to Boston in August

Is elected president of the Boston Handel and Haydn Society, September; begins work with the Hanover Street Church

1828

Continues church work and directorship of the Handel and Haydn Society in Boston; establishes first children's class in Boston

1829

Birth of son, William Mason, January 24

Takes charge of music at the July 4 commemoration with William L. Garrison (1805-1879) delivering his first antislavery address; John Greenleaf Whittier attends

1830

Meets George J. Webb and William B. Bradbury

Assists William C. Woodbridge at the American Institute of Instruction with a presentation by a boys' class

1831

Birth of son, Henry Mason, October 10

Moves to Bowdoin Street Church to work under Dr. Lyman Beecher again; "America" sung for the first time at July 4 commemorative service, Park Street Church

1832

Teaches at the Perkins Institute for the Blind (1832-36); has first contact with Andover Theological Seminary

Presents children's concert with 100 to 200 children participating, June 13

Presents first of his lectures at the American Institute of Instruction, August 27

1833

Helps organize the Boston Academy of Music, January 8; first annual report issued July 3

Teaches at the Chauncey Hall School (1833-34) and at Mt. Vernon School; opens singing school in Salem

Lectures at the third annual meeting of the American Institute of Instruction in New York City, May 4; lectures to Essex County Teachers' Association, Topsfield, assisted by his children's choir, May 25-26

1834

Joins Joseph A. Keller in teaching singing schools at Salem

Lectures to the American Institute of Instruction, August 22

Supervises preparation of William Smith Porter's book, *The Musical Cyclopedia: of the Principles of Music*

1835

Lectures in New York City; Boston, Newton, New Bedford, Massachusetts; Brunswick, Portland, Maine; Portsmouth, Exeter, New Hampshire; New Haven, Hartford, Connecticut

Teaches in private schools: Chauncey Hall; Fowle's Monitorial School for Girls; Mt. Vernon School; the Academy at Randolph, Massachusetts; the Female Seminary, Ipswich, Massachusetts

1836

Sets up first music class in an American Protestant seminary, Andover Theological Seminary

Initiates teachers' convention in Boston

1837

Organizes Musical Education Society at the Boston Academy of Music

Spends several months in Europe (April 25-November 1)

Teaches without salary at the Hawes School in Boston, beginning in November and continuing for the remainder of the school year

1838

Begins teaching music in the Boston Public Schools under the resolution passed August 28 by the School Committee

1841

Is music director-conductor of the Association of City Choirs, a group of 200 to 300 singers

Has charge of vocal music in all the grammar schools in Boston. Teaches at Fowle's Monitorial School

Lectures in New York City before the Lyceum of Rutgers Institute. Also lectures in Schenectady, Albany, Troy, New York; Groton, Westfield, Needham, Medfield, Plainfield, Chesterfield, Massachusetts; Keene, New Hampshire; Woodstock, Vermont

1843

Accepts church position at Central Congregational Church in December, beginning January 7, 1844

Travels to Rochester, New York, for Sixth Annual Music Convention; 518 persons enrolled

1844

Resigns his position at Andover Theological Seminary

1845

Is dismissed from the Boston Public Schools (fall)

Joins Horace Mann Institutes (work continues for seventeen years)

Assists William Russell with his book *Elements of Musical Articulation with Illustrations in Vocal Music by Lowell Mason* (published 1845)

1846

Is reinstated by the Boston Public Schools for half the supervision of the school music program

Convenes the teachers' convention at Tremont Temple and throws H. W. Day out of the meeting August 18

Makes trips of 2 to 8 days each to Lebanon, New Hampshire; Bennington, Vermont; Hartford, Connecticut; Cleveland, Ohio; Rochester, New York (twice)

1847

Teaches at the State Normal School, West Newton, Massachusetts (1847-51)

Convenes teachers' convention with 1000 attendees

Lectures at Pawtucket, Rhode Island Teachers Institute at the invitation of Henry Barnard, commissioner of Rhode Island Public Schools

1848

Marriage of Daniel Gregory Mason and Susan Belcher Headden, January 20

Birth of first grandchild, Lowell (Lolo), November 11

Goes to an Institute of Common School Teachers at Athol, Massachusetts

Attends his last institute with Horace Mann in the fall; works at an institute in Greenwich, Connecticut with G.B. Emerson

Convenes teachers' convention with 1000 attendees

1850

Teaches at an institute in Framingham, Massachusetts, April 15-20

Publishes articles in *The Choral Advocate and Singing Class Journal*

1851

Retires from Boston public schools and other work in Boston; last meeting of the teachers' convention with Mason and Webb, 1200 attendees

Considers George F. Root's plan for a three-month music teachers' institute

Prepares to travel extensively in Europe and then to relocate in New York City

Publishes the address on church music delivered to choir members July 8 at the farewell party

1852

Travels in England and Europe with Abby, part of the time with William and Henry

Death of his mother, May 26

Birth of granddaughter Abigail, November 8

1853

Gives keynote address at the first meeting of the New York Normal Musical Institute, April 25

Gives his third and fourth lectures to the American Institute of Instruction, New Haven, Connecticut, August 17-18

Became music director at Fifth Avenue Presbyterian Church, New York City in May

Publishes *Musical Letters from Abroad*

1854

Teaches at the Union Theological Seminary, New York City (1854-55)

Moves to Silver Spring estate, Orange, New Jersey

Helps son Henry and Emmons Hamlin establish Mason & Hamlin

1855

Receives honorary doctor of music degree from New York University

Publishes *Pestalozzian Music Teaching,* a series of sixty-one articles in *New York Musical Review and Gazette* (1855-57)

1856

Birth of grandson Walter, November 1 (?)

Death of his father, November 12

1857

Marriage of William Mason and Mary Isabelle Webb, March 12

Marriage of Henry Mason and Helen Augusta Palmer, December 24

1858

Death of grandson Walter, February 17

Birth of grandson George Webb Mason, April 7

Birth of grandson John Belcher Mason, October 10

Works with Root at the North Reading, Massachusetts Institute, June-July

Publishes a series of articles called "Choirs" in the *New York Musical Review and Gazette* (1858-59)

1859

Birth of grandson Edward Palmer Mason, June 13

1860

Goes into partnership with Root and Bradbury in book publishing

Goes to Massachusetts to attend the Waltham Institute but lumbago forces him to rest at the Webbs' home in Boston instead

Teaches and lectures in Chicago, part of the time with Bradbury, September-October

Teaches and lectures in St. Louis, Missouri and Louisville, Kentucky, October

1861

Birth of grandson Alan Gregory Mason, August 17

Birth of grandson Marion Otis Mason, October 20

Works in New England at the North Reading Normal School with Root (summer) and for five weeks at conventions and institutes (fall)

1862

Works with Root in Wooster, Ohio at a teachers' meeting

Spends three weeks in Massachusetts at institutes, November

1863

Birth of granddaughter Mary Wilhelmina Mason, April 15

Publishes *A Glance at Pestalozzianism,* an address delivered before the American Institute of Instruction in New Haven, Connecticut in 1853

1864

Birth of grandson Henry Lowell Mason, August 14

1865

Teaches at an institute in Massachusetts, November

1867

Celebrates his golden wedding anniversary, September 3

Assists T. F. Seward and W. B. Bradbury in the compilation of *The Temple Choir* (1867)

1868

Presents fifth and last lecture to the American Institute of Instruction, Pittsfield, Massachusetts, August

Teaches in a high school in Springfield, Massachusetts as a guest teacher

1869

Attends the National Peace Jubilee in Boston as a special guest, June

Death of Daniel Gregory Mason in Germany, June 24

1871

Continues writing letters, continues interest in education and the teachers' institutes

Publishes *The Pestalozzian Music Teacher; A Brief Presentation of the Elementary Principles of Music; Elements of Music, Presented in the Form of Interrogation*

1872

Writes to Melvin Lord on May 23 about George Lucas' visit

Assists T. F. Seward and C. G. Allen in the preparation of their book, *The Coronation*

Dies peacefully at home, August 11

Appendix B

Lowell Mason's Music Publications

The works below are listed with titles shortened for convenience. Coeditors are indicated in parentheses, as are certain other kinds of information. Works in which Mason only assisted or was acknowledged as "an inspiration" to the author or editor are not included.

Church Music

The Boston Handel and Haydn Society Collection of Church Music 1822
Select Chants, Doxologies.. 1824
Choral Harmony 1828-30
The Choir, or Union Collection 1832
Lyra Sacra.. 1832
Sacred Melodies (Webb) 1833
Sentences, or Short Anthems, Hymn Tunes, Chants 1834
The Sacred Harp or Eclectic Harmony (T. B. Mason) 1834
The Boston Collection of Anthems, Choruses 1834
The Boston Academy's Collection of Church Music.............................. 1835
Occasional Psalm and Hymn Tunes (serial) 1836
The Seraph (serial) 1838-40
The Modern Psalmist 1839
The Boston Anthem Book 1839
Carmina Sacra 1841
The Harp (T. B. Mason).. 1841
The Sacred Harp or Beauties of Church Music, Vol. 1 (T. B. Mason) 1841
Chapel Hymns 1842
Book of Chants 1842
Songs of Asaph 1843
Musical Service of the Protestant Episcopal Church............................. 1843
The Psaltery (Webb) 1845
The Choralist (serial) 1847
The National Psalmist (Webb) 1848
The Congregational Tune-Book (Webb)... 1848
Fifty-Nine Select Psalm and Hymn Tunes 1849
The Hymnist (William Mason) (serial, two issues) 1849
The Hymnist 1850
Cantica Laudis (Webb)... 1850
The New Carmina Sacra. 1850
Mason's Hand-Book of Psalmody. 1852

Congregational Church Music, Part I (Novello et al.) .... 1852-53?
The Hallelujah 1854
The Sabbath Hymn and Tune Book (Park, Phelps) 1859
The People's Tune Book 1860
The New Sabbath Hymn and Tune Book (Park, Phelps) 1866
Carmina Sacra Enlarged: The American Tune Book 1869
Congregational Church Music (Novello et al.) (Compressed Score Edition) 1869

Children's Books

The Juvenile Psalmist 1829
The Juvenile Lyre (Ives) 1831
Sabbath School Songs 1833
The Sabbath School Harp 1836
The Juvenile Singing School (Webb) 1837
The Juvenile Songster .... 1837-38?
Juvenile Music for Sunday Schools 1839
   (sometimes listed as *Juvenile Music* or
   Juvenile Music for Sabbath Schools)
Little Songs for Little Singers 1840
The Boston School Song Book 1841
The American Sabbath School Singing Book 1843
The Primary School Song Book (Webb) 1846
The Song-Book of the School-Room (Webb) 1847
The Song Garden, Parts I, II 1864
The Song Garden, Part III. 1866

Glee and Part-Song Books; Choral Works

Selections for the Choir of the Boston Academy 1836
The Boston Academy's Collection of Choruses 1836
The Odeon (Webb) 1837
The Lyrist (Webb) 1838
The Boston Glee Book 1838
The Gentlemen's Glee Book 1841
Twenty-One Madrigals, Glees, Part-Songs (Webb) 1843
The Vocalist (Webb) 1844
The Boston Chorus Book 1846
The Glee Hive (Webb) 1851
The Young Men's Singing Book (Root) 1855
The New Odeon (Webb) 1855
Asaph, or the Choir Book (William Mason) 1861

Individual, Sheet Music Publications

"Ordination" .... undated, composed 1812
"From Greenland's Icy Mountains" 1824
"Watchman! Tell Us of the Night" 1830
"Hymn for the Fatherless and Widow Society" 1832
"Lafayette Music, a Dirge, Requiem, and Ode" (Webb). 1834

"Select Pieces of Sacred Music"...1835
"Columbia's Birth-day, Again We Behold"...1836
"Collection of Anthems and Hymns" (three pieces)................................1836?
"I Will Extol Thee, My God, O King" 1836
"Thanksgiving Anthem" 1840
"Three Patriotic Songs"..1842
"I Was Glad When They Said Unto Me"..1842
Periodical Psalmody (serial, only one issue) 1842
"Songs of Chenaniah, No. 1" 1844
"Gloria in Excelsis" 1844
"Songs Prepared for the City Celebration" (July 4) 1845
"Christ Hath Arisen: A Carol for Easter-Day" 1863
"Duty's Call"...1868
"Our Labor Here Is Done".................................... undated, composed 1869
"With Loving Favor Crowned" .... undated, composed 1870
"Ode: Again the Voice of God" ....undated
"On Thy Church, O Power Divine"...undated
"Sentence: Come Unto Me" ....undated
"Wedding Hymn: Now the Sacred Seal" ....undated
"Christmas Carol" ....undated
"How Beautiful Upon the Mountains" ....undated
"I Love the Lord" (quadruple chant);
  "He That Dwelleth" ....undated
"Four Chants" ....undated

Miscellaneous

Church Psalmody (texts only) (Greene) 1831
Manual of Church Psalmody (texts only)
  (Greene, Babcock) 1832
Spiritual Songs for Social Worship (Hastings)...................................1832
Union Hymns, adapted to Social Meetings and Family Worship (texts only) (Green,
Babcock) 1834
Manual of the Boston Academy of Music 1834
The Musical Library (Webb) (serial) 1835-36
Lessons in Vocal Music..1838-39
Musical Exercises for Singing Schools 1838
Vocal Exercises and Solfeggios..1842
The Cherokee Singing Book (Guess)...1846
Large Musical Exercises 1851
Musical Notation in a Nutshell 1854
School Songs and Hymns...for the Massachusetts Teachers' Institutes 1854
The Singing School, or Elements of Musical Notation..............................1854
Guide to Musical Notation 1855
Sacred Songs for Family and Social Worship (Hastings)..........................1855
Mason's Normal Singer...for Singing Classes, Schools, and Social Circles 1856
Mason's Mammoth Exercises...1856
The Elements of Music and Its Notation, After the Interrogatory Manner..............1869

Notes

Frequently cited names and titles in the notes below are shortened to the following abbreviations:

LM   Lowell Mason

HLM   Henry Lowell Mason, grandson of Lowell Mason: Reference to him or to his manuscript biography at Yale University, Beinecke Rare Book and Manuscript Library

WmM   William Mason, son of Lowell Mason

BPL   Boston Public Library

JRME   *Journal of Research in Music Education*

DJM   *Dwight's Journal of Music*

MW   *The Musical World and New York Musical Times*

NEM   *New England Magazine*

Note: Unless otherwise indicated, the letters and other archival materials cited below are in the possession of Yale University as part of the Lowell Mason Papers now housed in the Beinecke Rare Book and Manuscript Library.

Chapter 1

1.   William Lyman Mason, *A Record of the Descendants of Robert Mason of Roxbury, Massachusetts* (Milwaukee: Burdick, Armitage & Allan, 1891) provides genealogical information. William, son of Timothy Battelle Mason, was Lowell Mason's nephew.

2.   Alexander W. Thayer, "Lowell Mason," *DJM* 39 (November 22, 1879): 186.

3.   LM to George and Mercy Prentiss Davis, June 1, 1852.

4.   LM to his grandson Lowell, III (Lolo), December 4, 1859.

5.   HLM, 53.

6.   HLM, 52.

7.   Ibid.

8.   William S. Tilden, *The History of the Town of Medfield, Massachusetts* (n.p., 1887), 206.

9.   Samuel F. Smith, "Recollections of Lowell Mason," *NEM* 11 (January 1895): 649.

10. Letter in the Rare Books Division, BPL. The "H. & H. Coll." refers to *The Boston Handel and Haydn Society Collection* (1822), Mason's first tunebook.

11. Herbert Chandler Thrasher, *250 Years of Music in Providence, Rhode Island, 1636-1886* (n.p., n.d.), 7.

12. James William Thompson, "Music and Musical Activities in New England, 1800-1838," (Ph.D. diss., George Peabody College for Teachers, 1962), 133, 140.

13. HLM, 66, quoting from "Memorial of Oliver Shaw" (Providence, RI: n.p., 1884).

14. Francis H. Jenks, "Lowell Mason," *NEM* 11 (January 1895): 655.

15. Lillian B. Miller, *Patrons and Patriotism: The Encouragement of the Fine Arts in the United States, 1790-1860* (Chicago: The University of Chicago Press, 1966), 12.

16. H. Earle Johnson, *Hallelujah, Amen! The Story of the Handel and Haydn Society of Boston* (Boston: Bruce Humphries, 1965), 43.

17. John Sullivan Dwight, "Music in Boston," in Justin Winsor's *The Memorial History of Boston* (Boston: Ticknor, 1881), 4: 417.

18. Louis C. Elson, *The National Music of America and Its Sources* (Boston: L. C. Page & Co., 1900), 276.

19. Medora F. Perkerson, *White Columns in Georgia* (New York: Rinehart & Co., 1952), 100. Many of the original homes of the 1700s remain. Unlike many Southern cities, Savannah escaped Sherman's armies. See chapter 15, Perkerson.

20. Robert Carse, *Ports of Call* (New York: Charles Scribner's, 1967), 296.

21. HLM, 80-83. Also quoted by Daniel Gregory Mason (grandson of LM) in "How Lowell Mason Travelled to Savannah," *NEM* 26 (April 1902): 238-40.

22. Summarized from various issues of the *Savannah Daily Gazette*, 1817, by Margaret Freeman LaFar, "Lowell Mason's Varied Activities in Savannah," *Georgia Historical Quarterly* 28 (September 1941): 115.

23. HLM, 90. Mr. Mason added that his grandfather's diary was before him as he wrote. Unfortunately, the diaries of the Savannah years have been lost. According to information provided the author, July 1970, by Helen Mason Endicott, daughter of HLM, a number of items were stolen from her father in his last years, including some primary materials on LM.

24. Thomas Gamble, "The Father of American Church Music—Lowell Mason," *Christian Observer*, June 25, 1919.

25. The story that Mason composed this tune within a half-hour seems to have been sanctioned by his widow; Hezekiah Butterworth's *The Story of the Tunes* (1890) cites Mrs. Mason as his reference for the story. HLM, 133, 135, 137 further identifies Miss Howard. In 1833 she married Francis R. Goulding (1810-1881) who became a popular writer of stories for boys.

26. HLM, 102; Douglas Moore, "The Activities of Lowell Mason in Savannah, Georgia, 1813-1827," (M.F.A. thesis, University of Georgia, 1967), 30.

27. LM to B. Mallon, Atlanta, Sept. 20, 1869.

28. Moore, "Activities of Lowell Mason," 32, quoting from *The Savannah Georgian*, Dec. 6, 1825.

29. LaFar, "Lowell Mason's Activities," 129; Moore, "Activities of Lowell Mason," 33, quoting from the *Columbian Museum & Savannah Daily Gazette*, 1818, 1819 issues, articles signed "L. Mason."

30. LaFar, 129, based on a report in *The Georgian*, April 15, 1823.

31. William H. Cumming to HLM June 16, 1909.

Chapter 2

1. "A Golden Wedding," *The Orange Journal*, Sept. 14, 1867.

2. HLM, 177.

3. Marion Davis Collamore to HLM, Nov. 12, 1938.

4. "Obituary," *The Georgian*, Oct. 10, 1820.

5. LM to Parker, as quoted by Moore, "Activities of LM," 12. Church history is drawn from Lowry Axley, *Holding Aloft the Torch* (Savannah: The Pigeonhole Press, 1958).

6. Moore, "Activities of LM," 12, quoting Adelaide Wilson, *Historic and Picturesque Savannah* (Boston: B. Photogravure Co., 1889).

7. Moore, "Activities of Lowell Mason," 13-14.

8. Ibid., 14.

9. Ibid., 15, from the issue of May 24, 1824.

10. Ibid., 18, from the *Daily Georgian*, Nov. 17, 1819.

11. Ibid., from *The Savannah Georgian*, Nov. 22, 1824.

12. HLM, 94.

13. John C. Swan, ed., *Music in Boston: Readings from the First Three Centuries* (Boston: Boston Public Library/National Endowment for the Humanities Learning Library Program, 1977), 28.

14. James Edward Dooley, "Thomas Hastings: American Church Musician" (Ph.D., diss., Florida State University, 1963), 51-52, from *The Western Recorder*, July 25, 1826 and Feb. 13, 1827.

Chapter 3

1. *The Columbian and European Harmony: or The Bridgewater Collection of Sacred Music* was a popular tunebook compiled by Nahum Mitchell, Benjamin Holt, and Bartholomew Brown (1772–1854). First issued in 1802, the book went through at least twenty-seven editions, ending in 1839. By that time more than 100,000 copies had been printed. Brown, a charter member of the Boston Handel and Haydn Society, knew Mason well, and Brown's books rivaled Mason's in sales. Frank J. Metcalf, *American Writers and Compilers of Sacred Music* (New York: Russell & Russell, 1967), 150-52.

2. "Review of First Number Boston Handel and Haydn Society Collection of Sacred Music," *The Euterpeiad*, 1 (June 24, 1820): 3.

3.   Johnson, *Hallelujah,* 22-23.

4.   W.S.B. Mathews, "Lowell Mason and the Higher Art of Music in America," *Music* 9 (Feb. 1896): 382.

5.   *The Euterpeiad,* 2 (Sept. 29, 1821): 7.

6.   LaFar, "Lowell Mason's Activities," 134, from the *Savannah Museum,* May 14, 1822.

7.   *The Euterpeiad,* 3 (May 11, 1822): 6-7. The article was signed "Middlesex," without further identification.

8.   *The Christian Advocate* 3 (June 1825): 271-76.

9.   Charles C. Perkins and John Sullivan Dwight, *From the Foundation of the Society through its 75th Season, 1815-1890,* vol. 1 of *History of the Handel and Haydn Society of Boston, Massachusetts,* (Boston, A. Mudge & Sons, 1883, 1893), 82.

10. *Report of a Committee of the Board of Trustees of the Handel and Haydn Society on the Subject of Existing Contracts Between Mr. Lowell Mason and Others for Editing and Publishing Sacred Music October 1834* (Boston: Benjamin H. Greene, 1834), 16-18. This source seems to be in error regarding restrictions placed on Mason's publishing; he did publish a number of musical works before 1832.

11. Theodore F. Seward, *The Educational Work of Dr. Lowell Mason* (n.p., 1879), 8.

12. LM, *Address on Church Music: Delivered by Request, on the Evening of Saturday, October 7, 1826, in the Vestry of Hanover Church, and on the Evening of Monday Following in the Third Baptist Church, Boston* (Boston: Hilliard, Gray, Little, & Wilkins, 1826). All quotes from the address come from this source.

13. H. D. Babbidge, *Noah Webster: On Being American* (New York: F. A. Praeger, 1967), 176.

14. *DJM,* 18 (Nov. 3, 1860): 252, reporting on a Mason lecture in Chicago during the Western tour, fall 1860.

15. The entire list, including amounts subscribed, is in Carol A. Pemberton, "Lowell Mason: His Life and Work" (Ph.D. diss., University of Minnesota, 1971), 115.

16. T. F. Seward, "Obituary," *The New York Musical Gazette,* September 1872.

17. Johnson, *Hallelujah,* 49.

18. Perkins and Dwight, *History,* 95, 99.

19. Amelia Bartlett Vincent, "Music in Boston, 1825-30" (M.A. thesis, Boston University, 1942), 42-43, quoting from Perkins and Dwight, *History.*

20. Vincent, "Music in Boston," 48-49, from *Columbian Sentinel,* Jan. 31, 1829.

21. Perkins and Dwight, *History,* 96, citing Frédéric Louis Ritter, *Music in America* (New York: Chas. Scribner's Sons, 1883). Perkins and Dwight concur with Ritter's assessment.

22. Perkins and Dwight, *History,* 112-13.

23. WmM, *Memories of a Musical Life* (New York: Century Co., 1901), 183.

24. HLM, 164. The Beechers were interested in music. LM taught music to at least one of their children, Charles (1815-1900). Lyman Beecher was a lifelong advocate of improved church music. See Milton Rugoff, *The Beechers* (New York: Harper & Row, 1981).

25.   Elnathan Duren, Jr. to HLM, May 22, 1913. Duren, born January 14, 1814, had clear recall though he was nearly 100 years old.

26.   William G. Lambert to LM, Jan. 25, 1831.

27.   HLM, 184.

28.   Ibid.

29.   Information from a conversation with Helen Mason Endicott, granddaughter of Helen Palmer Mason, daughter of HLM, July 1970.

30.   HLM, 185. Another member of the family, Mary Olive Woodman, married Mason's friend and associate, George Frederick Root, in 1845.

31.   Duren to HLM, May 22, 1913.

32.   HLM, 197A, from *The Boston Courier*, about 1848.

33.   George F. Root, *The Story of My Musical Life: An Autobiography* (Cincinnati: John Church & Co., 1891), 14.

34.   A younger sister, Lydia Beck, sent a copy of the invitation to HLM, Oct. 20, 1909.

35.   HLM, 196-97.

36.   Seward, *The Educational Work*, 5.

37.   *The Boston Evening Transcript*, July 14, 1854.

38.   HLM, 188.

39.   Louis F. Benson, *The English Hymn: Its Development and Use in Worship* (Richmond: John Knox Press, 1962 reissued from the 1915 edition), 377.

40.   Edith B. Card, "The Development of the American Hymn Tune 1800-1850," (M.M.Ed. thesis, Florida State University, 1957), 26.

41.   Dooley, "Thomas Hastings," 52.

42.   Henry Wilder Foote, *Three Centuries of American Hymnody* (Cambridge, MA: Harvard University Press, 1940), 210.

43.   WmM, *Memories*, 6.

Chapter 4

1.   Mary Cable and the American Heritage Editors, *American Manners and Morals* (New York: American Heritage Co., 1969), 114.

2.   Oliver W. Larkin, *Art and Life in America* (New York: Rinehart, 1949), 149.

3.   Judith Tick, *American Women Composers Before 1870* (Ann Arbor, MI: UMI Research Press, 1983), 34-35, summarizes this development.

4.   Russel B. Nye, *The Cultural Life of the New Nation: 1776–1830* (New York: Harper & Row, 1960), 162-63.

5.   HLM, 229.

6.   Ibid., 128. W.S.B. Mathews is cited as the source of this information. Mathews (1837-1912), organist, teacher, writer on music, knew LM and his associates well. In his later years

Mathews established himself as a music critic of the *Chicago Tribune* (1878-86) and as editor of the monthly journal *Music*. He also wrote a number of books, including the music history entitled *One Hundred Years of Music in America* (1889).

7.   Ellwood P. Cubberly, *Public Education in the United States* (New York: Houghton Mifflin, 1919), 354.

8.   Ibid., 355.

9.   Robert W. John, "Elam Ives and the Pestalozzian Philosophy of Music Education," *JRME* 8 (Spring 1960): 49, 45.

10. *American Journal of Education*, 1830: 419.

11. *Boston Musical Gazette* 1 (Dec. 12, 1838): 17. The Woodbridge speech was also printed in the *American Journal of Education* 1830-31.

12. For another interpretation of Mason's influence, see David Z. Kushner, "The 'Masonic' Influence on 19th-Century American Musical Education," *Journal of Musicological Research* 4 (1983): 443ff.

13. Lloyd F. Sunderman, "The Era of Beginnings in American Music Education (1830-1840)," *JRME* 4 (Spring 1956): 33.

14. Root, *Autobiography*, 52.

15. HLM, *Lowell Mason: An Appreciation of His Life and Work* (New York: The Hymn Society of America, 1941), 6.

16. Root, *Autobiography*, 52.

17. LM, *How Shall I Teach? or, Hints to Teachers* (New York: Mason Brothers, 1860).

18. LM, "The Pestalozzian Method of Teaching Music," *The Musical World and Times* 6 (May 14, 1853): 22.

19. Samuel L. Flueckiger, "Lowell Mason's Contribution to the Early History of Music Education in the United States" (Ph.D. diss., Ohio State University, 1936), 211, quoting LM, *A Glance at Pestalozzianism*.

20. Frances Doane, "The Influence of Pestalozzianism upon Lowell Mason's Work in Music Education" (M.A. thesis, University of Vermont, 1937), 48-49. This factor was a source of great satisfaction to LM in his later years. See "On Teaching Music," *The Choral Advocate and Singing-Class Journal* 1 (June 1850): 8-9.

21. LM, *Manual of the Boston Academy of Music*, 13.

22. LM, "The Pestalozzian Method," 23.

23. Howe (1810–1876), a graduate of Harvard Medical School, was a lifelong advocate of various causes. After his pioneer work at the Perkins Institute, he established an experimental school for the training of idiots. Later he was active in the abolitionist cause. With his wife, Julia Ward Howe, he issued *The Commonwealth*, an abolitionist paper. Julia Howe, famous as the author of "The Battle Hymn of the Republic," also worked for women's suffrage. Philanthropist Perkins (1764-1854) also endowed the Massachusetts General Hospital, the Boston Athenaeum, and the Boston Gallery of Art.

24. Louis C. Elson, *The History of American Music*, rev. ed. (New York: Macmillan, 1915), 78.

25. Samuel A. Eliot, "Music in America," *North American Review* 52 (April 1841): 330-31.

26. See the constitution of the Boston Academy of Music, the 1835 membership list, and an advertisement for a teachers' class (1838) in Pemberton, "Lowell Mason," (diss.) app. B, 514-16.

27. HLM, 254.

28. Ibid., 256.

29. Ibid., 258.

30. Ibid., 261-62.

31. Seward, *The Educational Work*, 14.

32. *Boston Musical Gazette* 1 (May 2, 1838): 1.

33. HLM, 260.

34. "Review of Concerts," *The Musical Reporter* 1 (Feb. 1841): 2.

35. *Boston Musical Gazette* 1 (May 2, 1838): 1.

36. HLM, 361.

37. Elson, *The National Music of America*, 287-88.

38. "Concerts," *The Musical Reporter* 1 (March 1841): 128. Swan, *Music in Boston*, includes an interesting portion of Thomas Ryan's autobiography, *Recollections of an Old Musician* (New York, 1899) in which he describes Webb and the academy orchestra about 1845.

39. HLM, 359, citing Appel, *Beethoven in America: First Performances in America.*

40. "The Twelfth Annual Report of the Boston Academy of Music," July 1844.

41. "The Second Annual Report of the Boston Academy of Music," May 1834, 22.

42. HLM, 289.

43. Ibid., 283.

44. Ibid., 277-78.

45. "The Fifth Annual Report of the Boston Academy of Music," 1837.

46. HLM, 304-8.

47. HLM, 315, citing Leonard Woods, *History of the Andover Theological Seminary.*

48. HLM, 319. See Pemberton, "Lowell Mason," (diss.), 196, for the exact wording.

49. HLM, 299.

50. The use of the plural verb indicates that the writer thought of the academy not as a single entity, but as a group in which members acted as individuals.

51. *The Musical Reporter*, 1 (May 1841): 227.

52. Howard E. Ellis, "Lowell Mason and the *Manual of the Boston Academy of Music*," *JRME* 3 (Spring 1955): 5-10, presents a detailed analysis of this matter.

Chapter 5

1. Robert W. John, "Origins of the First Music Educators Convention," *JRME*, 13 (1965): 207ff. gives a summary of conventions conducted by LM and his associates from 1834 through 1845, including names of those in attendance.

2. George Washington Lucas, *Remarks on the Musical Conventions in Boston* (Northampton, MA: G.W. Lucas, 1844), 4. For information on *The Bridgewater Collection,* see chapter 3, n. 1 of the present volume. The book is considered by some to be "the most important publication between Billings and Mason." J. Alexander Gilfillan, "Singing Schools in America" (M.M. thesis, Eastman School of Music, 1939), 49.

3. John, "Origins," 213; Lucas, *Remarks on the Musical Conventions.*

4. HLM, 349.

5. Johnson left an undated, handwritten account of this episode. The document is in the Medfield, Massachusetts Historical Society Collection. The remarks were apparently meant to correspond to a picture, but the picture has been lost or misplaced.

6. John S. Dwight, "Musical Conventions," *DJM* 1 (August 18, 1852): 149-50.

7. Metcalf, *American Writers and Compilers*, 283.

8. Root, *Autobiography*, 28.

9. Ibid., 43. No further identification is given. LM had several associates named Johnson.

Chapter 6

1. Quoted by HLM from the original letter owned by the American Antiquarian Society Library, Worcester, Massachusetts.

2. HLM states that this new oratorio was by Karl Loewe (1796-1869), a composer of lieder, operas, and songs.

3. HLM adds that the church was the Collegiate Church of St. Nicholas.

Chapter 7

1. W. L. Hubbard, ed., *The History of American Music*, vol. 8 of *The American History and Encyclopedia of Music* (New York: Irving Squire, 1908), 21.

2. HLM, 287.

3. Quoted in full in Pemberton, "Lowell Mason" (diss.), 517-24, from *The Boston Musical Gazette* November 28, 1838, and December 26, 1838. The report was drawn up by Davis (Seward, *The Educational Work*) .

4. *American Annals of Education and Instruction* 8 (Jan. 1838), 44.

5. *The Boston Musical Gazette* 1 (July 25, 1838), 53.

6. HLM, 331.

7. Ibid., 340.

8. Arthur L. Rich, *Lowell Mason, "the Father of Singing Among the Children"* (Chapel Hill: University of North Carolina Press, 1946), 25-26.

9.   James C. Johnson, "The Introduction of the Study of Music into the Public Schools of Boston and of America," *The Bostonian* 1 (March 1895): 630.

10.   HLM, 343, quoting Leah L. Nichols-Wellington (Class of 1846), *History of the Bowdoin School, 1821-1907.* (Manchester, NH: The Ruemely Press, 1912).

11.   Tilden, *The History of the Town of Medfield,* 289; W.S.B. Mathews, "Lowell Mason, a Father in American Music," *The Musician* 16 (November 1911): 721.

12.   Johnson's notes at the Medfield Historical Society (see chapter 5, n. 5).

13.   Rich, *Lowell Mason,* 27, quoting Horace Mann, "Singing in the Common Schools," *The Common School Journal.*

14.   "The Eleventh Annual Report of the Boston Academy of Music," July 1843.

15.   HLM, 397; Rich, *Lowell Mason,* 28. The term "political revolution" is Henry Lowell Mason's.

16.   HLM, 397, quoting from the *Boston Journal* of Oct. 11, 1845, where the entire letter appeared.

17.   HLM, 397-98, quotes both letters of Sept. 13, 1845.

18.   H. Earle Johnson, "Early New England Periodicals Devoted to Music," *The Musical Quarterly* 26 (1940): 153-61; Charles E. Wunderlich, "A History and Bibliography of Early American Music Periodicals, 1782-1852" (Ph.D. diss, University of Michigan, 1962).

19.   Samuel L. Flueckiger, "Why Lowell Mason Left the Boston Schools," *Music Educators Journal* 22 (Feb. 1936): 20.

20.   Johnson's notes (see chapter 5, n. 5) .

21.   Records of the Boston School Committee, Rare Book Division, BPL.

22.   Flueckiger, "Why Lowell Mason Left," 21, quotes the letter.

23.   HLM, 399.

24.   Martha R. McCabe, "Early American School Music Books," *School Life,* 24 (July 1939): 290ff states that *The Child's Song Book* (1830), apparently by Augustus Peabody, was the first work of this kind, but Robert W. John, "A History of School Vocal Instruction Books in the United States" (Ed.D., diss., Indiana University, 1953) concludes that Mason's book can be regarded as the first. Mason so regarded it; see his statements to that effect in *Mason's Normal Singer* (1856). The title page of the Peabody book indicates that it is for the use of "Schools and Families being a Selection of Favorite Airs and Hymns and Moral Songs, suitable for Infant Instruction"; no mention is made of primary schools. Therefore, LM could view *The Juvenile Lyre* as the first book specifically for those schools.

25.   John, "Elam Ives," 47-48.

26.   The full title of the work is *The Musical Cyclopedia: or the Principles of Music Considered as a Science and an Art, Embracing a Complete Musical Dictionary, and the Outlines of a Musical Grammar, and of the Theory of Sounds and Laws of Harmony with Directions for the Practices of Vocal and Instrumental Music, and a Description of Musical Instruments.*

27.   HLM, 312.

28. Ibid. Whittemore, Universalist minister at Milford and Cambridge, Massachusetts, wrote a number of books, including several collections of music. His correspondence with LM is a part of the Mason Papers at Yale University.

29. Harry Dichter and Elliott Shapiro, *Early American Sheet Music* (New York: R. R. Bowker, 1941), 217.

30. William Arms Fisher, *Notes on Music in Old Boston* (Boston: O. Ditson, 1918) and *One Hundred and Fifty Years of Music Publishing in the United States, 1783-1933* (Boston: O. Ditson, 1933). See also Thompson, "Music and Musical Activities," 177, 379-83.

31. A study of the texts was undertaken by Walter R. Jones, "An Analysis of Public School Music Textbooks before 1900" (Ed.D. diss., University of Pittsburgh, 1954).

Chapter 8

1. HLM, 344, quoting Leah L. Nichols-Wellington.

2. The three songs were "Thrice Hail, Happy Day," "When Stern Oppression's Iron Rod," and "God Bless Our Native Land." The latter had appeared in 1842 in Mason's "Three Patriotic Songs."

3. HLM, 430-32.

4. Carol Brink, *Harps in the Wind: The Story of the Singing Hutchinsons* (New York: Macmillan, 1947), 14-15.

5. James M. Trotter's *Music and Some Highly Musical People* (Boston: Lee and Shepard, 1878; reprinted by Johnson Reprint Corp., New York, 1968), 111-12. For more information about Williams' career, see Eileen Southern, *Biographical Dictionary of Afro-American and African Musicans* (Westport, CT: Greenwood Press, 1982), 405.

6. HLM, 413-14.

7. Included in the Lowell Mason Papers at Yale are sixteen letters from Mann to Mason, dated 1844-55.

8. Ibid., 439-40.

9. Ibid., 419.

10. "Obituary: Marie Mason," *Orange Chronicle,* Nov. 12, 1881, says 1844; "Obituary: Lowell Mason, [Jr.]" *Orange Chronicle,* Oct. 24, 1885, says 1847.

11. WmM, *Memories,* 25-26, referring to Mary Isabelle Webb, born Aug. 1, 1833.

12. Figures based on data from *Historical Statistics of the U.S. Bureau of the Census* (U.S. Government Printing Office, 1975) and the Consumer Price Index. At this writing, no figures were available beyond 1983.

13. LM, *An Address on Church Music, delivered July 8, 1851 in Boston* (New York: Mason & Law, 1851), 6, 20.

14. From the diary of one of Lydia A. Beck's sisters, as related to HLM by Lydia in letters Oct. 20, 1909 and July 23, 1914. Two of Lydia Beck's sisters were members of Mason's church choirs (see chapter 3).

15. Jenks, "Lowell Mason," 652, includes a picture of the vase. A detailed description is provided in Pemberton, "Lowell Mason," (diss.), 282.

16. Root, *Autobiography*, 85-88.

17. Ibid.

Chapter 9

1. WmM, *Memories,* 46-47.

2. LM, *Musical Letters from Abroad,* (Boston: O. Ditson, 1853; reprinted by DaCapo Press, New York, 1967), 81.

3. Ibid., 279.

4. Ibid., 285.

5. Ibid., 230.

6. Ibid., 239.

7. See, for example, the account of the four-hour program at the Birmingham Festival of Sept. 1853. Ibid., 226ff.

8. Ibid., p. 23 includes his account of the Symphony No. 8; p. 267, the Pastoral Symphony; p. 241, the Ninth Symphony.

9. In this regard Letter 12 in *Musical Letters* is of interest. Writing from Leipzig on March 13, 1852, LM described a concert in which Robert and Clara Schumann presented some of Robert's works. Musicians from miles around had journeyed to hear the performance—"*the very* Listz [*sic*] *himself* came from Weimar to listen," but the Masons did not attend though they were in the city at the time. Why not? Mason asks and answers his own question; "Why? *It was given on Sunday Morning...at 11 o'clock,"* and the Masons were in church, 83.

10. He says that the *Messiah* chorus, "His Yoke is Easy" should "float in the air.... It should be light, bouyant, spiritual, not subjected to the laws of gravitation.... Although we should not dare to say it, lest we might be regarded as musically heretical, yet we do not like Mozart's Trombones in this chorus." *Musical Letters,* 283.

11. Ibid., 202.

12. Ibid., 84.

13. Ibid., 236.

14. Ibid., 83.

15. Ibid., 232.

16. Eva J. O'Meara, "The Lowell Mason Library of Music," *The Yale University Library Gazette* 40 (Oct. 1965): 62.

17. Eva J. O'Meara, "The Lowell Mason Papers," *The Yale University Library Gazette* 45(Jan. 1971): 124.

18. LM, *Musical Letters,* 143-44.

19. HLM, 459, reporting a statement by G. F. Root.

20. A handbill distributed in London in December 1852, announcing eight lectures on Congregational Psalmody, preserved in one of LM's scrapbooks at Yale University. The handbill is quoted in full in Pemberton, "Lowell Mason" (diss.), app. E, 528-29.

Chapter 10

1. *MW* 6 (May 7, 1853): 289.

2. HLM, 389, quoting Jacob Henry Hall's sketch of Bradbury in *Biography of Gospel Song and Hymn Writers* (New York: Fleming H. Revell, 1914).

3. W. W. Killip to HLM, July 16, 1909.

4. *MW* 7 (Dec. 10, 1853): front page.

5. *DJM* 3 (April 16, 1853): 15.

6. Mazie Pauline Carder, "George Frederick Root, Pioneer Music Educator: His Contributions to Mass Instruction in Music" (Ed.D. diss., University of Maryland, 1971), 126.

7. *DJM* 39 (August 1879): 30.

8. Killip to HLM, July 16, 1909.

9. Killip to HLM, July 31, 1909.

10. Ibid.

11. Flueckiger, "Lowell Mason's Contributions," 173-74.

12. Carder, "George Frederick Root," 128, quoting A. W. Thayer, "The Normal Music School at North Reading," *DJM* 11 (July 25, 1857): 133. Thayer states that Root excelled in teaching class voice and harmony.

13. HLM, 441-42.

14. Root, *Autobiography,* 144.

15. Thompson, "Music and Musical Activities," 125, citing Joyce E. Mangler, "Music in King's Church, St. John's Providence, 1722-1850," Part II of "Early Music in Rhode Island Churches," *Rhode Island History XVII* concerning Law's advocacy of chant.

16. These points, among others, are covered in *Musical Letters from Abroad:* congregational tunes must be plain and easy (115, 301), within a moderate vocal range (163), and rhythmically simple (155); singing must be assisted by an organ and choir (138-39); congregational music must not be an exercise in artistry, but rather "religiously edifying" (125); congregational participation in hymns and chants is important (167); chorales are too difficult (301), but simple anthems could be learned with a bit of instruction (257).

17. *DJM* 36 (May 13, 1876): 228-30. See also "Church Music in New York," *The New York Tribune* April 29, 1876; "Boston Church Choirs," *The Boston Herald* May 14, 1876; *DJM* May 27, 1856 issue.

18. LM, *Musical Letters,* 114.

19. Elfrieda A. Kraege, "The Early Organs of the Fifth Avenue Presbyterian Church," *The Tracker* 18 (Winter 1974): 4.

20. John K. Ogasapian, "Lowell Mason as a Church Musician," *Journal of Church Music* 21 (Sept. 1979): 9, with the ending quotation from *DJM* Oct. 27, 1855.

21. Ogasapian, 10. The report was Thomas Hutchinson's *American Musical Directory,* 1861.

22. George Blagden Bacon, *Sermon, Commemorative of Lowell Mason* (New York: Cushing, Bardua & Co., 1872), 18-19.

23.   Austin Phelps (1820-1890), Professor of Sacred Rhetoric in 1859, became the school's president ten years later. He issued books on many subjects during his career, including *Hymns and Carols* with David Furber. *Appleton's Cyclopedia* IV, 752.

24.   Leonard Ellinwood, *The History of American Church Music* (New York: Morehouse-Gorham, 1953), 68.

25.   Benson, *The English Hymn,* 475-76.

26.   Rich, *Lowell Mason,* 107-8, based on "Lowell Mason," in vol. II of S. A. Allibone, *A Critical Dictionary of English Literature and British and American Authors* (Philadelphia: J.B. Lippincott Co., 1897), 1237-38.

27.   HLM, 197, quoting "Oliver Ditson," in *The Boston Musical Herald, a Magazine Devoted to the Art Universal* (Jan. 1889). Figures computed on U.S. Government sources. See chapter 8, n. 12.

28.   *DJM* 5 (Sept. 16, 1854): 190-91.

29.   WmM, *Memories,* 183.

30.   Daniel Gregory Mason, *Music in My Time and Other Reminiscences* (New York: Macmillan, 1938), 7-8.

31.   Information on Hamlin from *Dictionary of American Biography*, vol. 8, 196. For more information on instrument manufacturing at the time, see Christine M. Ayars, *Contributions to the Art of Music in America by the Music Industries of Boston, 1640-1936* (New York: H. Wilson Co., 1937).

32.   Information provided the author by Elizabeth Mason Ginnel, daughter of Edward Palmer Mason, August 1984.

33.   A. W. Thayer, "From My Diary," *DJM* 12 (Feb. 27, 1858): 380.

34.   The first honorary doctorate in music was granted to Henry Dielman by Georgetown University, 1849. *Grove's Dictionary, American Supplement,* 185-86, 286.

35.   David L. Pierson, *History of the Oranges in 1921: Reviewing the Rise, Development and Progress of an Influential Community* (New York: Lewis Historical Publishing Co., 1922) II: 311.

36.   "The Germania Musical Society," *DJM* 5 (Sept. 16, 1854): 189. The article is unsigned. It appears to understate the number of volumes owned by LM, considering the holdings of his library at the time of his death. Information on the nation's libraries is taken from the *Newport Daily News.*

37.   *DJM* 39 (Nov. 22, 1879): 196. Thayer was graduated from Harvard in 1843 and worked for six years as a librarian there. Later he was a U.S. Government Consul in Trieste, appointed by President Lincoln. His lifelong work on a definitive biography of Beethoven formed the core of his career. Though he left the fourth and final volume unfinished upon his death, his contribution was enormous.

38.   O'Meara, "The Lowell Mason Library," 63.

39.   Ibid, 66-67. Thayer seems to have used the verb "catalogue" in a broad sense.

40.   Thayer, *DJM,* 39 (Dec. 6, 1879), 196.

41.   O'Meara, "The Lowell Mason Papers," 125.

42. O'Meara, "The Lowell Mason Library," 68.

43. Ibid., 65, 71. Verified in correspondence with Music Librarian Harold E. Samuel, July 1984.

44. O'Meara, "The Lowell Mason Library," 74.

Chapter 11

1. *DJM*, 4 (Oct. 8, 1853): 5.

2. Published by H. W. Gray, New York, 1945.

3. Ritter, *Music in America*, 176-77.

4. Ibid.

5. HLM, *Hymn Tunes of Lowell Mason: a Bibliography* (Cambridge: The University Press, 1944), reaches this conclusion, but Ellen Jane Lorenz Porter casts some doubt on the totals in "A Hymn-Tune Detective Stalks Lowell Mason," *Journal of Church Music* 24 (Nov. 1982): 7-11, 31-32.

6. HLM, *Lowell Mason: An Appreciation*, 10, quoting George B. Bacon.

7. W.S.B. Mathews, "Lowell Mason and the Higher Art of Music in America," *Music* 9 (April 1896): 586. This assertion was made in reference to *Cantica Laudis* (1850).

8. *MW* 5 (Jan. 29, 1853): 66.

9. Arlene E. Gray, "Lowell Mason's Contribution to American Church Music" (M.M. thesis, Eastman School of Music, 1941); Lillian Pope Howell, "Lowell Mason, Composer of Hymn Tunes" (M.S.M. thesis, Southern Baptist Seminary, 1948). The conclusions reached by Gray and Howell correspond closely to one another and to those of other researchers. Their analyses focused on tunes representative of Protestant musical expression at the time in which they were written, tunes representative of a variety of musical types, and tunes that proved durable.

10. Robert M. Stevenson, *Protestant Church Music in America* (New York: W. W. Norton, 1966), 84-85 discusses the "set piece" and Mason's use of the "set piece."

11. Edited by Johannes Riedel, published by Augsburg Publishing Co. in the Lutheran Brotherhood Choral Series (LB11-6), Minneapolis, 1957.

12. LM, "Preface," *The Sabbath Hymn and Tune Book* (1859). He had made a similar statement in the preface of *The National Psalmist* (1848), 4.

13. Howell, "Lowell Mason," 44ff.

14. Gray, "Lowell Mason's Contribution," 273.

15. Hamilton C. MacDougall, *Early New England Psalmody* (Brattleboro, VT: Stephen Daye Press, 1940), 169.

16. Gray, "Lowell Mason's Contributions," 84.

17. Howell, "Lowell Mason," 54.

18. Ibid., 47ff.

19. Stevenson, *Protestant Church Music*, 82.

20. Gray, "Lowell Mason's Contributions," 238, 255; Howell, "Lowell Mason," 47ff. Howell found one instance of a minor key in the sixty tunes analyzed; Gray found none in the twenty-five she used.

21. Howell, "Lowell Mason," 55.

22. Gray, "Lowell Mason's Contributions," 256-57.

23. Howell, "Lowell Mason," 62.

24. Gray, "Lowell Mason's Contributions," 243.

25. *MW* 5 (Jan. 22, 1853): 49. LM had written from London, Dec. 5, 1852, citing a review published in November 1852. His entire response was printed in this issue.

26. Jones, "An Analysis," using these books by LM: *The Juvenile Lyre* (with Ives) 1831; *The Juvenile Singing School,* 1839 ed.; *The Boston School Song Book,* 1843; *The Song-Book of the School-Room* (with Webb), 1847; *The Singing School,* 1854; and *Mason's Normal Singer,* 1856. Jones provides much statistical detail about LM's songs for children, although Mason's work was not the focal point of his research.

27. Ibid., 142.

28. Ibid., 111.

29. For identification of some of these arrangements, see Stevenson, *Protestant Church Music,* 77.

30. Porter, "A Hymn-Tune Detective," shows side-by-side examples of original tunes and Mason's arrangements with brief analysis. Porter demonstrates that after Mason's "arranging," tunes may have "very slight resemblance to their supposed classic source," 10.

31. J. Vincent Higginson, "Notes on Lowell Mason's Hymn Tunes," *The Hymn* 18 (1967): 40. Higginson notes LM's fondness for the first, fifth, eighth modes and the Tonus Perigrinus, all but the latter having a strong feeling of the major mode.

32. This is the position HLM took. See also Armin Haeussler, *The Story of Our Hymns: the Handbook to the Hymnal of the Evangelical and Reformed Church* (St. Louis: Eden Publishing House, 1952), 213. The same point is made convincingly by Porter, "A Hymn-Tune Detective."

33. "Lowell Mason as a Church Musician," *New York Evening Post,* August 15, 1872.

Chapter 12

1. Collamore to HLM, Nov. 12, 1938.

2. Charles A. Savage, ed., *The Thirty-Fifth Anniversary of the Orange Valley Church,* (Newark: L. J. Hardem, 1896), 27.

3. Ibid.

4. Ibid., 28.

5. Emma Rhodes, a daughter in the family, in a letter to HLM, Aug. 3, 1917.

6. The piano was given to the Medfield Historical Society and remains in the society's building.

7. LM to D. G. Mason, Feb. 28, 1858.

8. LM to D. G. Mason, March 24, 1863.

9. Frederick Root to HLM, June 20, 1909. The statement about teachers being promoted downward is quoted in Charles L. Gray, "Vignettes of Music Education History," *Music Educators Journal* 48 (1962): 56.

10. Flueckiger, "Lowell Mason's Contributions," 182-83, quoting George B. Bacon, "Exercises at the Opening of 'The Lowell Mason Library of Music.' "

11. Letters to HLM Aug. 9 and Aug. 14, 1919. Foster (1851-1935) is identified by HLM only as a Doctor of Divinity.

12. Constance Hyde to HLM Aug. 15, 1909. She indicated that the child had been her father, William Augustus Smith, D.D., a Methodist minister in Illinois.

13. Letter dated March 25, 1865. BPL.

14. Abigail Mason to Hattie Mason Hillyer, daughter of Johnson Mason, Jr., Sept. 6, 1866.

15. From a clipping on file at Yale, apparently from the Oswego, New York newspaper. Discussion of the attendants' identities is in Pemberton, "Lowell Mason," (diss), 416.

16. Patrick S. Gilmore, *History of the National Peace Jubilee and Great Musical Festival Held in Boston, June, 1869, to Commemorate the Restoration of Peace Throughout the Land* (Boston: P. S. Gilmore, 1871), 341-42.

17. "Obituary," *The New York Times,* as printed in *The New York Times Index,* May-Aug. 1869, 471.

18. LM to G. B. Bacon, Aug. 5, 1870.

19. Seward, "Obituary," 130; Rich, *Lowell Mason,* 169.

20. Seward, "Obituary," 130.

21. Collamore to HLM, Nov. 12, 1938.

22. LM to Melvin Lord, Dec. 2, 1871. BPL.

23. LM wrote "Allan" though the boy's name was Alan, showing very slight confusion at that moment. This grandchild was later afflicted with a mental disorder and spent most of his life in a sanitarium.

24. LM to J. W. Dickinson, Dec. 15, 1871.

25. Letter in the Rare Book Division, BPL.

26. Flueckiger, "Lowell Mason's Contributions," 183, quoting Bacon, "Exercises."

27. LM, Jr., to G. B. Bacon from Weisbaden, Aug. 18, 1872.

28. *Commercial Advertiser,* Aug. 18, 1872.

29. "Obituary," *Orange Chronicle,* Aug. 17, 1872.

30. Ibid.

31. Mary B. Scanlon, "Dr. Lowell Mason in Music Education," (M.A. thesis, Eastman School of Music, 1940), 115. The detail about Caroline Webb comes from Mary Sturgis Gray, "George James Webb: His Life and Compositions," manuscript biography, 1937, BPL.

32. Savage, *The Thirty-Fifth Anniversary,* 28.

33. Seward, "Obituary," 129.

34. "Obituary," *New York Evening Post*. Other writers provided a more comprehensive view, but with praise of LM. See, for instance, the tribute published in *The New York Musical Gazette* of February 1873, quoted in Pemberton, "Lowell Mason," (diss.), app. G, 534.

Epilogue

1. Richard Storrs Willis, *MW* 5 (Jan. 29, 1853): 66.

2. Ibid.

Bibliography

Adams, Charles F. *Familiar Letters of John Adams and His Wife Abigail Adams, During the Revolution with a Memoir of Mrs. Adams*. Boston: Houghton Mifflin, Co., 1875.

Alcott, William, "William Channing Woodbridge." *American Journal of Education* 5 (June 1858): 51-64.

"America's Momentous Contribution to Public School Music," Editorial. *Etude* 50 (April 1932): 237.

Axley, Lowry. *Holding Aloft the Torch: A History of the Independent Presbyterian Church of Savannah, Georgia*. Savannah: The Pigeonhole Press, 1958.

Ayars, Christine Merrick. *Contributions to the Art of Music in America by the Music Industries of Boston, 1640-1936*. New York: H. Wilson Co., 1937.

Bacon, George Blagden. *Exercises at the Opening of The Lowell Mason Library of Music in the Yale Divinity School, May 11, 1875: an Address*. New Haven, n.p., 1875.

_____. "Lowell Mason." *Congregational Quarterly* (January 1873): 1-15.

_____. *Sermon, Commemorative of Lowell Mason*. New York: Cushing, Bardua & Co., 1872.

Baldwin, Sister Mary F. X. "Lowell Mason's Philosophy of Music Education." M.A. thesis, Catholic University of America, 1937.

Baltzell, Winton James. *A Complete History of Music for Schools, Clubs, and Private Reading*. Philadelphia: Theodore Presser, 1905.

Barnard, Henry. "Educational Labours of Lowell Mason." *American Journal of Education* 4 (1857): 141-48.

_____. "Lowell Mason." *American Journal of Education* 4 (1858): 146.

Barry, William. *History of Framingham, Massachusetts, Including the Plantation, from 1640 to the Present Time*. Boston: James Munroe & Co., 1847.

Benson, Louis F. *The English Hymn: Its Development and Use in Worship*. Richmond: John Knox Press, 1962.

Benton, Rita. "Early Musical Scholarship in the United States." *Fontes* 11 (1964): 12-21.

Birge, Edward Bailey. *History of Public School Music in the United States*. Boston: O. Ditson Co., 1928. Reprint. Washington, D.C.: Music Educators National Conference, 1966.

_____. "One Hundred Years of School Music." *Music Educators Journal* 22 (September 1935): 19.

_____. "Public School Music, 1838-1938." *Music Educators Journal* 24 (February 1938): 13-14.

Blagden, George W. *An Address, Delivered Before the Associate Choirs of the Evangelical Churches, Boston, in the Bowdoin Street Church, October 24, 1840*. Boston: Perkins & Marvin, 1840.

Bode, Carl, ed. *American Life in the 1840s*. New York: Anchor Books, 1967.

_____. *The Anatomy of American Popular Culture, 1840-1861*. Los Angeles: University of California Press, 1959.

Boston Academy of Music Annual Reports. Boston: Perkins & Marvin, 1833-46.

Boston Academy of Music. *Programmes of Concerts. May 15, 1833-February 27, 1847.* Boston Public Library, 1833-47.

Brandon, G. "Some Classic Tunes in Lowell Mason Collections." *The Hymn* 18 (1967): 78-79.

Brayley, A. W. "The Inception of Public School Music in America." *The Musician* 10 (November 1905): 483-85.

Brayley, George. "Early Instrumental Music in Boston." *The Bostonian* 1 (November 1894): 185-96.

Britton, Allen P. "Music Education: An American Specialty." *Music Educators Journal* 48 (June/July 1962): 27-29, 55-63.

_____. "Music In Early American Public Education: A Historical Critique" in *Basic Concepts in Music Education.* Chicago: University of Chicago Press, 1958.

_____. "Theoretical Introductions in American Tune Books." Ph.D. diss., University of Michigan, 1949.

Brooks, Henry M. *Olden-Time Music: A Compilation from Newspapers and Books.* Boston: Ticknor & Co., 1858.

Brooks, Van Wyke. *The Flowering of New England.* New York: E. P. Dutton & Co., 1936.

Bulkley, C. H. A. *Alliance of Music and Religion: Address at the Music Teachers Institute of Nunda, Livingston County, New York, August 28-September 7, 1850.* New York: Swain & Ray, 1850.

Burk, Cassie, and others. *America's Musical Heritage.* New York: Laidlaw Bro., 1942.

Burnham, Collins B. "Olden-Time Music in the Connecticut Valley." *New England Magazine* 24 (March 1901): 12-27.

Card, Edith B. "The Development of the American Hymn Tune 1800-1850." M.M.Ed. thesis, Florida State University, 1957.

Carder, Mazie Pauline. "George Frederick Root, Pioneer Music Educator: His Contributions to Mass Instruction in Music." Ed.D. diss., University of Maryland, 1971.

Chase, Gilbert. *America's Music from the Pilgrims to the Present.* rev. 2d ed. New York: McGraw-Hill, 1966.

Clark, Francis. "School Music in 1836, 1886, 1911, and 1936." *NEA Proceedings* (1924): 603-11.

"Conventions of Teachers of Vocal Music." *American Annals of Education and Instruction* 6 (October 1836): 473-74.

Cook, Wanda. "Methodology in Public School Music, a Survey of Changes in the Aims and Procedures of Music Teaching in the Public Schools of the United States During the Past One Hundred Years." M.M. thesis, Michigan State University, 1939.

Cooke, George Willis. *John Sullivan Dwight, Brook-Farmer, Editor, and Critic of Music: A Biography.* Boston: Small, Maynard & Co., 1898.

Cornwall, N. W. *Music: As It Was, and As It Is.* New York: D. Appleton & Co., 1851.

Crawford, Richard A. *Andrew Law, American Psalmodist.* Evanston: Northwestern University Press, 1968.

Cubberly, Ellwood P. *Public Education in the United States.* New York: Houghton Mifflin, 1919.

Curwen, J. Spencer. *Studies in Worship Music.* First Series. 3d ed. London: J. Curwen & Sons, 1901.

Dale, Edward Everett. "The Singing School" in *Dictionary of American History,* vol. 5: 82-83. New York: Charles Scribner's Sons, 1940.

Dearing, Rachel R. *Commemorative Booklet: Westborough's 250th Anniversary Committee.* Westborough, MA; n.p., 1967.

Dickey, Frances M. "The Early History of Public School Music in the United States." *Papers and Proceedings of the MTNA* (1914): 185-209.

Doane, Frances. "The Influence of Pestalozzianism upon Lowell Mason's Work in Music Education." M.A. thesis, University of Vermont, 1937.

Dooley, James Edward. "Thomas Hastings: American Church Musician." Ph.D. diss., Florida State University, 1963.

Douglas, Winfred, and Leonard Ellinwood. *Church Music in History and Practice: Studies in the Praise of God.* New York: Charles Scribner's Sons, 1962.

Doxey, Mary Bitzer. "Lowell Mason, Modern Music Educator." M.M. thesis, University of Mississippi, 1957.

Durgin, Cyrus W. *A Condensed History of the Handel and Haydn Society of Boston, Massachusetts.* Boston: The Handel and Haydn Society, 1955.

"Eclectic Academy of Music in Cincinnati," *American Annals of Education and Instruction* 4 (June 1834): 289.

Edwards, Ann Miller. "History of Vocal Music in the Public Schools of the United States from 1830-1930." M.A. thesis, Stanford University, 1947.

E. J. "Reasons Why Sacred Music Should Be Made a Branch of Education in Common Schools." *The Family Minstrel: A Musical and Literary Journal.* 1 (June 15, 1835): 74.

Eliot, Samuel A. *Address Before the Boston Academy of Music on the Opening of the Odeon, August 5, 1835.* Boston: Perkins, Marvin & Co., 1835.

_____. "Mason's Address on Church Music: A Critical Review." *North American Review* 24 (January 1827): 244-46.

_____. "Music in America." *North American Review* 52 (April 1841) : 320-38.

Ellinwood, Leonard. *The History of American Church Music.* New York: Morehouse-Gorham Co., 1953.

Ellis, Howard Eber. "The Influence of Pestalozzianism on Instruction in Music." Ph.D. diss., University of Michigan, 1957.

_____. "Lowell Mason and the *Manual of the Boston Academy of Music.*" *Journal of Research in Music Education* 3 (Spring 1955): 3-10.

Elson, Louis C. *The History of American Music.* rev. ed. New York: Macmillan, 1915.

_____. *The National Music of America and Its Sources.* Boston: L. C. Page & Co. Inc., 1900.

Essex [pseud.]. *The Sabbath Hymn Book Reviewed.* Boston: J. P. Jewett & Co., 1858.

Ewen, David. *Music Comes to America.* New York: T. Y. Crowell Co., 1942.

"Exercises at the Opening of 'The Lowell Mason Library of Music' in the Yale Divinity School, May 11, 1875." n.p., n.d.

Fisher, William Arms. *Music Festivals in the United States.* Boston: The American Choral and Festival Alliance, Inc., 1934.

_____. *Notes on Music in Old Boston.* Boston: O. Ditson, 1918.

_____. *One Hundred and Fifty Years of Music Publishing in the United States, 1783-1933: An Historical Sketch with Special Reference to the Pioneer Publisher, Oliver Ditson Co., Inc.* Boston: O. Ditson, 1933.

_____. *Ye Olde New-England Psalm-Tunes 1620-1820.* Boston: O. Ditson Co., 1930.

Flueckiger, Samuel Lehman. "Lowell Mason's Contributions to the Early History of Music Education in the United States." Ph.D. diss., Ohio State University, 1936.

_____. "Why Lowell Mason Left the Boston Schools." *Music Educators Journal* 22 (February 1936): 20-23.

Foote, Henry Wilder. *Musical Life in Boston in the Eighteenth Century.* Worcester: American Antiquarian Society, 1940.

_____. *Three Centuries of American Hymnody.* Cambridge: Harvard University Press, 1940.

Gamble, Thomas. *Stories of Savannah.* Papers, manuscripts. Savannah Public Library, n.d.

Gilfillan, J. Alexander. "Singing Schools in America." M.M. thesis, Eastman School of Music, 1939.

Gilman, Samuel. *Memories of a New England Village Choir with Occasional Reflections by a Member.* Boston: S. G. Goodrich & Co., 1829.

Gilmore, Patrick S. *History of the National Peace Jubilee and Great Musical Festival Held in Boston, June, 1869, to Commemorate the Restoration of Peace Throughout the Land.* Boston: P. S. Gilmore, 1871.

Goldman, Richard Franko, and Roger Smith. *Landmarks of Early American Music.* New York: G. Schirmer, 1943.

Goodrich, Henry A. *Church Organs: Some of the Early Builders in New England.* Fitchburg, MA: Fitchburg Historical Society, 1902.

Goodwin, Thomas. *Sketches and Impressions.* New York: G.P. Putnam, 1887.

Gould, Nathaniel D. *History of Church Music in America: Comprising its History and Peculiarities at Different Periods, with Cursory Remarks on its Legitimate Use and Its Abuse; with Notices of Schools, Composers, Teachers, and Societies.* Boston: Gould & Lincoln, 1853.

Gray, Arlene E. "Lowell Mason's Contribution to American Church Music." M.M. thesis, Eastman School of Music, 1941.

Gray, Mary Sturgis. "George James Webb: His Life and Compositions." Manuscript. Boston Public Library, 1937.

Hadden, J. Cuthbert. "Lowell Mason, American Educator and Musical Pioneer." *Etude* 28 (March 1910): 165.

_____. "Lowell Mason and Psalmody Reform." *The Choir Herald* 16 (November 1912): 21, 23.

Harrington, Joseph, Jr. "Music in Schools." *American Institute of Instruction.* 1838.

Hastings, George H. *Illustrations of the Original Use of the Sacred Lyrics.* Philadelphia: Perkins & Purves, 1843.

Hastings, Thomas. *Dissertation on Musical Taste: or General Principles of Taste Applied to the Art of Music.* Albany: 1822; New York: Mason Brothers, 1853.

_____. *The History of Forty Choirs.* New York: Mason Brothers, 1853.

_____. "The Principles and Claims of Devotional Music: A Prime Essay." *American Biblical Repository* (April 1842): 361-75.

Higginson, J. Vincent. "Notes on Lowell Mason's Hymn Tunes." *The Hymn* 18 (1967): 37-42.

Hodges, Edward. *An Essay on the Cultivation of Church Music.* New York: J. A. Sparks, 1841.

Holt, H. E. "Music in Public Schools." *Education* 4 (January 1884): 262-70.

Hood, George. *History of Music in New England with Biographical Sketches of Reformers and Psalmists.* Boston: Wilkins, Carter & Co., 1846. Reprint. New York: Johnson Reprint Co., 1970.

Hooker, Edward W. *An Address Delivered before the Hastings and Mason Musical Association at Pittsfield, December 25, 1837.* Pittsfield: Phineas Allen & Son, 1838.

_____. *Music as a Part of Female Education.* Boston: T. R. Marvin, 1843.

Howard, John Tasker. *Our American Music.* rev. 4th ed. New York: T. Y. Crowell Co., 1965.

Howe, Granville L., and W.S.B. Mathews. *A Hundred Years of Music in America: An Account of Musical Effort in America During the Past Century, with Historical and Biographical Sketches of Important Personalities.* Chicago: G. L. Howe, 1889.

Howell, Lillian Pope. "Lowell Mason, Composer of Hymn Tunes." M.S.M. thesis, Southern Baptist Seminary, 1948.

Hubbard, W. L., ed. *The American History and Encyclopedia of Music.* Vol. 8, *The History of American Music.* New York: Irving Squire, 1908.

Hughes, Charles W. *American Hymns Old and New: Notes on the Hymns and Biographies of the Authors and Composers.* New York: Columbia University Press, 1980.

Ives, Elam, Jr. *American Elementary Singing Book.* Hartford: F. J. Huntington, 1832.

_____. Letter to William Woodbridge, *American Journal of Education* (1830): 419.

Jackson, George Pullen. *Down-East Spirituals and Others.* Locust Valley, NY: J. J. Augustin, 1939. Reprint. New York: Da Capo Press, 1975.

_____. *White Spirituals in the Southern Uplands: The Story of the Fasola Folk, Their Songs, Singings, and the "Buckwheat" Notes.* Chapel Hill: University of North Carolina Press, 1933.

Jackson, George Sturtevant. *Early Songs of Uncle Sam*. Boston: Bruce Humphries, Inc., 1933.

Jenks, F. H. "Lowell Mason." *New England Magazine* 11 (January 1895): 651-67.

John, Robert W. "Elam Ives and the Pestalozzian Philosophy of Music Education." *Journal of Research in Music Education* 8 (Spring 1960): 45-50.

———. "A History of School Vocal Instruction Books in the United States." Ed.D. diss., Indiana University, 1953.

———. "Origins of the First Music Educators Convention." *Journal of Research in Music Education* 13 (1965): 207-19.

———. "The Second Hundred Years." *Music Educators Journal* 51 (1965): 103–4.

Johnson, Artemas Nixon. *Church Music*. New York: S. T. Gordon, 1844.

Johnson, Frances Hall. *Music Vale Seminary, 1835-76*. New Haven: Yale University Press, 1954.

Johnson, H. Earle. "Early New England Periodicals Devoted to Music." *Musical Quarterly* 26 (1940): 153-61.

———. "George K. Jackson, Doctor of Music, 1745-1822." *Musical Quarterly* 29 (January 1943): 113-21.

———. *Hallelujah, Amen! The Story of the Handel and Haydn Society of Boston*. Boston: Bruce Humphries, 1965.

———. *Musical Interludes in Boston 1795-1830*. New York: Columbia University Press, 1943.

———. "Notes on Sources of Musical Americana." *Notes*, Series II. 5 (March 1948): 169-77.

Jones, F. O., ed. *Handbook of American Music and Musicians*. Canaseraga, NY: F. O. Jones, 1886.

Jones, Merilyn. "Lowell Mason's Contributions to American Music." *American Music Teacher* 27 (June/July 1978): 24–7.

Jones, Walter R. "An Analysis of Public School Music Textbooks before 1900." Ed.D. diss., University of Pittsburgh, 1954.

Julian, John, ed. *A Dictionary of Hymnology: Setting Forth the Origin and History of Christian Hymns of All Ages and Nations*. London: John Murray, 1892. Reprint. New York: Dover Publications, 2 vols., 1957.

Kinnear, William B. "Lowell Mason—Some Teaching Peculiarities." *Musical Courier* 103 (July 11, 1931): 6.

Klein, Sister Mary Justina. *The Contribution of Daniel Gregory Mason to American Music: A Dissertation . . .* Washington, DC: Catholic University of America Press, 1957.

Kouwenhoven, John Atlee. "Some Unfamiliar Aspects of Singing in New England, 1620-1810." *The New England Quarterly* 6 (September 1933): 567-88.

Kraege, Elfrieda A. "The Early Organs of the Fifth Avenue Presbyterian Church." *The Tracker* 18 (Winter 1974): 3-10.

Kushner, David Z. "The 'Masonic' Influence on 19th-Century American Musical Education." *Journal of Musicological Research* 4 (1983): 443-54.

LaFar, Margaret Freeman. "Lowell Mason's Varied Activities in Savannah." *Georgia Historical Quarterly* 28 (1941): 113-37.

Lahee, Henry C. *Annals of Music in America: A Chronological Record of Significant Musical Events, from 1640 to the Present Day, with Comments on the Various Periods into Which the Work is Divided*. Boston: Marshall Jones Co., 1922.

———. "A Century of Choral Singing in New England." *New England Magazine* 26 (March 1902): 102-17.

Lang, Paul Henry. *One Hundred Years of Music in America*. New York: G. Schirmer, 1961.

Lawrence, Clara E. "Early School Music Methods." *Music Educators Journal* 25 (December 1938): 20-22.

Lawrence, Sarah B. "The Great Peace Jubilee." *New England Magazine* 32 (1905): 161-72.

Leavitt, Joshua. *The Christian Lyre: Adapted for Use in Families, Prayer Meetings, and Revivals of Religion*. 2 vols. New York: Jonathan Leavitt, 1831.

Linscott, Robert N., ed. *State of Mind: A Boston Reader*. Clinton, MA: The Colonial Press, 1948.

"The Lowell Mason House at Medfield, Massachusetts," *The Libretto* 4 (November 1928): 1.

Lowens, Irving. *Music and Musicans in Early America*. New York: W.W. Norton & Co., 1964.

———. "Our Neglected Musical Heritage." *The Hymn* 3 (April 1952): 51-52.

Lucas, George Washington. *Remarks on the Musical Conventions in Boston*. Northampton, MA: G.W. Lucas, 1844.

McCabe, Martha R. "Early American School Music Books." *School Life* 24 (July 1939): 290-91, 319.

McConathy, Osbourne, and others. "Evolution of Public School Music in the United States." *MTNA Proceedings 1922*, Pittsburgh, PA, 158-93.

McCusher, Honor. *Fifty Years of Music in Boston: Based on Hitherto Unpublished Letters in the Boston Public Library*. Boston: Trustees of the Library, n.d., Reprint in *More Books*, the Bulletin of the Library, 1937.

McCutchan, Robert Guy. *Our Hymnody: A Manual of the Methodist Hymnal*. 2d ed. New York: Abingdon Press, 1937.

MacDougall, Hamilton C. *Early New England Psalmody: An Historical Appreciation 1620-1820*. Brattleboro, VT: Stephen Daye Press, 1940.

"Mason and Webb's 'Lyrist.' " *North American Review* 46 (1838): 553.

Mason, Daniel Gregory. "How Young Lowell Mason Travelled to Savannah." *New England Magazine* 26 (April 1902): 236-40.

———. "Lowell Mason." *Music Educators National Conference Yearbook* (1937) Chicago: MENC, 352ff.

———. "Some Unpublished Journals of Dr. Lowell Mason." *The New Music Review and Church Music Review* 9 (November 1910): 577-81; 10 (December 1910): 16-18; 10 (January 1911): 62-67.

Mason, Henry Lowell. *Hymn Tunes of Lowell Mason: a Bibliography*. Cambridge: The University Press, 1944.

———. *Lowell Mason: An Appreciation of His Life and Work*. New York: The Hymn Society of America, 1941.

———. "Lowell Mason Biography." Manuscript. Beinecke Rare Book and Manuscript Library, Yale University, 1957.

Mason, Lowell. *Address on Church Music: Delivered by Request, on the Evening of Saturday, October 7, 1826, in the Vestry of Hanover Church, and on the Evening of Monday Following in the Third Baptist Church, Boston*. Boston: Hilliard, Gray & Company, 1826.

———. *An Address on Church Music, delivered July 8, 1851, in Boston*. New York: Mason & Law, 1851.

———. *A Brief Presentation of the Elementary Principles of Music, In Perceptive or Didactic Form*. New York: C. H. Ditson & Co., 1871.

———. *A Glance at Pestalozzianism; Delivered Before the American Institute of Instruction in New Haven*. New York: Mason Brothers, 1863.

———. *How Shall I Teach? or, Hints to Teachers as to the Use of Music and Its Notation*. New York: Mason Brothers, 1860.

———. *Manual of the Boston Academy of Music, for Instruction in the Elements of Vocal Music, on the System of Pestalozzi*. Boston: Carter, Hendee & Co., 1834.

———. *Musical Letters from Abroad: including Detailed Accounts of the Birmingham, Norwich, and Dusseldorf Musical Festivals of 1852*. Boston: O. Ditson, 1853. Reprint. New York: Da Capo Press, 1967.

———. *The Pestalozzian Music Teacher: or Class Instructor in Elementary Music, in Accordance with the Analytic Method*. New York: C. H. Ditson & Co., 1871.

———. *Song in Worship, an Address with an Introduction by the Reverend Reuen Thomas*. Boston: Marvin & Son, 1878.

Mason, William. *Memories of a Musical Life*. New York: Century Co., 1901.

Mason, William Lyman. *A Record of the Descendants of Robert Mason of Roxbury, Massachusetts.* Milwaukee: Burdick, Armitage & Allan, 1891.

Mathews, William Smythe Babcock. "Lowell Mason, a Father in American Music." *The Musician* 16 (November 1911): 721-22.

_____. "Lowell Mason, American Congregational Musician." *Music* 4 (September 1893): 527-30.

_____. "Lowell Mason and the Higher Art of Music in America." *Music* 9 (February 1896): 378-88; 9 (April 1896): 577-91.

_____. "The Lowell Mason Centennial." *Music* 1 (February 1892): 400–408.

Metcalf, Frank J. *American Psalmody or Titles of Books, Containing Tunes Printed in America from 1721-1820.* New York: C. F. Heartman, 1917. Reprint. New York: Da Capo Press, 1968.

_____. *American Writers and Compilers of Sacred Music.* New York: Abingdon Press, 1925. Reprint. New York: Russell & Russell, 1967.

_____. "Lowell Mason." *The Choir Leader* 23 (March 1916): 29-30, 34.

Miller, Josiah. *Our Hymns: Their Authors & Origins: A Companion to the New Congregational Hymn Book.* London: Jackson, Walford & Hodder, 1866.

Moore, Douglas. "The Activities of Lowell Mason in Savannah, Georgia, 1813-1827." M.F.A. thesis, University of Georgia, 1967.

Moore, John W. *Appendix to Encyclopaedia of Music.* Boston: O. Ditson, 1875.

_____. *Complete Encyclopaedia of Music: Elementary Technical, Historical, Biographical, Vocal, and Instrumental.* Boston: O. Ditson & Co., 1854.

More Old Houses in Westborough, Massachusetts and Vicinity with Their Occupants. Westborough Historical Society, 1908.

Morgan, Hazel N. "Music in American Education." *MENC Source Book II.* Chicago: Music Educators National Conference, 1955.

Morison, Samuel Eliot. *The Intellectual Life of Colonial New England.* New York: New York University Press, 1956.

Mott, Frank Luther. *A History of American Magazines.* 4 vols. Cambridge: Harvard University Press, 1938.

Mowry, William A. "Reminiscences of Lowell Mason." *Education* 13 (February 1893): 335-38.

"Music in the Common Schools." *American Annals of Education and Instruction* 1 (July 1831): 330.

"Music in the Public Schools." *American Annals of Education and Instruction* 8 (January 1838): 44.

"Music in Schools." *The Common School Journal* 4 (September 1842): 257-60.

Nesnow, Adrienne. "Lowell Mason Papers." A register compiled under a grant from the National Endowment for the Humanities. New Haven: Yale University, 1982.

Nye, Russel B. *The Cultural Life of the New Nation: 1776-1830.* New York: Harper & Row, 1960.

Ogasapian, John K. "Lowell Mason as a Church Musician." *Journal of Church Music* 21 (September 1979): 6-10.

O'Meara, Eva J. "The Lowell Mason Library of Music." *The Yale University Library Gazette* 40 (October 1965): 57-74.

_____. "The Lowell Mason Papers." *The Yale University Library Gazette* 45 (January 1971): 123-26.

Paige, Paul Eric. "Musical Organizations in Boston: 1830-1850." Ph.D. diss., Boston University, 1967.

Parker, John R., ed. *Musical Biography, or Sketches of the Lives and Writings of Eminent Musical Characters. Interspersed with an Epitome of Interesting Musical Matter.* Boston: Stone and Fovell, 1824.

Pemberton, Carol Ann. "Lowell Mason: His Life and Work." Ph.D. diss., University of Minnesota, 1971.

Perkins, Charles C., and John Sullivan Dwight. *History of the Handel and Haydn Society of Boston, Massachusetts.* Boston: A. Mudge & Sons, 1883, 1893.

Perrin, Phil D. "Pedagogical Philosophy, Methods, and Materials of American Tune Book Introductions: 1801-1860." *Journal of Research in Music Education* 18 (Spring 1970): 65-69.

Pichierri, Louis. *Music in New Hampshire, 1623-1800.* New York: Columbia University Press, 1960.

Pierce, E. H. "The Rise and Fall of the 'Fugue-Tune' in America." *Musical Quarterly* 16 (April 1930) : 214-28.

Pincherle, Marc. "Elementary Musical Instruction in the Eighteenth Century." *Musical Quarterly* 34 (January 1948): 61-67.

"Pioneers in Music Education: Hartford, Connecticut." *Music Educators Journal* 25 (October 1938): 22-25.

Place, C. A. *The Early Forms of Worship in America.* Worcester: American Antiquarian Society, 1930.

Porter, Ellen Jane Lorenz. "A Hymn-Tune Detective Stalks Lowell Mason." *Journal of Church Music* 24 (November 1982): 7-11, 31-32.

Porter, William S. *The Musical Cyclopedia: or the Principles of Music Considered as a Science and an Art; Embracing a Complete Musical Dictionary, and the Outlines of a Musical Grammar....* Boston: James Loring, 1834.

Pratt, Waldo S., ed. *American Supplement,* vol. 6 of *Grove's Dictionary of Music and Musicians,* 3d ed. New York: Macmillan, 1935.

Proceedings of the Musical Convention Assembled in Boston, August 16, 1838. Boston: Kidder & Wright, 1838.

Report of a Committee of the Board of Trustees of the Handel and Haydn Society on the Subject of Existing Contracts between Mr. Lowell Mason and Others for Editing and Publishing Sacred Music. October 1834. Boston: Benjamin H. Greene, 1834.

"Report of the Boston School Committee, August 24, 1837." *The Boston Musical Gazette,* November 28, December 26, 1838.

"Review of the *Boston Handel and Haydn Society Collection...* by Lowell Mason and the Society." *The Christian Advocate.* 3 (June 1825): 271-76.

"Reviews of Lowell Mason's *Musical Letters from Abroad." Musical Opinion* 91 (March 1968): 327; *Pan Pipes* 60 (1968): 49; *Response* 9 (1967): 94-95; *Response* 9 (1968): 184-85.

Rice, Charles I. "Boston, the Cradle of Public School Music in America." *NEA Journal of Proceedings and Addresses.* (1910): 798-803.

Rich, Arthur L. *Lowell Mason, "the Father of Singing Among the Children."* Chapel Hill: University of North Carolina Press, 1946.

_____. "Lowell Mason, Modern Music Educator." *Music Educators Journal* 28 (January 1942): 22-23.

Ritter, Frédéric Louis. *History of Music in the Form of Lectures.* 2 vols. New York: C.H. Ditson & Co., 1870-74.

_____. *Music in America.* New York: Charles Scribner's Sons, 1883.

Roorbach, Orville A. *Bibliotheca Americana: Catalogue of American Publications, Including Reprints and Original Works, from 1820 to 1861.* 4 vols. Reprint. New York: Peter Smith, 1939.

Root, George Frederick. *The Story of My Musical Life: An Autobiography.* Cincinnati: John Church Co., 1891.

Ross, James H. "Lowell Mason, American Musician." *Education* 14 (March 1894): 411-16.

Routley, Eric. *The Music of Christian Hymnody.* London: Independent Press, 1957.

Rugoff, Milton. *The Beechers: An American Family in the Nineteenth Century.* New York: Harper & Row, 1981.

Sabin, Robert. "Early American Composers and Critics." *Musical Quarterly* 24 (April 1938): 210-18.

Scanlon, Mary Browning. "Dr. Lowell Mason in Music Education." M.A. thesis, Eastman School of Music, 1940.

_____. "Lowell Mason's Philosophy of Music Education." *Music Educators Journal* 28 (January 1942): 24-25.

_____. "Thomas Hastings." *Musical Quarterly* 32 (April 1946): 265-77.

Seward, Theodore F. *The Educational Work of Dr. Lowell Mason.* n.p., 1879.

Silver, Edgar O. "The Growth of Music Among the People." *NEA Journal of Proceedings and Addresses* (1891): 813-20.

"Singing in the Common Schools." *The Common School Journal* 3 (June 1841): 189-90.

Smith, Samuel F. "Recollections of Lowell Mason." *New England Magazine* 11 (January 1895): 648-51.

Smith, William. *The Reasonableness of Setting Forth the Most Worthy Praise of Almighty God According to the Usage of the Primitive Church; with Historical View of the Nature, Origin, and Progress of Metre Psalmody.* New York: T. & J. Swords, 1814.

Sonneck, Oscar G. "The History of Music in America: A Few Suggestions" in *Miscellaneous Studies in the History of Music.* New York: Macmillan Co., 1921.

_____. *Suum Cuique: Essays in Music.* New York: G. Schirmer, 1916.

Stevenson, Arthur L. *The Story of Southern Hymnody.* Salem, VA: Arthur L. Stevenson, 1931. Reprint. New York: American Musicological Society, 1975.

Stevenson, Robert M. *Patterns of Protestant Church Music.* Durham: Duke University Press, 1953.

_____. *Protestant Church Music in America: A Short Survey of Men and Movements from 1564 to the Present* New York: W. W. Norton, 1966.

Sunderman, Lloyd Frederick. "Boston and the Magna Charta of American Music Education." *Education* 69 (March 1949): 425-37.

_____. "Early Music Education in Massachusetts." *Education* 72 (September 1951): 45-67.

_____. "The Era of Beginnings in American Music Education (1830-1840)." *Journal of Research in Music Education* 4 (Spring 1956): 33-39.

_____. "A History ꞌof Public School Music in the United States, 1830-1890." Ph.D. diss., University of Minnesota, 1939.

_____. "Sign Posts in the History of American Music Education." *Education* (May 1942): 515-50.

Sweet, William Warren. *Makers of Christianity from John Cotton to Lyman Abbott.* New York: Holt & Co., 1937.

Thayer, A. W. "Lowell Mason." *Dwight's Journal of Music* 39 (November 22, 1879): 186-87; 39 (December 6, 1879): 195-96.

Thompson, Florence W. "Music Vale." *Congregational Quarterly* 3 (1897): 19-22.

Thompson, James William. "Music and Musical Activities in New England, 1800-1838." Ph.D. diss., George Peabody College for Teachers, 1962.

Thrasher, Herbert Chandler. *Oliver Shaw.* Reprinted from *Books at Brown,* vol. 8, no. 4, 1945-46. Providence: Friends of the Library, 1946.

Tilden, W. S. "Early Life of Lowell Mason: Address of William S. Tilden, President of the Medfield Historical Society, at Chenery Hall, Medfield, Friday, January 8, 1892, the Centennial Anniversary of the Birth of Dr. Lowell Mason" in William Mason, *Memories of a Musical Life* (see above): 275-90.

Trotter, James M. *Music and Some Highly Musical People.* Boston: Lee & Shepherd, 1878. Reprint. New York: Johnson Reprint, 1968.

Upton, George P. *Musical Memories: My Recollections of Celebrities of the Half Century: 1850-1900.* Chicago: A. C. McClurg & Co., 1908.

Vincent, Amelia Bartlett. "Music in Boston, 1825-30." M.A. thesis, Boston University, 1942.

Vital Records of Westborough, Massachusetts, to the end of the Year 1843. Worcester: Franklin P. Rice, Trustee of the Systematic History Fund, n.d.

Warrington, James. *Short Titles of Books Relating to or Illustrating the History and Practice of Psalmody in the United States 1620-1820.* Philadelphia: J. Warrington, 1898.

Waters, Edward N. "John Sullivan Dwight, First American Critic of Music." *Musical Quarterly* 21 (January 1935): 69-88.

Watkins, Cole. "A Study of Some American Developments in Congregational Church Song as Influenced by Social and Cultural Factors of the American Scene." M.M. thesis, DePauw University, 1939.

Willis, Richard Storrs. *Our Church Music: A Book for Pastors and People.* New York: Dana, 1856.

―――."A Tribute to Lowell Mason." *The Musical World and New York Musical Times* 5 (January 29, 1853): 66.

Wilson, Bruce Dunbar. "A Documentary History of Music in the Public Schools of the City of Boston, 1830-1850." Ph.D. diss., University of Michigan, 1973.

Wingard, Alan Burl. "The Life and Works of William Batchelder Bradbury, 1816-1868." D.M.A. diss., Southern Baptist Theological Seminary, 1973.

Winicker, A. C. *Explanatory Notes to a New System of Teaching the Science of Music.* Columbus, OH: Scott & Couglass, 1839.

Winsor, Justin, ed. *The Memorial History of Boston, Including Suffolk County, Massachusetts, 1630-1880.* 4 vols. Boston: Ticknor & Co., 1881.

Woodbridge, William C. "Music as a Branch of Instruction in Common Schools." *American Journal of Education* (1830): 417-20.

―――. *On Vocal Music as a Branch of Common Education.* Boston: Hilliard, Gray, Little & Wilkins, 1831.

Wunderlich, Charles Edward. "A History and Bibliography of Early American Music Periodicals, 1782-1852." Ph.D. diss., University of Michigan, 1962.

Index